Every
Little
Thing

Reference Series

Tom Schultheiss, Series Editor

**Available only through Popular Culture, Ink., P.O. Box 1839, Ann Arbor, Michigan 48106
Phone 1(800) 678-8828 or (313) 973-1460.**

Remembrances Series
Tom Schultheiss, Series Editor

Trivia Series
Tom Schultheiss, Series Editor

**Available only through Popular Culture, Ink., P.O. Box 1839, Ann Arbor, Michigan 48106
Phone 1(800) 678-8828 or (313) 973-1460.**

Every Little Thing

The Definitive Guide to
Beatles Recording Variations,
Rare Mixes & Other Musical Oddities,
1958-1986

by
William McCoy
and
Mitchell McGeary

Popular Culture, Ink.
Ann Arbor, Michigan
1990

Book design and layout by William McCoy, Diane Bareis,
and Tom Schultheiss.
Cover design by Diane Bareis.
All cover art is copyright © 1990 by Popular Culture, Ink.
All Rights Reserved.

ISBN 1-56075-004-9
LC 89-92321

Published by Popular Culture, Ink., P.O. Box 1839,
Ann Arbor, MI 48106 USA

"The best rock-and-roll books in the world."

Contents

List of Illustrations

ALBUMS

EPs

SINGLES (7-inch)

SINGLES (12-inch)

Introduction

The Beatles were certainly a prolific recording group. In their first twenty-seven months with EMI Records, they taped sixty-nine songs which were commercially released plus countless alternate versions, demos and original numbers that remain "in the can."

During 1962 and much of 1963, Beatles records were issued only in the United Kingdom, on the Parlophone label. But in late 1963/ early 1964, "Beatlemania" spread like wildfire through Sweden, France, the United States and Australia. In no time at all the whole world fell victim. EMI's foreign branches were soon clamoring for the latest Beatles records as well as for the group's back catalog. In the course of supplying master tapes to subsidiaries on short notice, many alternate mixes and a few alternate takes inadvertently slipped out of EMI's London vaults.

This book contains the first complete listing of variations between the British and foreign pressings of Beatles and solo Beatle recordings, and between the mono, stereo and quadraphonic editions. There are also several references to film material and prerecorded tapes.

The first part of the book, "Getting Closer," takes an in-depth look at several bodies of Beatles recordings that have rarely received close attention before. Here for the first time are detailed examinations of the Tony Sheridan cuts made in Hamburg, Germany in 1961 and the Star Club tape from 1962, complete with session information, listings of original releases, track differences and reissues. The "White Album" chapter includes a track-by-track comparison of the surprisingly different mono and stereo editions of this 1968 double-LP. "Rarities . . . and Box Sets" traces the creation of EMI's **Rarities** albums and provides descriptions of all commercially released Beatles multi-disc packages from around the world.

Also included are chapters on half-speed mastered albums and compact discs, the reissuing of the Beatles original British mono LPs and EMI's special twentieth anniversary releases, along with stories about several one-of-a-kind Beatle discs and a close-up look at the making of John Lennon's **Rock 'N' Roll** album.

"Every Little Thing," the second part of the book, consists of a detailed, song-by-song listing of all known recording variations to both group and solo tracks. It contains concise descriptions of the differences, with original catalog numbers given whenever possible, plus a little bit of background information about each cut.

There's also a comprehensive bibliography covering not only books and articles about the Beatles but also several informative pieces about the recording and audio industries. Finally, a glossary is provided for those who may not be familiar with recording jargon.

While exploring little known areas of the Beatles legacy, we think this book also illustrates a larger issue and that is that recording artists, even a group as big as the Beatles, are not necessarily in control of their most precious work, their records.

Rock 'n' roll is not just a music, it's a sound--a sound. . .a sound that jumps out of a record's grooves and often can't be recreated "live." The Beatles and producer George Martin spent many hours crafting their sound, yet millions of record buyers outside of England never fully experienced it. Their commitment to quality was often lost to the demands of mass production.

EMI/Parlophone Records in England handled the Beatles' material admirably, but as far as foreign releases were concerned, the group was at the mercy of the local affiliates. Many foreign pressings were made from second- or third-generation dubs rather than true stereo master tapes. In America, Dave Dexter, Jr. and Bill Miller of Capitol Records attempted to improve the early albums by "re-processing" them for stereo. This meant taking a twin-track tape (with the instruments on one channel and the voices on the other), re-equalizing it by dividing the sound spectrum so that the bass signals were on the left and the treble was on the right, then adding reverb or echo to the entire track for stereo effect and to mask the lack of definition. All of this was carried out without the consent or knowledge of the Beatles or George Martin. Far from enhancing the material, this method could turn clear, well-balanced original re-cordings into a thumping, crashing onslaught of sound. Fortunately, the infectious nature of the Beatles' music and the spirit with which they performed it triumphed over Capitol's efforts.

This book is designed for both the casual Beatles fan and the serious collector. While containing information on over 200 recording variations, we hope it will also provide some fun for less scholarly Beatlemaniacs by sending them back to their record players to *hear* exactly which version of a particular song they own. After all, that's what record collecting should be about: the music.

Finally, a word of warning. Don't get caught up in listening to your records too closely. It's easy to start trying to isolate every sound and lose sight of the music. As rock journalist Paul Gambaccini recounted in his book *Paul McCartney: In His Own Words* (New York: Flash Books, 1976):

> "There's the famous example of John and Yoko's 'Wedding Album' where the reviewer reviewed the tone of the test pressing and said that the subtle fluctuations in this tone were very arty."

Beatles 4-Ever,
William McCoy
Mitchell McGeary

Acknowledgements

Our special thanks to Jos Remmerswaal for starting this project back in 1976. Remmerswaal, a writer for *Beatles Unlimited*, a bi-monthly fanzine from the Netherlands, compiled about a quarter of the raw data used in the second part of this book and published it in *BU* as an eight-part, serialized article titled "Here, There and Everywhere."

These articles were then expanded and rewritten in the United States by Mitchell McGeary, author of *The Beatles Discography* (Lacey, WA: Ticket to Ryde, 1975), and published in *Goldmine*, an American record collectors magazine. After receiving many additions and corrections, McGeary prepared an updated version which was included in issue #30 of *Strawberry Fields Forever*, the premier Beatles fanzine.

Again, more mail followed as readers began comparing their own records. McGeary handed over the bundle of letters to William McCoy, a fellow collector and contributor to *Strawberry Fields Forever*, to edit. In 1979, this joint project materialized as a booklet, *Every Little Thing: The Beatles on Record* (Lacey, WA: Ticket to Ryde, 1979). Sold by mail, it was quite successful and demand soon required a second edition.

While the material was being revised and broadened for this book, two other authors tackled the subject in short pieces. However, both works dealt only with recordings by the group; neither writer looked at the solo careers of John, Paul, George and Ringo.

J.P. Russell, in his book *The Beatles on Record* (New York: Charles Scribner's Sons, 1982), included a chapter titled "Recording Oddities" that covered recording variations in thirty-five Beatles songs. Russell's form was similar to *Every Little Thing* but his choice of titles was not as comprehensive.

The October 1982 issue of *Record Collector*, a British magazine, carried a well-researched, seven-page article by Nick Piercey called "The Beatles-The Alternate Takes." Piercey's piece, arranged chronologically, was broader in scope and was written in a concise, easy to understand style.

Here at last is the first extended look at the Beatles recording variations. Special thanks must go to the hundreds of Beatles collectors worldwide who supplied us with pertinent information. To avoid repetition, each contributor has been mentioned only once.

CONTRIBUTORS

"Here, There and Everywhere"
Torbjorn Alm, T. Askeroi, Wolfgang Baum, Willi Braam, Rogier Bruggemans, Eva Marie Brunner, Renaat Develtere, Eddie Dieckman, Mark Edmond, Joel Glazier, Bengt Gustavasson, Arno Guzek, Satoshi Iino, Jan-Willem Koene, Jochen Kummer, Alain V. Lauwe, Frank Leenheer, Niels Lund, Piotr Metz, Emiel Mijnhout, Richard Nuzum, Sandra Pereira de Oliveira, Michael Pope, Raymond Richard, R. Rosierse, Gerhard Ruffer, Loek Ruijters, Franco Settimo, Eddy Smits, Annabel Wagner Smitt, Paul Tidey and Evert Vermeer.

Goldmine
Len Backman, John Borrelli, Bill DeYoung, Andy Fesco, Jim Harkey, Tim Jenson, Richard Klein, Jeff Kleinbaum, Darlene McIndile, Anthony Pavick, Joe Pope, Jason Schumate, Leon Sloan, John Stolicny, John Vandenberg and David Wilkie.

Every Little Thing: The Beatles on Record
Fred Grady, Sterling Harwood, Steve Johnson, Tom Jones, Ross Klein, Fred Lark, John Miller, Terry Morrison, Peter Olafson, Mike Sarafian, John Schmidt and Robbie White.

Additional contributors
Jim Brady, Steve Camilli, John Carsell, Stuart Cob, Bob Craig, Ross Dorsett, Susan Godfrey, Golden Films, John A. Guisinger II, Mark Haverkos, D. Herron, Marcus Hirter, Sebastian Kempgen, Bill Kern, Frank Kern, Robert E. Koski, Paul Krasnick, Mark Lawyer, Donald Leighty, Felice Lipsky, Joe Long, LSR Records Inc., Dan McGuire, the Martins, Thomas J. Meenach III, Peter Mildren, Tom Miller, Michael Mulhausen, Mick Murphy, Albert Navarro Jr., Rick Rann, Charles Reinhart, Marlene Rock, Wayne Rogers, Brad Rovoanpera, Scheherazade Records, David Schwartz, Gary Smith, Gene Stern, Robert F. Stricker Jr., Supersound Record Service, Eric Swedberg, Sue Thorne, Rene Van Haarlem, Mark Wallgren, Rusty White, Larry Wisherd and John Wisniewski.

Photos of record covers and labels were taken by Ray Honda, from the collection of William McCoy, with additional photo material supplied by Mitch McGeary.

A word of thanks to Gary Wright for always being on the other end of the phone ready to check running times and read label credits from his own record collection.

Special thanks go to Tom Schultheiss at Popular Culture, Ink. for never doubting this project even as deadlines came and went.

An honorable mention also goes to free-wheeling disc jockey M. Dung, host of the "Sunday Night Idiot Show" on San Francisco's KFOG-FM. In February 1984, when radio stations across America were doing mini-tributes to the Beatles, all playing the same songs over and over, M. Dung chose instead to play a half hour's worth of rarer tracks including the mono version of *I'm Only Sleeping*, which is missing some of George's "backwards" guitar, and six cuts from the mono "White Album." A true collector at heart.

Final thanks for inspiration go to Harry Castleman and Walter J. Podrazik, authors of *All Together Now* (Ann Arbor, MI: Pierian Press, 1975). In the introduction of their definitive Beatles discography, they wrote:

> "We totally ignored a favorite topic among Beatles collectors: recording oddities . . . The mono/stereo differences are very numerous and nearly impossible to catalog."

Beatles fans are not the sort to back down from a challenge, especially if it means searching for more information about their favorite rock 'n' roll band. It was in response to the above quotation that this project was born.

Getting Closer

The Beatles And Tony Sheridan
Germany: Polydor E 76-586 (EP)

A German record club pressing from 1963. "My Bonnie" begins with
Tony Sheridan's English spoken intro.

1

Tony Sheridan
and
The "Beat Brothers"

In April 1961, the Beatles (John Lennon, Paul McCartney, George Harrison, Stuart Sutcliffe and Pete Best) left their hometown Liverpool for a second trip to Hamburg, Germany. They'd been hired to perform at the Top Ten Club, a large beat venue located in the heart of the city's notorious red light district. It was during this three-month engagement that the group made their first commercial recordings.

Prior to the historic session, however, Stu Sutcliffe left the band. Deeply in love, he'd decided to marry fiancée Astrid Kirchherr, live in Hamburg and attend the State Art College. Although only a rudimentary bass player at best, Stu possessed exceptional talent as a painter. Paul McCartney, who'd been alternating between piano and lead guitar, took over as the group's new bassist.

As part of their agreement with Top Ten manager Peter Eckhorn, the Beatles occasionally provided backing for singer/guitarist Tony Sheridan (real name: Anthony Esmond Sheridan McGinnity). An ex-art student from Norwich, Sheridan was well known to teenagers in England as a former regular on "Oh Boy," British television's first rock 'n' roll program.

One evening, Alfred Schacht, the European director of coordination for the Aberbach music publishing company, visited the Top Ten Club to meet with Tony Sheridan, whom he represented. (Aberbach, a major publisher, licensed a great many American rock 'n' roll songs, including Ray Charles's *What'd I Say, Sweets For My Sweet* by Doc Pomus and Mort Shuman, and the Little Richard screamer *Rip It Up*.) After listening to a set, Schacht also took an interest in the Beatles.

A few days later, Schacht had some business with Bert Kaempfert, the popular West German orchestra leader and a & r man. Schacht told Kaempfert about this new group he'd seen and asked if he'd be interested in producing them on a record. Schacht was hoping to sign the Beatles to a publishing contract.

Bert Kaempfert later accompanied Schacht to the Top Ten and

was also impressed by John, Paul, George and Pete. The next morning at 11:00 a.m., Tony Sheridan and the Beatles met Schacht and Kaempfert at the Aberbach offices in Hamburg. After a bit of discussion, Schacht came up with a publishing deal for George and John to handle their first (and only) joint composition, *Cry For A Shadow*, an instrumental whose title was meant as a slight dig at the Shadows, the backing band for England's biggest home-grown rock star, Cliff Richard.

Kaempfert then signed both Tony Sheridan and the Beatles to recording contracts with Deutsche Grammophon Records. According to the terms, the Beatles would record four singles over the next twelve months. They'd be paid a flat fee for backing Sheridan but would receive royalties for any of their own records Deutsche Grammophon chose to release.

Fourteen years later, Hal Fein, the former owner of Roosevelt Music publishing company in New York, offered a different version of how the Beatles got their first recording contract. Roosevelt Music was the publisher of *Take Out Some Insurance On Me Baby* (also titled *If You Love Me Baby*), one of the songs recorded by Tony Sheridan and the Beatles, and still later was the American publisher of *Cry For A Shadow*. In a 1975 article in *Modern HiFi & Music*, Fein said *he* had accompanied Kaempfert to the Top Ten Club and had convinced him to sign the Beatles to a contract with Bert Kaempfert Productions, a company supposedly owned jointly by he and Kaempfert. Fein contended that Brian Epstein had to later persuade Kaempfert to let the Beatles out of this agreement in order that Epstein could then sign the group to a personal management contract in December 1961.

Hal Fein's story was quickly refuted by John Lennon. In a letter to Robert Weinstein, the author of the article, John said that although he could recall clearly working with Bert Kaempfert and backing Tony Sheridan, he had no recollection of anyone named Hal Fein.

Even though the Beatles were about to make their first commercial recordings, the group didn't regard the impending session as a step forward in their career. Afterall, they would only be playing behind Tony Sheridan and, when any records were released, John, Paul, George and Pete would be billed as the "Beat Brothers." Deutsche Grammophon felt the word "Beatles" would be too confusing to record buyers in Germany and in the rest of Europe where the discs would later be distributed.

The modest session took place one morning in June, not in a proper recording studio but on the stage at a local primary school. On hand were Tony Sheridan, singing and playing lead guitar, John Lennon and George Harrison on rhythm guitars, Paul McCartney playing bass, Pete Best on drums and Bert Kaempfert producing. In a 1971 BBC Radio interview, Tony Sheridan said that Stu Sutcliffe was also present at the session "as a friend" but did not take part.

When the session began, Bert Kaempfert had no idea what he wanted the group to record. He asked everyone what they could play that might appeal to the German public. The Beatles ran through a few Lennon-McCartney originals but to Kaempfert's ears the songs weren't commercial. Tony Sheridan suggested a rock 'n' roll version of *My Bonnie Lies Over The Ocean.* He reckoned all the kids in Europe learned the number at school, and just recently a group of seamen had requested it at the Top Ten. As Sheridan explained in the video "rockumentary" "The Compleat Beatles" (US: Delilah Films, 1982), he'd started singing *My Bonnie* because Gene Vincent did it, and Vincent had included it in his repertoire after hearing a Ray Charles recording of it. (The Ray Charles rendition was first issued in September 1959 on his Atlantic Records LP, **What'd I Say.**)

So, *My Bonnie* became the A-side of Tony Sheridan and the Beat Brothers' first single. From there the band played through more rock versions of standards, plus George and John's number and some ballads that Sheridan sang in his best Elvis Presley voice.

The exact number of tracks recorded is not known. Only eight songs have ever been released. Six of them feature Tony Sheridan as lead singer: *My Bonnie, The Saints, Why* (a Tony Sheridan composition written in Hamburg with the aid of another popular Liverpool beat group, Gerry and the Pacemakers), *Sweet Georgia Brown, Nobody's Child* and *If You Love Me Baby* (with a slightly edited version issued under the number's original title, *Take Out Some Insurance On Me Baby*).

The remaining two cuts feature just the Beatles. They are *Ain't She Sweet* with John singing lead, and *Cry For A Shadow*, the instrumental that, according to the Liverpool pop bi-weekly *Merseybeat*, was almost called the *Beatle Bop.* The Beatles demonstrated their lack of regard for these recordings by selling the rights back to Deutsche Grammophon after the session, thereby forfeiting any future royalties. They were paid a flat fee of 300DM each (about $62) for their work. In 1964, with Beatlemania sweeping the world, *Ain't She Sweet* and *Cry For A Shadow* were both issued as singles in Australia and, in July, both entered the Australian Top Twenty. Deutsche Grammophon executives no doubt smiled all the way to the bank.

Concerning unreleased tracks, John Lennon told biographer Hunter Davies that the Beatles performed a total of five songs at the session, none of which suited Deutsche Grammophon. In fact, in his June 1975 letter to *Modern HiFi & Music*, John said Bert

Kaempfert found the Beatles "too bluesy." Subtracting *Ain't She Sweet* and *Cry For A Shadow* from the five Beatles numbers leaves three unreleased cuts. Reminiscing about the session some fifteen years later, Tony Sheridan offered these comments regarding what tapes may still be locked away in Deutsche Grammophon's vaults:

"I seem to remember that we also recorded *Kansas City*, and a couple of Chuck Berry songs . . . I think John sang *Rock And Roll Music* and *Some Other Guy*. But as you can appreciate, it was quite some time ago."*

Sheridan believed the reason Deutsche Grammophon never released the other tracks was because ". . . John's voice was a bit dodgy . . . due to overwork."

Despite the primitive state of multi-track recording in 1961, these numbers were taped in stereo. Dividing the mix, Tony Sheridan's voice and lead guitar were placed on the left channel while the Beatles' back-up vocals and Paul's bass were put on the right. Pete Best's drums, along with George and John's rhythm guitars, were spread across both channels. This positioning varied slightly from song to song, depending on the arrangement. To fully appreciate the exuberance in these early Beatles performances, listen to *My Bonnie* playing just the right channel. You'll hear everything but Tony Sheridan's lead singing, with a nineteen-year-old Paul McCartney belting out his background vocal in a brash, uninhibited style that's sorely missing in the majority of today's studio-crafted rock music.

There is, however, one track that has never been issued in true stereo. It's a re-recorded version of *Sweet Georgia Brown* (see "**Differences**," p. 16). In late 1963, Deutsche Grammophon's English subsidiary, Polydor Records, brought Tony Sheridan back into the studio to re-cut his vocal on this song. In an attempt to cash in on the Beatles' staggering popularity, Sheridan taped a set of updated lyrics that made direct references to the Beatles, their hair and their fan club. This re-recorded version was apparently intended to be put out only as a single because no true stereo mix has ever been released.

A SHORT HISTORY OF RELEASES

The Beatles always downplayed the importance of the Hamburg recordings. Originally, Deutsche Grammophon had intended to issue these records just on the European continent. In 1961, there were no plans to put out these tracks in the Beatles' (and Tony Sheridan's) native England.

New Musical Express, September 6, 1975.

6

Nevertheless, the release of these recordings did mark a turning point in the Beatles' career. First, the mere making of a disc by any Liverpool beat group was cause for celebration. No Merseyside band had done it before. Second, the availability of these records in local music shops was a source of pride for Beatles fans in both Liverpool and Hamburg. But third and most important, the demand in Liverpool for the Beatles' first single brought them to the attention of their future manager, Brian Epstein.

My Bonnie b/w *The Saints* by Tony Sheridan and the Beat Brothers was issued in Germany (Polydor 24-673) in June 1961, the same month it was recorded. The disc became a slow but steady seller and, in December, entered the German Top Twenty after selling a reported 180,000 copies. Because of this chart success, *My Bonnie* was supposedly played once on Radio Luxembourg during its weekend country-by-country survey of pop hits. (In the 1950's, Radio Luxembourg was the only station English listeners could tune in to hear rock 'n' roll; BBC Radio refused to include rock records in its one weekend pop program.)

In September 1961, German Polydor issued a Tony Sheridan EP titled **My Bonnie**. It contained both sides of the single plus two more Hamburg tracks, *Why* and the Beatles' instrumental *Cry For A Shadow*. Deutsche Grammophon apparently viewed the later two cuts as filler because when German Polydor put out Tony Sheridan's first album, **My Bonnie** (Polydor HiFi 46-612; Stereo 237-112), the only Beatles-backed numbers included were *My Bonnie* and *The Saints*. The rest of the LP was made up of fresh songs recorded earlier that year with a different backing band that featured another Britisher, Roy Young, on electric organ, and a saxophone player from Scotland, Rikki Barnes. (Roy Young first accompanied Tony Sheridan on "Oh Boy" and then traveled with him to Hamburg where he sat in with many groups, including the Beatles, and sometimes even headlined his own *ad hoc* combo.)

Back in Liverpool, the Beatles were appearing regularly at the Cavern, a dank, underground club that presented only jazz when it opened in 1957 but was now the city's main showcase for beat groups. Bob Wooler, the Cavern's resident disc jockey and a staunch supporter of the Beatles, plugged the *My Bonnie* single as often as possible even though it was available only as a German import. Just before the Beatles would take the stage, he'd urge the fans to ask their local record shops to order the disc.

According to legend, Brian Epstein was first made aware of the Beatles on Saturday, October 28, 1961, when Raymond Jones, an eighteen-year-old lad from Huyton, walked into Liverpool's North End Music Store (NEMS), which Epstein managed, and asked for a copy of *My Bonnie* by the Beatles. Epstein knew he didn't have the record in stock and according to his autobiography*, he'd never heard of it or of the Beatles. But his diligent search for the German disc led to an eventual meeting with John, Paul, George and Pete on November 9 during a lunchtime session at the Cavern, which turned out to be located only 200 yards from NEMS. The twenty-seven-year-old Epstein stood mesmerised as he watched the Beatles work through their afternoon performance. Subsequent visits convinced him that the Beatles could have a very successful future if they were handled properly.

To satisfy the group's growing following in Liverpool, Brian Epstein ordered a full stock of the *My Bonnie* single from Germany and by December 1961 had sold well over 100 copies. Brian's interest and desire to get involved with the band grew so great that by the end of December he'd become their personal manager.

It's at this point in the Beatles' career that most biographers focus on Brian Epstein's efforts to secure a recording contract for the group. Using his retail contacts, Brian did manage to get Mike Smith, an a & r man for Decca Records, to come up to Liverpool and see the Beatles in person at the Cavern. This favorable presentation led to a formal audition at the Decca studios in London on January 1, 1962.

But Epstein's first move, as chronicled in *Merseybeat*, was persuading Polydor Records in England to release *My Bonnie* b/w *The Saints* as a domestic single. More importantly, he prodded Polydor into correcting the record's label credits to read "Tony Sheridan and the Beatles." This U.K. single (Polydor NH 66-833), issued on January 5, 1962, was the first commercial disc to bear the "Beatles" name.

(On September 1, 1983, an original copy of this record, signed on both the label and on the sleeve by John, Paul, George and Pete, was put up for auction at Sotheby's in London where it sold for £120, or about $192.)

Brian also put together a series of promotional handout photos of the Beatles to accompany the single. This set supposedly included some striking shots of the group taken in Hamburg by Jurgen Vollmer, one of their few close German friends. In early 1975, John Lennon chose Jurgen's photo of himself standing in a downtown Hamburg doorway to be the cover for his **Rock 'N' Roll** LP and, in 1981, a large collection of Jurgen's prints, not only of the Beatles but also of their Hamburg surroundings, was published in an intriguing book titled *Rock 'n' Roll Times* (New York: Google Plex Books).

Not one to miss a trick, Brian Epstein redesigned the Beatles

---

**A Cellarful Of Noise* (New York: Doubleday, 1964.)

8

local concert posters. Placards for their Merseyside dates now billed the group as "Polydor Recording Artists."

On April 10, 1962, just three days before the Beatles were to begin another engagement in Germany, they were stunned by the news that Stu Sutcliffe had died in Hamburg of a brain tumor. He was twenty-two.

The next release of the Tony Sheridan recordings came on April 23, 1962, when Decca Records in the United States and Canada issued *My Bonnie* b/w *The Saints* (Decca 31382). (U.S./Canadian Decca were in no way affiliated with the Decca label in England.) Bert Kaempfert had a contract with Decca dating back to November 1960, when the label put out his first number one hit, the instrumental *Wonderland By Night* (originally *Wunderland Bei Nacht*.)

My Bonnie and *The Saints* were licensed to Decca by Deutsche Grammophon in Germany so the tracks were still credited to "Tony Sheridan and the Beat Brothers." With no promotion, the record was lost in obscurity. Today, these discs rank as the highest-valued Beatles singles issued in North America, but novice collectors beware: excellent counterfeit copies of the American, pink-label promotional single are in circulation.

Of the eight Hamburg recordings eventually issued, it's interesting to note that initially Deutsche Grammophon only considered *My Bonnie, The Saints, Why* and *Cry For A Shadow* suitable for release and, as mentioned earlier, the latter two tracks were apparently viewed as just filler for an EP. Following the 1962 German release of Tony Sheridan's **My Bonnie** (Polydor HiFi 46-612; Stereo 237-112), no other Hamburg tracks were put out until after the Beatles became world famous.

Sweet Georgia Brown, Nobody's Child, Take Out Some Insurance On Me Baby (also titled *If You Love Me Baby*) and *Ain't She Sweet* were not released until early 1964, just as Beatlemania was sweeping America. Much to the Beatles' and Brian Epstein's dismay, Deutsche Grammophon signed two licensing agreements that brought all eight Hamburg recordings flooding onto the American market. MGM Records was granted the U.S. release rights to the first four Hamburg tracks, while Atlantic Records was given the four previously unissued numbers. Between 1964 and late 1966, MGM and Atlantic (and their subsidiaries) used these eight cuts (and a large quantity of horrendous cover material by unknown artists) to create a total of five albums and four singles.

An apparently unauthorized compilation of Hamburg tracks appeared in America in the mid-sixties under the title **The Savage Young Beatles** (Savage BM 69). Four of the cuts featured John, Paul, George and Pete (*Cry For A Shadow, Sweet Georgia Brown, Why,* and *If You Love Me Baby*) while the other four were later Tony

The Beatles With Tony Sheridan And Their Guests
US: MGM S/E 4215 (LP)

The Savage Young Beatles
US: Savage BM 69 (pirated LP)

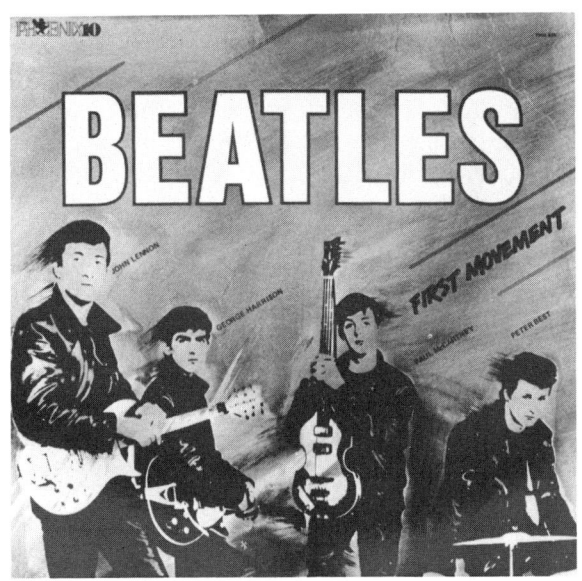

First Movement
US: Phoenix 10 - PHX 339 (LP)

Sheridan recordings (*Let's Dance, What'd I Say, Ruby Baby* and *Ya Ya*.) This was the only Hamburg album to bear a cover photo of the original Beatles (correctly picturing Pete Best on the drums); all of the other labels tried to pass off these early tracks as current material.

In March 1982, this package was reissued in the United States with a slightly different jacket design and title: **First Movement** (Phoenix 10 - PHX 339). The release is of questionable value. The record was pressed from a mono dub of the original album, not a stereo master tape. Also, there's an irritating jump in volume midway through the opening track, *Cry For A Shadow*.

Unlike the original issue, this album lists running times for the songs, although some differ by a second or two from the accepted times given on most other releases. The liner notes also credit the Beatles as Tony Sheridan's backing band on the four cuts the group *did not* play on.

One bit of information included on **First Movement** that can't be found in many other places is the name of the current American publisher of the George Harrison-John Lennon instrumental, *Cry For A Shadow*. It's Talisman Music/BMI.

In October 1983, Phoenix's parent company, Audiofidelity Enterprises, Inc., pressed a picture disc version of **First Movement** (US: Audiofidelity PD 339). However, no title appeared on the record label, just the word "Beatles."

In July 1982, **The Savage Young Beatles** was released in England by Charly Records (Charly CFM 701) as a 10-inch LP. Again, the original cover graphics were changed a bit. One point of interest for collectors is that Charly, a record company that is respected for the care it takes in reissuing original rock 'n' roll material, got former Beatles press officer Tony Barrow to write the liner notes for this album. Barrow provided a few bits of new information about some of these early cuts, but in the process he included several inaccuracies that only further confused the story behind these legendary recordings.

While giving a brief rundown on the Beatles' career, Barrow said that Stu Sutcliffe played with the group until shortly before his death when, in fact, Stu left the band in May 1961 just prior to the Polydor session. Barrow also incorrectly assumed that all of the tracks were recorded at roughly the same time. Therefore, he points out that the Beatles as a group were not present on all eight cuts. But he then goes on to say that individual members of the band "shared the instrumental backing with other musicians" on the remaining numbers.

It was established long ago that all of the Tony Sheridan-Beatles recordings were taped in June 1961 during one early morning session.

Since the four non-Beatles-backed cuts were cover versions of American rock 'n' roll hits, none of which had even been released by this time, it's impossible for the Beatles, either as a group or as individuals, to have played on any of these tracks.

The original recording of *Ya Ya* by Lee Dorsey (US: Fury 1053) was released in August 1961, three months after the Beatles cut their numbers. In fact, Polydor first issued Tony Sheridan's cover version in October 1962 (Germany: Polydor 21485). *Let's Dance* was a Chris Montez record (US: Monogram 505) that came out in July 1962, two months after the Beatles were signed to Parlophone Records in England. *Ruby Baby* was first issued by the Drifters in May 1956 but Sheridan's cover was based on the January 1963 rendition by Dion (US: Columbia 42662). By this time, the Beatles already had *Love Me Do* in the British charts. Tony Barrow did offer the news that Sheridan's backing group on this recording was Joey Dee's Starlighters, the resident twist band at New York's famed Peppermint Lounge. In January 1963, the Starlighters were performing for the first time in Hamburg, at the Star Club. *What'd I Say*, the Ray Charles classic from 1959 (US: Atlantic 2031), was probably recorded at the same time judging by the instrumental track.

Otherwise, Barrow contributed a unique story about *Take Out Some Insurance On Me Baby* (which is listed on this release as *Take Out Some Insurance*). He implied that Ringo Starr might have played drums with the Beatles on this track. Barrow said that when this session took place, Ringo was in Hamburg working in the resident band at the Top Ten Club along with Tony Sheridan. A check of all the known facts instead indicates that Ringo performed at the Top Ten in early *1962*, at least eight months after the Beatles recorded this song. In June 1961, Ringo was preparing for another summer season at Butlin's holiday camp in England with Rory Storm and the Hurricanes.

DIFFERENCES

Ain't She Sweet (Jack Yellin-Milton Ager)
This song was first issued May 29, 1964 on a British single (Polydor NH 52-317). On July 6, 1964, Atlantic Records put it out in the United States and Canada on one of its subsidiary labels, Atco. But before Atco mastered the disc, a session drummer was hired to enhance the rather primitive sound of the original recording by overdubbing a louder drum track. This new version was first released on a single (Atco 6308) and was later included on two albums, **Ain't She Sweet** (Atco SD 33-169) and **The Amazing Beatles And Other Great English Group Sounds** (Clarion 601). All other pressings have only Pete Best on drums.

Ain't She Sweet
US: Atlantic OS 13243 (45)

A 1983 reissue containing Atlantic's augmented
version of "Ain't She Sweet."

(Attention collectors: several counterfeit editions of the Atlantic single are in circulation. One is a standard, black vinyl disc that comes in a counterfeit picture sleeve; a second issue is pressed on red vinyl but comes without a sleeve.)

In December 1983, two months prior to the twentieth anniversary of the Beatles' first trip to America, the doctored version of *Ain't She Sweet* was reissued on a single, this time on the Atlantic label as part of its "Oldies Series" (Atlantic OS 13243).

In a 1971 BBC Radio interview, Tony Sheridan said that a slightly remixed version of *Ain't She Sweet* was released on a single in Australia (Polydor NH 52-317) in May 1964 and went on to become a number one hit. The B-side was *If You Love Me Baby* with Sheridan singing lead. Since it also was a "Beatles" record, it garnered quite a lot of airplay as well. This unexpected exposure and chart success enabled Sheridan, then a resident performer at the Star Club in Hamburg, to book a series of personal appearances in Australia while the record was at the top of the charts.

Polydor Records in Chile issued an edited version of *Ain't She Sweet* on a single (Polydor 52-317). The track was shortened to 1:30 by fading it out right after the instrumental break. All other pressings run 2:12.

Cry For A Shadow (Harrison-Lennon)
On the German double-album, **Die Wilden 60er Jahren**, this track was shortened to 1:20. All other pressings run 2:22.

If You Love Me Baby (Charles Singleton-Waldenese Hall)
This is the alternate title of *Take Out Some Insurance On Me Baby*.

Polydor Records in Chile issued an edited version of this song on a single (Polydor 52-317). The track was shortened to 1:36 by fading it out right after the instrumental break. All other pressings run 2:52. (See *Take Out Some Insurance On Me Baby*, p. 19.)

My Bonnie (J. T. Woods-H. J. Fuller)
The version issued on the original German single (Polydor 24-673) and on the original German **My Bonnie** EP (Polydor Records) runs 2:41 and begins with Tony Sheridan's thirty-five-second, German language introduction. Both pressings were put out in 1961.

The version issued on the original British single (Polydor NH 66-833), on the original U.S. and Canadian singles (Decca 31382), and on the original German **My Bonnie** album (Polydor HiFi 46-612; Stereo 237-112) runs 2:41 and starts with Sheridan's thirty-five-second spoken introduction, this time in English. (The labels on the U.S. and Canadian singles incorrectly list the running time of *My*

Bonnie as 2:58.) All four pressings were put out in 1962.

The British **My Bonnie** EP (Polydor H 21-610) and the German **The Beatles and Tony Sheridan** EP (Polydor E 76-586), both issued in 1963, also contain the English intro.

All commercial pressings released between 1964 and 1979 run 2:06 and have no spoken introduction. However, in October 1978, Polydor Records in Germany put out a numbered, limited edition promotional single of *My Bonnie* b/w *Cry For A Shadow* (Polydor 2801-033) for sale at "Roll Over Beatles," the first Beatles fan convention to be held in Cologne. Both tracks were issued in stereo and *My Bonnie* contained the German language introduction. Only 500 copies were pressed.

Beginning in 1980, many re-releases (primarily those issued by Polydor, as opposed to budget label editions) began appearing, opening with the English introduction and pressed in stereo. Two such releases were a German single put out as part of Polydor's "Golden Greats" series (Polydor 2135-501), and the version found on the Japanese **The Beatles 1961** album (Polydor MPF 1024).

Even bootleggers got into the act. On **Indian Rope Trick** (Fan Records Limited), a special version of *My Bonnie* was created by editing both the English and German intros back-to-back at the start of the song.

In December 1982, Staffan Olander of Polydor Records in Sweden issued a limited edition, six-track EP of Beatles rarities (Polydor 2230-114) available only by mail order. Included were both the German and English spoken introductions to *My Bonnie*, minus the song. Only 500 copies were pressed.

Nobody's Child (Mel Foree-Cy Coben)

This song was first issued January 31, 1964 on a British single (Polydor NH 52-906). On July 6, 1964, Atlantic Records put it out in the United States and Canada on one of its subsidiary labels, Atco. But before Atco mastered the disc, two edits were made, shortening the track from 3:52 to 2:54.

Atlantic engineers first omitted the body of the second verse, leaving only the first and last two lines. They also condensed the closing, cutting out Tony Sheridan's final two guitar chords but still ending the track with a note from Paul's bass.

This new version was first released on a single (Atco 6308) and was later included on two albums, **Ain't She Sweet** (Atco SD 33-169) and **The Amazing Beatles And Other Great English Group Sounds** (Clarion 601). All other pressings contain the original, full-length recording.

Sweet Georgia Brown (Ben Bernie-Maceo Pinkard-Kenneth Casey)

The Beatles 1961
Japan: Polydor MPF 1024 (LP)

A 1980 reissue in true stereo. Includes the non-Beatles version of
"Sweet Georgia Brown." Also "My Bonnie" is preceded
by the English spoken intro.

Sweet Georgia Brown
US: Atlantic OS 13243 (45)

A 1983 reissue featuring Atlantic's augmented version of "Sweet
Georgia Brown."

Contrary to popular belief, the first recording of this song put out under Tony Sheridan's name did not include the Beatles as Sheridan's backing band, even though Sheridan and the Beatles taped this number in June 1961. This first version, issued in June 1962 on the German **My Bonnie** LP (Polydor HiFi 46-612; Stereo 237-112) and then in October 1962 on the German **Ya Ya** EP (Polydor 21485), has Tony Sheridan singing the song's original lyrics, contains no backing vocals and, like many of Sheridan's other records, includes a saxophone. In 1980, this recording was accidentally re-released on the Japanese **The Beatles 1961** (Polydor MPF 1024) but was credited to "Tony Sheridan and the Beatles." The running time of this track is 2:28; the true Beatles-backed version is only 2:03.

The Sheridan-Beatles version was first issued January 31, 1964 on a British single (Polydor NH 52-906). Prior to release, Polydor Records had Tony Sheridan re-record his lead vocal, replacing the original words by Ben Bernie, Maceo Pinkard and Kenneth Casey with a set of "hip," updated lyrics that made direct references to the Beatles, their hair and their fan club. To the best of our knowledge, the original Sheridan-Beatles recording of *Sweet Georgia Brown* has never been put out.

On June 1, 1964, Atlantic Records issued a third version of the song in the United States and Canada. This new version also used Tony Sheridan's updated vocals, but before Atlantic released the recording, a session drummer and lead guitarist were hired to augment the original track in hopes of making the record sound more commercial. This version was first put out on a single (Atco 6302) and was later included on two albums, **Ain't She Sweet** (Atco SD 33-169) and **The Amazing Beatles And Other Great English Group Sounds** (Clarion 601).

In December 1983, two months prior to the twentieth anniversary of the Beatles' first trip to America, the doctored version of *Sweet Georgia Brown* was reissued on a single, this time on the Atlantic label as part of its "Oldies Series" (Atlantic OS 13243).

One year earlier, Staffan Olander of Polydor Records in Sweden issued a limited edition, six-track EP of Beatles rarities (Polydor 2230-114), available only by mail order. Included was the non-Beatles-backed version of *Sweet Georgia Brown*. Only 500 copies were pressed.

Take Out Some Insurance On Me Baby (Charles Singleton-Waldenese Hall)
    This is the original title of *If You Love Me Baby*. In reference to the Tony Sheridan recordings, it was first used June 1, 1964 by Atlantic Records in the United States and Canada. As it turned out,

The Beatles-Circa 1960-In The Beginning
US: Polydor 24-4504 (LP)

the recording issued by Atlantic was slightly different from the version available under the tune's other name. Prior to the American release, Atlantic hired a session drummer and lead guitarist to over- dub additional rhythm parts. Atlantic also made one edit on Tony Sheridan's lead vocal track to keep the song from being offensive, particularly to the hundreds of thousands of parents it was counting on to buy this record for their children.

In the final chorus of *If You Love Me Baby*, Sheridan sings, "Take out some insurance on me baby . . . some *god damned* insurance on me baby." On the Atlantic Records cut, Sheridan's vocal track was edited to play, "Take out some insurance on me baby . . . *ooh*, some insurance on me baby."

This sanitized version was first put out on a single (Atco 6302) and was later included on three albums, **Ain't She Sweet** (Atco SD 33-169), **The Amazing Beatles And Other Great English Group Sounds** (Clarion 601) and **The Original Discoteque Hits** (Clarion 609).

In 1970, Polydor Records in the United States reissued the Tony Sheridan-Beatles material on **The Beatles - Circa 1960 - In The Beginning** (Polydor 24 - 4504). However, the original *If You Love Me Baby* recording was listed as *Take Out Some Insurance On Me Baby*, creating confusion among collectors. Charly Records in England did the same thing in 1982 when it released its 10-inch version of **The Savage Young Beatles** (Charly CFM 701). In fact, here the title was shortened to *Take Out Some Insurance*. (See *If You Love Me Baby*, p. 15.)

WAS IT BERNARD PURDIE?

As detailed in the preceding section, Atlantic Records augmented three of the four Hamburg tracks before releasing them in the United States and Canada on its various subsidiaries. When the songs were first issued on **Ain't She Sweet** (Atco SD 33-169), the label and jacket notes listed the performers as simply "the Beatles." Atlantic obviously hoped to cash in on the group's overwhelming record sales in America by implying that all four cuts were recorded by John, Paul, George and Ringo. No mention was made as to the year these tracks were taped or that Pete Best, not Ringo Starr, played drums. However, later stereo issues of **Ain't She Sweet** were corrected to credit three of the four songs as being by "the Beatles with Tony Sheridan."

The studio musicians Atlantic employed certainly could have made names for themselves by telling the press how they'd been hired to play on a "Beatles" record. Such a story did appear in print, but fourteen years after the fact.

Ain't She Sweet
US: Atco SD 33-169 (LP)

Contains doctored versions of "Ain't She Sweet," "Sweet Georgia
Brown" and "Take Out Some Insurance On Me Baby."
Also, only the stereo edition lists Tony Sheridan as lead
vocalist on three of the four tracks.

In the February 1978 issue of *Gig*, a New York-based rock musician's newspaper, Bernard Purdie, a black, veteran east coast session drummer, claimed he once was contracted to overdub percussion parts on various early Beatles records. But Purdie, who frequently worked on Atlantic Records sessions, made no mention of the Hamburg material.

Purdie contended that in the summer of 1963, at least six months before the Beatles came to America, he was hired by Brian Epstein to overdub drums on twenty-one tracks off the Beatles' first three British albums, presumably to improve on Ringo's playing. Purdie said these sessions took place at Capitol Records' 46th Street studios in New York, lasted for nine days, and that he was paid his customary "double session fee of $130 an hour" along with a check "in five figures" to keep his "mouth shut." The end of Purdie's story had a perfect out should anyone ask him to substantiate his claims: "The manager did everything. Epstein instigated everything that had to be done. He was the one who told me to keep my mouth closed. He was the one," Purdie told *Gig* staff writer Steve Weitzman.

Since Brian Epstein died in 1967, and since, according to Purdie, Beatles' producer George Martin was never aware of what Epstein was supposed to have done, there appears, at first glance, no way to confirm or refute Purdie's remarks. (Ironically, Purdie was employed by Martin in September 1977 to play on the soundtrack of the Robert Stigwood motion picture "Sgt. Pepper's Lonely Hearts Club Band.") But from just these few excerpts, Beatles fans can have a field day picking this story apart.

How could Bernard Purdie have been working on drum tracks from the first three Beatles albums when the group had recorded only two LPs by that time? If Brian Epstein did indeed have the drum tracks redubbed, why is there no difference between the original English pressings with only Ringo and the later 1963 pressings that Purdie claimed include both Ringo and himself? And more importantly, how was Brian Epstein supposed to have gotten the Beatles master tapes out of EMI's vaults, taken them to the United States for nine days, and then returned them unnoticed? Finally, why was Epstein supposedly tampering with the Beatles' sound, an area he felt never needed improving in any way?

When claims as highly implausible as these are published, the question arises as to why anyone of Purdie's professional stature would want to damage their reputation with such an incredible tale as this if there weren't some thread of truth to it. What we are going to do is look at the part of Purdie's account that seems to have some basis in fact.

Bernard Purdie started his career as a New York studio musician in 1961. His first job was accompanying Mickey and Sylvia (*Love Is Strange*). Following a short stint with his own club band, Purdie decided to work solely as a session drummer. "Pretty" Purdie, as he was later nicknamed, had no desire for the limelight. Instead, he enjoyed the demands of working with different musicians on every job as well as the lucrative earnings top studio men could make. Purdie has since played on thousands of records and has backed a wide variety of artists, including Tim Rose, Gato Barbieri, the Monkees, Marvin Gaye, Steely Dan, the Animals, Jeff Beck and James Brown.

Purdie was no stranger to Atlantic Records. As the premier rhythm and blues label in New York, Atlantic employed him on numerous sessions, including many with King Curtis. Purdie's biggest commercial success came from his seven-year association with one of Atlantic's greatest talents, Aretha Franklin. It was Curtis who originally hired Purdie to back the "queen of soul."

In the early sixties, Purdie was the most sought-after session drummer in New York. According to *Rolling Stone*, "Purdie was in the studio nearly every day, the equivalent of L.A.'s Hal Blaine and Nashville's Kenneth Buttrey. . . ." So in 1964, when Atlantic needed a studio percussionist to overdub parts on the Beatles' Hamburg recordings, and also someone who wouldn't care about the notoriety that doing anything associated with the Beatles would bring, Bernard Purdie would have been a logical choice.

If we continue with the assumption that Purdie was indeed the session man Atlantic used, the rest of his remarks fall into place. First, Purdie mentioned that he worked on finished tapes. This would certainly be true. Bert Kaempfert had spread Pete Best's drums across both the right and left channels, leaving no way to isolate them.

Purdie also said there was a guitar player hired to do overdubbing: "After I was finishing up one day, the engineer said they had another guitar player coming in later to do overdubs and they were paying him good money to keep his mouth shut too."

There was a new lead guitar part added to both *Sweet Georgia Brown* and *Take Out Some Insurance On Me Baby* on all Atco and Clarion pressings.

But the telltale remark that strongly suggests Purdie was the drummer playing on Atlantic Records' Beatles cuts was his description of exactly how he worked on the original tapes: "They had four tracks and they put me on two separate tracks. I would listen to what Ringo (sic) had played and then overdub on top of it to keep it happening," explained Purdie.

And this was precisely what was done. Pete Best's original drum line had not been recorded too loudly. Also, Pete's playing was competent but not flashy. He didn't possess Ringo's strong backbeat. In Atlantic's attempts to make these records sound similar to current Beatles releases, its drummer imitated Ringo's "Merseybeat."

Purdie's claim that he didn't work on all of the Beatles tracks would be correct. There was no overdubbing on *Nobody's Child*, just editing.

Finally, Purdie's statement that he and the guitar player were paid to keep their mouths shut may not be false. We doubt they were paid in "five figures," but consider Atlantic's position. The Beatles were the hottest recording act in the world. Atlantic had purchased four early "Beatles" records and was trying to market them as new material. If its session players made public their stories, implying the Beatles didn't play on their own records, they would have first created a furor around John, Paul, George and Ringo. But you can be sure Brian Epstein and the Beatles' attorneys would have set the record straight. Then all attention would have shifted back to Atlantic Records. Everyone would have known that what Atlantic was selling were not bonafide Beatles records, and that Atlantic had tampered with the original tapes. Atlantic would not only have suffered the loss of sales of its various Beatles singles and albums, the label would also have gained a tainted image in the eyes of all record buyers. After all, if Atlantic was capable of fooling with its Beatles records, the label might be just as guilty of such ploys with its other artists.

However sensational, Purdie's revelations in *Gig* failed to stir up much of a fuss. Ringo chose to ignore Purdie's claims, as did the rest of the media, and they were soon forgotten.

In 1984, Purdie gave a far less detailed version of his story to Max Weinberg in *The Big Beat: Conversations With Rock's Great Drummers* (Chicago: Contemporary Books). Here too, Purdie said that he played on twenty-one early Beatles tracks but again made no mention of the Hamburg material. Weinberg, the commanding drummer with Bruce Springsteen's E Street Band and a former student of Purdie's, simply reported what Purdie had told him and left it to the reader to decide as to the validity of Purdie's tale.

REISSUES

The eight Hamburg tracks have been reissued around the world on singles, EPs and LPs more times than any of the Beatles other recordings. They have also been exploited in every way imaginable. The most distasteful campaign was devised by Polydor Records of Canada in 1969. A rumor was then sweeping the rock world that Paul McCartney had been killed in an automobile accident in

November 1966 and had been replaced in the Beatles by one William Campbell, the supposed winner of a McCartney look-alike contest in England. Polydor reissued the Hamburg cuts on an album titled **Very Together** (Canada: Polydor 242-008). The front cover showed a row of four candles, with only three burning. The snuffed-out candle was supposed to represent the "late" Paul McCartney. The album cover received quite a lot of attention from the press and today is considered a collector's item, but sales of the record were actually quite poor.

By the mid-seventies, as the Hamburg tracks continued to be re-released, many collectors also took an interest in the other Tony Sheridan material recorded in Germany without the Beatles. Most early Hamburg compilation albums included a few of these solo Sheridan cuts as filler. Songs most often used were *Let's Dance, What'd I Say, Ruby Baby* and *Ya Ya*. In fact, there are even recording variations to two of these songs. On **The Savage Young Beatles** (US: Savage BM 69), Tony's spoken introduction on *Ya Ya* was omitted, shortening the track from 2:24 to 2:02, as was his count-off (". . . two, one, two, three . . .") on *Let's Dance*. In the late-seventies, the value of these solo recordings began to increase.

In 1982, Polydor Records in New Zealand issued a two-record set titled **The Beatles' First**. One album was the traditional coupling of Tony Sheridan-Beatles material, while the second disc featured eleven solo Tony Sheridan cuts recorded in 1961-1963. Included were such hard-to-find titles as *Skinny Minny, Save The Last Dance For Me* and *I've Got A Woman*.

At the same time, Polydor in Germany and Japan began releasing singles with a Tony Sheridan-Beatles track on one side and a solo Sheridan cut on the other. One example is *My Bonnie* b/w *Skinny Minny* (Germany: Polydor 2135-501).

Tony Sheridan, who was still living in Germany, started to get annoyed at the number of his early recordings that were being reissued. By this time he no longer earned anything from these tracks, since his contract with Deutsche Grammophon had expired over a decade before. In mid-1962, Dirk Summers, a promoter who tried unsuccessfully to stage a Beatles reunion concert three years earlier, persuaded Sheridan to let him try and negotiate a deal with Polydor Records for some of the money Sheridan felt he deserved.

On August 17, 1982, Summers, who now billed himself as Tony Sheridan's new "manager," held a press conference in Hollywood along with Sheridan's attorneys to announce they had filed a $1 billion fraud suit against Polydor International, many of its subsidiaries and licensees, the three remaining Beatles, and the estate of John Lennon. In "Mailgrams" sent to the news media, Summers promised to unveil "a scandal so shocking in its magnitude that the whole world will be stunned by its duplicity."

What the suit actually contended was that nineteen Tony Sheridan recordings made in Germany with a local backing band during "1960-1961" had later been reissued around the world by Polydor as Beatles records. The suit charged that Sheridan, who Summers referred to as "one of the world's truly great performers," had been denied royalties from these discs as well as public recognition as an artist. Summers also maintained that these Sheridan tracks, including *Ruby Baby, Skinny Minny, Let's Twist Again, Swanee River* and *You Are My Sunshine,* were some of the Beatles' all-time best-selling records.

George Harrison, Paul McCartney, Ringo Starr (who had not yet joined the Beatles when they backed Sheridan on record), and John Lennon's estate were excluded from the damage claims but were still cited in the action because they were central to the case. Sheridan's attorneys felt that Polydor had probably not paid them any royalties either for the records in question. It's a known fact that the Beatles were paid a flat fee to back Sheridan and that they also sold the rights to their own tracks back to Deutsche Grammophon shortly after the session because they weren't satisfied with the results and were more in need of a little spending money.

The list of Polydor affiliates named in the suit were as follows: Polydor International, Phillips-Seaman (sic) Corp., Decca Records, MGM Records, Atco Records, Clarion Records, Vee Jay Records, Brunswick Records, Savage Records, Impact Records, Polydor, Polydor S. A., Lingasong Ltd., Double H. Licensing Corp., K-tel, Deutsche Grammophon Gesellschaft, Swan Records, Metro Records and Belinda Recording Co.

In examining each of these labels, it's interesting to note that several of them never issued any Tony Sheridan material. Vee Jay and Swan were two independent companies that released the Beatles' early EMI recordings in the United States before Capitol Records picked up their option.

Double H. Licensing Corporation owns the worldwide distribution rights to the Beatles' Star Club tape. Lingasong Ltd. released the Star Club material in England but neither company has ever issued any Tony Sheridan tracks.

All of the other labels did release singles or albums by Tony Sheridan, both with and without the Beatles, but most of them gave full credit where it was due. Decca Records in the United States and Canada issued just one Tony Sheridan-Beatles single, *My Bonnie* b/w *The Saints.* The records are highly sought-after collector's items because the labels read "Tony Sheridan and the Beat Brothers," not the Beatles. Credits are also given to Deutsche Grammophon in Germany as the source of these two tracks.

Ad for "The World's Largest Beatle Festival."

MGM Records, and a subsidiary, Metro, also licensed its Tony Sheridan-Beatles material from Deutsche Grammophon and gave full label credit to Sheridan.

Atco and Clarion Records did fail to mention Tony Sheridan as the lead singer on their early mono pressings of several Beatles albums, but this was corrected on the later stereo editions and all material was licensed from Deutsche Grammophon.

The only company that seems liable for prosecution is Savage Records. **The Savage Young Beatles** (US: Savage BM 69) contains eight Tony Sheridan tracks, four with the Beatles and four without. However, the entire album is credited to just the Beatles. There is a small mention of "T. Sheridan" (sic) in the liner notes and on the front cover, but there is no differentiation made as to which material was recorded with the Beatles and which was not. Also, Savage Records appears to have released these tracks without the authorization of Deutsche Grammophon.

At the end of the press conference, Dirk Summers was asked why Tony Sheridan had waited twenty years before trying to straighten out this matter. Summers claimed they had tried to negotiate an out-of-court settlement with Polydor but the talks fell through so they were forced to file suit. Polydor denied any knowledge of the talks, or of the reissues in question.

The real reason for filing suit at this time seems to have been to publicize "The World's Largest Beatle Festival," a Beatles fan convention Summers was promoting eleven days later at the Hollywood Palladium. Not coincidentally, Tony Sheridan was scheduled to perform. Summers listed himself as "host" and "the first Beatle producer" in the preliminary press hand-outs for this event.

POSTSCRIPT

On June 22, 1980, Bert Kaempfert died of a stroke at his vacation home in Majorca. He was fifty-six.

Kaempfert, who began playing piano at age six, achieved international acclaim as a composer and arranger with his hits *Wonderland By Night, Spanish Eyes* and *Strangers In The Night*. He referred to his soft, big-band style as "music" that doesn't disturb you." *Spanish Eyes*, as sung by Al Martino, and *Strangers In The Night* by Frank Sinatra, sold more than 10 million records worldwide.

After producing the Beatles' first commercial recordings in June 1961, Kaempfert didn't see the group again until June 26, 1966 at a backstage party between their two, sold-out performances at Hamburg's Ernst Merck Halle.

Kaempfert is survived by his wife, Hanne, and two daughters, Marion and Doris.

The Beatles Live! At The Star-Club
In Hamburg, Germany; 1962
Germany: Bellaphon BLS-5560 (LP)

2

The
Star Club Tape

On December 18, 1962, the Beatles (now John, Paul, George and Ringo) began their fifth and final engagement in Hamburg's St. Pauli district. For the next two weeks, the group performed at the Star Club, the best of all the beat establishments along Grosse Freiheit (a street made up of beer joints, porno movie theaters, cheap restaurants and transvestite bars). Since its opening eleven months earlier, the Star Club had presented such legendary American rock 'n' rollers as Fats Domino, Jerry Lee Lewis (who later cut a "live" album there) and Gene Vincent.

But had it been possible, the Beatles would've cancelled this booking. *Love Me Do* (UK: Parlophone R 4949), their debut single on Parlophone Records, was slowly climbing up the British charts. The group felt to leave England now and not be able to promote their disc could spell disaster for them as a recording act. Unfortunately, their agreement with Manfred Weissleder, the owner of the Star Club, had been made in April, one month before Parlophone signed them. Even so, manager Brian Epstein was supposedly paid 1,000 marks under the table to guarantee the band's appearance.

The Beatles certainly regarded their return to the seamier side of Hamburg as a step backward in their career. Their physical appearance and stage manner had changed considerably since their early stints at the Indra, the Kaiserkeller and the Top Ten Club. Gone were the black leather jackets and cowboy boots, plus the swearing, smoking and mock fighting that had first brought them to the attention of the German rockers. The group now wore matching suits, neatly trimmed "Beatle" haircuts and, at the insistence of Brian Epstein, eschewed all food and drink while on stage. Another reason the Beatles resented this holiday engagement was that, for the first time in their lives, they'd be separated from their relatives during Christmas and New Year's.

To make matters worse, the Beatles weren't even top of the bill for most of this run. An American instrumental group, Johnny and the

Hurricanes (*Red River Rock*) were the headliners. (In 1965, Hurricanes' leader Johnny Paris formed his own record label, Atila, and issued an album of his group, **Live At The Star Club**.)

For three nights, the Beatles were elevated to the main attraction, sharing the stage with two other Liverpool bands, "Kingsize" Taylor and the Dominoes, and Cliff Bennett and the Rebel Rousers. (In July 1966, Paul McCartney produced the Rebel Rousers' recording of the Beatles' *Got To Get You Into My Life*, which became a hit single in Britain.)

"Kingsize" Taylor and the Dominoes were a rhythm and blues band led by the burly Ted Taylor, a butcher's apprentice. During their Star Club sets, Taylor made a private tape of his group, along with the Rebel Rousers and the Beatles. The recording was produced from the audience using a single handheld microphone. The sound quality was rough at best since Taylor's portable Grundig tape machine could only run at 3 3/4 inches per second.

The Beatles were recorded all three nights. Their performance was loose and lacking in spirit but under the circumstances that was to be expected. Below is the complete track listing of the Beatles' portion of the tape, as first reported in *Melody Maker* in July 1973:

> *Be-Bop-A-Lula* (vocal by Star Club bouncer Horst Fascher)/*I Saw Her Standing There/Hallelujah! I Love Her So* (vocal by Horst Fascher)/*My Girl Is Red Hot/Sheila/ Kansas City/Shimmy Shake/Red Sails In The Sunset/Ain't Nothing Shakin' (Like The Leaves On A Tree)/Little Queenie/Long Tall Sally/Till There Was You/A Taste Of Honey/Falling In Love Again/I Remember You/Ask Me Why/Your Feet's Too Big/Besame Mucho/To Know Her Is To Love Her* (two versions)/*Roll Over Beethoven/Everybody's Trying To Be My Baby/Sweet Little Sixteen/I'm Gonna Sit Right Down And Cry Over You/Talkin' 'Bout You/Mr. Moonlight/Matchbox/Roll Over Beethoven* (second version).

After returning from Hamburg in January 1963, Ted Taylor supposedly took his tape to a recording engineer in Liverpool to see if it could be brought up to commercial standards for some sort of release. Taylor claimed he'd obtained the rights to the Beatles' performance "for the price of a few drinks." (In fact, Taylor didn't possess legal ownership due to the Beatles' contract with Parlophone Records, but this will be examined in detail later.) In early 1963, Taylor offered the raw recording to Brian Epstein, but Brian saw no commercial value in the tape and was only prepared to pay £20 (about $48) for it. Taylor turned down Epstein's bid, took the tape home and stuck it away in a kitchen cabinet where it remained for ten years.

STAR CLUB TAPE RE-DISCOVERED

The existence of the Star Club recording was all but forgotten until the early 1970s, but there's a dispute as to how the tape resurfaced. A July 13, 1973, UPI story headlined "Butcher May Have Fortune In Beatles Tape," reported that Ted Taylor, by now a self-employed neighborhood butcher in Liverpool, had found the legendary recording while cleaning out a cupboard in his house.

"I was thinking about this rock 'n' roll revival going on. Suddenly [I] remembered I had this tape from the old days and I reckoned it must be worth something," said Taylor.

However, in 1975, Allan Williams, the Beatles' first manager, offered a more sensational account of how *he* relocated the recording. In Williams's version, Ted Taylor was supposed to have left the tape with the Liverpool engineer he took it to in January 1963. Williams contended that in 1972, by mere chance, he ran into this unnamed technician who told him the Star Club recording might still be sitting in his long-vacated office. According to Williams, the engineer, Taylor, and he met one afternoon for a drink, then went over to the "derelict office" and, while digging through the debris, uncovered the tape.

Whichever story you choose to believe, Williams and Taylor then became partners and prepared to approach Apple Records about purchasing and releasing the recording. Taylor was hoping to get $250,000 in advance plus a percentage of the royalties, but it was acknowledged at the time that the four Beatles would have to give their consent before the tape could be issued.

It wasn't until 1975 that Allan Williams actually spoke with George Harrison and Ringo Starr about persuading Apple to buy the recording. In the meantime, Williams had teamed with *Daily Mirror* reporter and long-time friend William Marshall to write a book about his experiences with the Beatles, titled *The Man Who Gave The Beatles Away* (New York: Macmillan, 1975). Williams was looking to earn a small fortune from the sales of the book and the tape. In fact, Williams's meeting with George and Ringo became the book's final chapter. The two ex-Beatles turned down his offer of the recording although they both requested copies for themselves. Apple was all but closed down by now and the remaining lawyers and accountants certainly didn't want to get embroiled in the legalities of releasing this long-forgotten tape.

News of the Star Club recording disappeared until Allan Williams's book was published and he began making personal appearances to

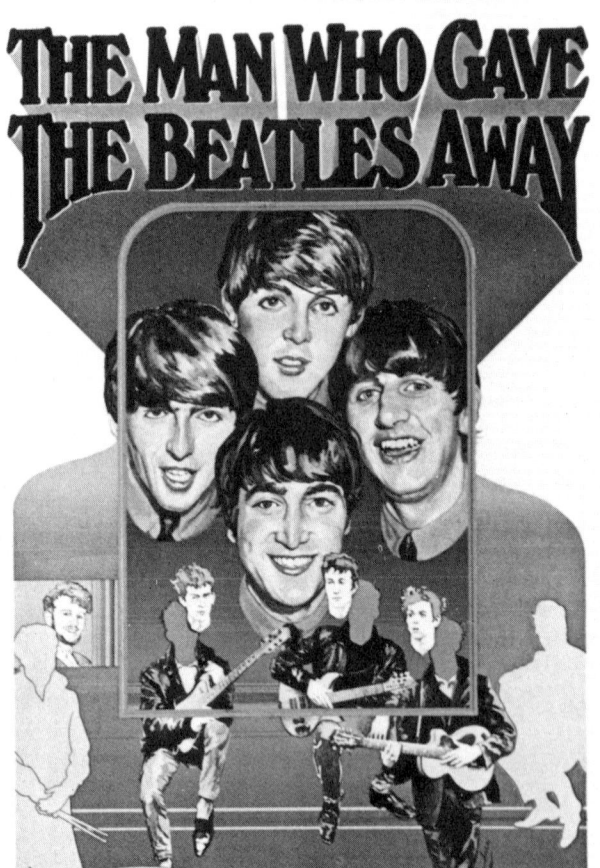

THE MAN WHO GAVE
THE BEATLES AWAY

ALLAN WILLIAMS AND WILLIAM MARSHALL

THE HARD DAYS AND VIOLENT NIGHTS THAT
BEGAN THEIR METEORIC RISE-"THE ONLY BOOK THAT CAN GIVE
EYEWITNESS INSIGHT INTO THE MAKING OF THE BEATLES"
-JOHN LENNON

with 52 pages of photos

Ballantine/Nonfiction 🄱🄱 27074 $1.95

Cover of *The Man Who Gave The Beatles Away.*

promote it. On February 6, 1976, Williams was the featured guest at the Southport Arts Centre in London, speaking in one of its "Rockumentary" series events aptly titled "The Man Who Gave The Beatles Away." Besides discussing the group's early career and autographing copies of his book, Williams screened two early television specials about Liverpool beat music, "And The World Listened" and "The Mersey Sound" (BBC-TV, 1963), and played portions of the Star Club tape.

Williams continued to look for a buyer for the recording. He even travelled to Holland where he tried to make a deal with a European bootlegger and later a Dutch pornographer, but again with no luck.

In March 1976, Williams and Taylor finally sold the Star Club recording to Paul Murphy, managing director of Lingasong Records in England, for an undisclosed sum. Murphy then tried to market the tape to Apple and EMI Records, but was also unsuccessful.

Murphy next attempted to use public opinion to force some record company into buying the recording. In a statement to the press, Murphy threatened to cut the tape up into tiny pieces, seal the pieces in plastic and sell them as souvenir key rings. In the April 24 issue of *New Musical Express*, Murphy said this seemed to be the only way for him to realize any commercial benefit from the tape as long as it couldn't be issued or sold.

Following this announcement, Allan Williams and Ted Taylor, who still claimed part ownership of the tape, filed an injunction to prevent it from being destroyed. One point that was never made clear was whether Murphy intended to cut up the original master tape or his own, two-inch, sixteen-track copy.

On August 28, the first British Beatles fan convention was held at St. Andrews Hall in Norwich with over 2,000 people attending. As part of the festivities, Allan Williams appeared and played some of the Star Club tape.

In the fall of 1976, Paul Murphy sold the worldwide distribution rights of the Star Club recording to Double H Licensing Corporation in New York. With the impending commercial release of this material, a dispute arose over the tape's true owner.

Allan Williams contended that Ted Taylor had recorded the Beatles' shows between Christmas 1961 and New Year's Day 1962 while the group was under contract to Deutsche Grammophon Records. In order to guarantee full, legal ownership of the Star Club tape, Double H Licensing announced it had purchased the Beatles' original Deutsche Grammophon agreement. This seems highly unlikely, though, since the group's German contract expired in mid-1962, at which time all of their recordings, both those made alone and backing Tony Sheridan, became the full property of Deutsche Grammophon.

A major point Williams and Murphy also failed to check was that the Star Club didn't open for business until January 1962.

Allan Williams then changed his story and claimed the tape had actually been recorded during the Beatles' April 1962 Star Club engagement, on a night when Ringo Starr (then a member of Rory Storm and the Hurricanes) just happened to be substituting for the Beatles' regular drummer, Pete Best. (Ringo didn't officially join the Beatles until mid-August.)

Saying the recording was made in April 1962 meant that Williams, Taylor and now Paul Murphy were still its legal owners since the Beatles weren't signed by Parlophone until May 9. Supporting this idea, the liner notes on the subsequent albums all implied the tape was recorded no later than early May 1962. On the original German release, English music critic Chris White wrote that the tape had been made during one of the Beatles' early Hamburg engagements but gave no dates. On the Pickwick International reissues, annotator Howard Brinkman said flatly that the tapes were produced during the "Beatles' third stint in Hamburg . . . in April-May 1962." (The Beatles' April-May seven-week season at the Star Club actually marked the group's fourth trip to Germany.)

The Beatles and EMI/Apple correctly maintained the Star Club tape was recorded between Christmas 1962 and New Year's Day 1963, making EMI its true owner.

There are two simple ways to prove this recording was made during the holidays in late 1962. First, it was common practice at the Star Club for members of the audience to send notes up on stage, requesting their favorite songs. On the tape, Paul McCartney reads such a message that begins "very best wishes and *seasonal greetings*" and then asks him to sing *A Taste Of Honey*. John is later heard mumbling "Christmas comes but once a year and when it comes it brings good cheer." Even with the Beatles' off-beat sense of humor, we doubt they'd be making these remarks in the middle of April. And second, one of the songs the Beatles played was *Sheila*, a cover version of the Tommy Roe hit. Roe didn't release his own recording of this song until May 1962, making it impossible for the tape to have been made in April as Allan Williams maintained.

When Double H Licensing formally announced its intent to release the Star Club tape, the Beatles quickly filed suit. Besides contending Double H didn't have the legal right to issue the recording, the group's attorneys were also acting on behalf of EMI Records, which was planning to release its own, official "live" album, **The Beatles At The Hollywood Bowl.** But the British High Court ruled that since the Beatles had already passed up two opportunities to gain possession of the tape and had not expressed any reservations over the issuing of this material until it came into direct competition with its own, Double H did indeed have the legal right to put out the recording. The Beatles appealed, but to no avail.

A SHORT HISTORY OF RELEASES

Lee Halpern, president of Double H Licensing Corporation, hired Larry Grossberg, an independent record producer and engineer, to prepare the Star Club tape for commercial release. An extreme amount of post-production work was necessary to make this primitive recording suitable for sale to the public. Grossberg used New York's Sound Ideas recording studio to do the resulting $100,000 "clean-up" job. The entire tape went through rigorous equalization, remixing, editing and noise reduction. In fact, this largely experimental project turned out to be the most thorough "salvaging" job ever performed on any sound recording to date.

(For a complete rundown on all of the technical methods employed by Grossberg, we recommend an article by Charles Repka in the August 1977 issue of *High Fidelity*, "Resurrecting The Beatles: Star Club To Stereo.")

Several of the songs had to be edited before they could be issued. It turned out Ted Taylor had missed the start of a number of tunes when making his recording. No beginning existed for the Beatles' cover version of the Frank Ifield hit *I Remember You*, so Grossberg restructured the verses and chorus of the song to create an introduction out of the material that was on tape.

Ain't Nothing Shakin' (Like The Leaves On A Tree) was also joined in progress. The track began halfway into the song, at the instrumental break. Grossberg masked this with some crowd noise and between-songs tinkering by the Beatles to make it sound as if they just suddenly launched into the middle of this Eddie Fontaine hit.

Taylor's original tape also contained two takes each of *Roll Over Beethoven* and *To Know Her Is To Love Her*. According to Grossberg, the finished versions of these songs were actually composite tracks produced by editing the best parts of the two takes together.

Before the material was released, the running order of the songs was changed. In album form, the Star Club material was presented as an idealized Beatles concert rather than a chronological recording of several performances. Many of the transitions, stage announcements and crowd noises were put on tape loops, then spliced back into the final record at more appropriate times.

Larry Grossberg took another liberty during post-production. It seems the audience had shown more vocal encouragement for Star Club bouncer Horst Fascher when he joined the Beatles onstage to sing *Be-Bop-A-Lula* and *Hallelujah! I Love Her So*, than it did for John, Paul, George and Ringo. However, for the purposes of this 1977 release, Grossberg equalized the crowd's response to Fascher to that of the Beatles.

(There's an interesting musical note regarding *Be-Bop-A-Lula* involving the two guitar breaks in the song. On the first, George Harrison simply covered the original solo on the Gene Vincent hit. But on the second, he lifted a solo, note-for-note, from *Woman Love*, Vincent's flipside to *Be-Bop-A-Lula*, rather than again copying the record. Since the two songs are similar, the second solo fit in just fine.)

In the first week of April 1977, **The Beatles Live! At The Star-Club In Hamburg, Germany; 1962** was issued in Germany (Bellaphon BLS-5560) as a two-record set. Paul Murphy hadn't yet arranged a U.K. licensing deal and the Beatles were seeking an injunction to block the importing and sale of the album in Britain. But an injunction was ultimately denied and 100,000 copies of the double-LP were flown into England, reaching the stores two weeks ahead of EMI's **The Beatles At The Hollywood Bowl** (UK: Parlophone EMITV 4). With the Star Club set now cleared for U.K. release, Murphy issued the records on his own Lingasong label in England (UK: Lingasong LNL 1) on May 25, 1977, while Double H Licensing Corporation retained the worldwide distribution rights.

Below is the complete track listing of the original German release:

(Side One) *I Saw Her Standing There/Roll Over Beethoven/Hippy Hippy Shake/Sweet Little Sixteen/Lend Me Your Comb/Your Feet's Too Big/*(Side Two)*Twist And Shout/Mr. Moonlight/A Taste Of Honey/Besame Mucho/ Reminiscing/Kansas City/* (Side Three) *Ain't Nothing Shakin' (Like The Leaves On A Tree)/To Know Her Is To Love Her/Little Queenie/Falling In Love Again/Ask Me Why/Be-Bop-A-Lula* (vocal by Star Club bouncer Horst Fascher)/*Hallelujah! I Love Her So* (vocal by Horst Fascher) /(Side Four) *Red Sails In The Sunset/Everybody's Trying To Be My Baby/Matchbox/Talkin' 'Bout You/Shimmy Shake/Long Tall Sally/I Remember You.*

In comparing the track listing of the original Star Club tape with the Bellaphon Records release, the first thing one discovers is the records contain four songs not listed on the tape: *Hippy Hippy Shake, Lend Me Your Comb, Twist And Shout* and *Reminiscing*.

Murphy and Halpern were well aware of the growing Beatles collectors market when they issued the Star Club recordings. Halpern sold the U.S. release rights to Atlantic Records but the double-album wasn't actually put out until June 28, 1977. By that time, most Americans had already purchased the original German set. (Pirated copies of the Bellaphon package, titled **Stars Of '63** — Gamma Alpha Records; also Contraband Music CBM 4749/4750 — surfaced in the United States shortly after the German release.) To guarantee sales of the domestic edition, Halpern issued a slightly different version of the records, containing four previously unreleased tracks: *I'm Gonna Sit Right Down And Cry Over You, Where Have You Been All My Life* (another song not listed on the original tape), *Till There Was You* and *Sheila*. This difference was clearly noted on a brightly colored sticker affixed to the album's front cover.

(*Where Have You Been All My Life* was a hit in April 1962 for Arthur Alexander, one of the Beatles' favorite American rhythm and blues artists. The B-side of Alexander's single on Dot Records was *Soldier Of Love*, a lively song the Beatles performed July 16, 1963 on their BBC Radio series "Pop Go The Beatles," but which they never released on record.)

These four cuts were obviously left off the original German release because of their poor sound quality. Despite $100,000 in enhancement, both *Sheila* and *Till There Was You* were barely audible. *Where Have You Been All My Life* was artificially lengthened by repeating the instrumental break, and *I'm Gonna Sit Right Down And Cry Over You* was completely re-edited. Ted Taylor had apparently caught just the first half of the latter number on tape, so the entire track was played through twice and a final chord was spliced on to give the song an ending.

American collectors had to buy two, double-album packages in order to own all of the commercially released Star Club cuts, yet they were really getting the second set for just four new songs.

Halpern was a little more considerate to German fans. In the winter of 1977, Bellaphon Records compiled a single album of the Star Club tracks, one entitled **Live Im Star-Club 1962** (Germany: Bellaphon BI 15223), designed to appeal to both the serious collector and the casual record buyer. For the collector, the record contained the four songs that had previously been available just in the United States: *I'm Gonna Sit Right Down And Cry Over You, Where Have You Been All My Life, Till There Was You* and *Sheila*. Because of this domestic issue, German collectors didn't have to pay exorbitant prices to obtain these four tracks on an American import.

For the casual record buyer, this album was marketed through television with the emphasis on the remainder of the cuts, all familiar Beatles titles later made world famous by the group on EMI Records: *Twist And Shout, Roll Over Beethoven, Ask Me Why, Long Tall Sally, I Saw Her Standing There, A Taste of Honey,* and *Mr.*

LINGASONG
Records

Campbell
Connelly
& Co. Ltd.

Electronically
Reprocessed

NB 1
(LNL 1)
NB 1 B
℗1977
Lingasong
Limited

FALLING IN LOVE AGAIN
(Hollander, Connelly)
THE BEATLES

Falling In Love Again
UK: Lingasong NB 1 (45)

Moonlight. The only song on the album that didn't fit into either category was Chuck Berry's *Sweet Little Sixteen*.

The release of the Star Club recordings was welcomed by collectors everywhere. Here for the first time since 1970 was a wealth of previously unissued Beatles material. Included on the two albums were tracks that wouldn't be recorded by Parlophone for several months, such as *I Saw Her Standing There, A Taste Of Honey,* and *Twist And Shout*. After hearing these excellent renditions, it's no wonder the Beatles took just thirteen hours to put their first album on tape. There were also tracks, *Your Feet's Too Big* for one, that otherwise existed just on demos. And there were even songs most people never knew the Beatles performed, such as Paul's singing *Falling In Love Again*, a tune immortalized by Marlene Dietrich. In fact, the Star Club tape offered the Beatles' only known recordings of *Falling In Love Again* and *I Remember You*.

Chris White's liner notes hailed the music as "raw, vital, and exciting." Even if this wasn't one of the Beatles' better performances or recordings, it did give fans the world over a chance to hear the group in a club setting, not confined to performing the same ten or eleven songs each set, and with the freedom to do or say anything they pleased. Where else could John Lennon be heard changing a line to *Mr. Moonlight* from "Here I am on my knees begging if you please," to "Here I am on my *nose* . . ." and also altering the title of the Joe South/Billy Land song *Shimmy Shake* to *Shitty Shitty*?

Two releases of special interest to collectors are the U.S. promotional copies of the Star Club set (Atlantic/Lingasong 2-7001), pressed on red and blue vinyl, and the only original single, *Twist And Shout* b/w *Falling In Love Again* (UK: Lingasong NB 1).

One song on the Star Club tape that's never been commercially released is *My Girl Is Red Hot*, the Billy Lee Riley number. However, a thirty-second excerpt of this cut, with George singing lead, surfaced on two identical bootlegs, **The Beatles Vs. Don Ho** (US: Melvin Records MM08) and **Silver Lining**.

There were several cuts released from the Star Club tape that weren't included in the original track listing published in *Melody Maker*. There's also at least one song on tape that wasn't listed and has never been issued. It's *Please Please Me*, the Beatles' second single for Parlophone (UK: Parlophone R 4983). The group recorded this Lennon-McCartney number on November 26, 1962, prior to leaving for Hamburg, yet the disc was not issued until January 11, 1963. Since the record's B-side, *Ask Me Why*, another Lennon-McCartney composition, was performed at the Star Club and was included on the Star Club recording, it's safe to assume the Beatles also played *Please Please Me* to test the audiences' reaction to their next single. Because the song was never mentioned as being on the

The Beatles, The Historic First Live Recordings
US: Pickwick PTP-2098 (LP)

Rare Beatles
UK: Phoenix PHX 1011 (LP)

Star Club recording, it was assumed Ted Taylor had simply not captured the number on tape. But a fair quality, unmixed copy of *Please Please Me* from the Star Club, possibly an audience tape made during one of Allan Williams's personal appearances at which he may have played the Star Club master, is circulating among private collectors in Europe.

REISSUES

In 1979, after all the original Star Club records were out-of-print, Pickwick International acquired the tape for release in the United States and Canada. Again, more remixing was done as Pickwick felt the Beatles' vocals were still too weak.

The first Pickwick releases were two single albums; **The Beatles First Live Recordings, Hamburg, Germany 1962 - Volume One** (US: Pickwick SPC-3661) and **Volume Two** (US: Pickwick SPC-3662). In compiling **Volume One**, Pickwick accidentally included a "Kingsize" Taylor and the Dominoes track off the original tape, *Hully Gully,* the Olympics' hit. No mention was made in either the liner notes or on the record label that this cut was not by the Beatles. In 1980, Pickwick reissued these two volumes in one two-record set, **The Beatles, The Historic First Live Recordings** (US: Pickwick PTP-2098).

Pickwick resequenced the songs for its own packages and chose to focus just on the music. In doing so, the individual tracks were faded in and out, eliminating many of the off-the-cuff remarks and much of the by-play between the Beatles and the audience. Two bits that were left off the Pickwick albums were John reciting the original rhyming words to the first line of *I Saw Her Standing There* ("She was just *seventeen*; teenage *queen* . . . You know what I *mean*"), and Paul greeting "Tony ('My Bonnie') Sheridan" who happened to be in the audience with "a *flash* of whiskey."

"Give us a *flash*," said John as the Beatles launched into Carl Perkins's *Matchbox*, with John, not Ringo, singing lead.

In 1981, Audiofidelity Enterprises Limited in London acquired the Star Club tape for European release. Rather than following Pickwick's running order, the original German Bellaphon set was used as a guide. Audiofidelity also mixed the tape back to its original mono state and kept all the between-songs patter. In fact, the resulting LPs were unbanded; each side played continuously with no fade-outs between numbers.

On July 17, 1981, Phoenix Records, a subsidiary of Audiofidelity, issued two individual albums of Star Club material: **The Beatles/Early Years 1** (UK: Phoenix PHX 1004) and **The Beatles: Early Years 2** (UK: Phoenix PHX 1005). As mentioned before, the track order of the original Bellaphon release was followed, but included only the first five songs on each side rather than the six or seven cuts that appeared on the German package. The remaining material, plus the four songs not on the original Bellaphon album, were also gathered together but not released until January 22, 1982 on **Rare Beatles** (UK: Phoenix PHX 1011).

The jackets on all three albums were confusing. They featured standard portrait shots of the Beatles taken in 1963 by Dezo Hoffman. No mention was made on any of the front covers that the records consisted of early "live" recordings from the Star Club or that all of the material had been previously issued.

On August 14, 1981, Audiofidelity Enterprises released all thirty Star Club tracks on a two-record set, **The Beatles Historic Sessions** (UK: Audiofidelity AFE LD 1018). On this compilation, Audiofidelity took the basic running order of the first two single albums and tacked back on at least two of the left-over tracks (from **Rare Beatles**) at the beginning and/or end of each side.

Despite having the Bellaphon and Pickwick albums for reference, Audiofidelity made several mistakes in the liner notes. First, Stuart Sutcliffe was listed as a member of the Beatles on these recordings. Stu died of a brain tumor on April 10, 1962 and had quit the group a year before his death. And second, *Reminiscing*, the Buddy Holly number sung by George, was referred to on both the jacket and on the record label as *Can't Help It/Blue Angel*.

One other quirk: Even though Audiofidelity included the jokes and comments between tracks from the original Bellaphon package, John's remarks before the start of *I Saw Her Standing There* were for some reason deleted from this two-record set.

Another interesting packaging of the Star Club material came out in America in the summer of 1982. A company called Collectable Records licensed the Star Club tape and issued the thirty tracks on fifteen singles. Each record came in its own unique picture sleeve, featuring an early black-and-white photo of the Beatles. Below is a complete listing of all the records in the set:

Col	1501	*I'm Gonna Sit Right Down And Cry Over You/ Roll Over Beethoven*
	1502	*Hippy Hippy Shake/Sweet Little Sixteen*
	1503	*Lend Me Your Comb/Your Feet's Too Big*
	1504	*Where Have You Been All My Life/Mr. Moonlight*
	1505	*A Taste Of Honey/Besame Mucho*
	1506	*Till There Was You/Everybody's Trying To Be My Baby*
	1507	*Ain't Nothing Shakin' (Like The Leaves On A Tree)/Kansas City*

1508	*To Know Her Is To Love Her/Little Queenie*
1509	*Falling In Love Again/Sheila*
1510	*Be-Bop-A-Lula/Hallelujah! I Love Her So*
1511	*Red Sails In The Sunset/Matchbox*
1512	*Talkin' 'Bout You/Shimmy Shake*
1513	*Long Tall Sally/I Remember You*
1514	*Ask Me Why/Twist And Shout*
1515	*I Saw Her Standing There/Can't Help It (Blue Angel)**

Finally, for the collector who wants all of the Star Club material (including *Hully Gully* by "Kingsize" Taylor and the Dominoes), in the best available sound quality and the sturdiest packaging, we recommend **Rare Beatles: Live At The Star-Club, Hamburg '62** (Japan: Trio Records AW-20003/4). This limited edition, two-record set was pressed on green virgin vinyl and came with a complete lyric sheet in both Japanese and English. Only 10,000 copies were made.

Since the copyright on the Star Club tape is held exclusively by Double H Licensing Corporation, you can bet these recordings will continue to be remixed, resequenced and offered to the public as long as there are still Beatles fans around. These thirty tracks may someday rival the Tony Sheridan material for having been reissued so many times. In fact, in early 1983, a compilation was issued in Italy titled **La Grande Storia Del Rock: Birth Of The Beatles** (Curcio: Volume 46). It consisted of eight Tony Sheridan-Beatles tracks and eight cuts from the Star Club tape.

---

* actually *Reminiscing.*

Red Sails In The Sunset/Matchbox
US: Collectable Col 1511 (45)

Ob-La-Di, Ob-La-Da/While My Guitar Gently Weeps
Japan: Apple AR-2207 (45)

One of two singles pulled from the "White Album" in 1968. This
Japanese pressing was issued in stereo on red vinyl.

3

The
White Album

On November 22, 1968, Apple Records in England released **The Beatles** (Apple-mono PMC 7067/8; stereo PCS 7067/8). The album merits a special place in the annals of rock 'n' roll for a number of reasons. First, it marked the only time the group issued two full records of new material. In fact, **The Beatles** stands as the first all-new double-album put out by anyone in rock music. It was also the band's first long player for their newly-formed Apple label.

The "White Album," as it soon became known because of its stark white jacket, consists of thirty songs, most of which were written in the spring while the Beatles attended the Maharishi Mahesh Yogi's Academy of Meditation in Rishikesh, India. Work on the record began the night of May 30 at EMI's Abbey Road studios in London with the first take of *Revolution* #1, John's entry into the political arena, and ended early on the morning of October 14 with the completion of *Julia*, Lennon's "song of love" to both his late mother and his new "ocean child," Yoko Ono.

Reviewers gave the album instant, almost universal praise. Tony Palmer of London's *Observer* hailed Lennon and McCartney as "the greatest songwriters since Schubert," while *Rolling Stone's* Jann Wenner felt the record represented nothing less than "the history and synthesis of Western music." Looking back, critics seem to have been awed by the diversity the Beatles displayed. In all the excitement, they failed to recognize that the group had grown apart.

The Beatles were no longer just musicians, they were now also businessmen in charge of a small but complex company, Apple Corps, Ltd. After Brian Epstein's death in August 1967, no one else was appointed to take care of the multitude of details in the group's day-to-day affairs. Recording sessions for the White Album were often interrupted so one or more of the band could confer with their lawyers.

Personal problems also hindered the Beatles' work. Paul could no longer collaborate with John in the same way he had in the past;

Yoko was now forever at John's side. As a result, some of Paul's music sounded overly sentimental, lacking the bite John used to give it. Conversely, John's songs were now rougher, without the polish Paul so often added.

The world failed to hear the White Album as it really was, more a collection of solo tracks than a group effort. Paul recorded *Wild Honey Pie, Blackbird, Why Don't We Do It In The Road* and *Mother Nature's Son* entirely on his own, playing all the instruments on each cut. John spent time with Yoko working on their avant-garde, electronic collage *Revolution #9*, and George brought in Eric Clapton from Cream to play lead guitar on *While My Guitar Gently Weeps*. On the other songs, the Beatles acted as sidemen for each other. Ringo, bored by the proceedings and annoyed at Paul's penchant for retakes, walked out of the sessions on August 16 after telling John and Paul he was quitting the group. Paul ended up playing drums on *Back In The U.S.S.R.*

This was also the first Beatles album not recorded entirely at Abbey Road. *Dear Prudence, Martha My Dear, Honey Pie* and *Savoy Truffle* were all cut at London's Trident Studios.

With over thirty tracks "in the can," producer George Martin tried hard to persuade the Beatles to pick the best twelve or fourteen songs and put out a strong single album. But the group was adamant about wanting to release a two-record set. Many suspected the only reason they gave EMI a double-album was to lessen their obligations to the label. By delivering two records, they needed to make only one more LP to fulfill their contract.

Despite the uneven quality of certain cuts, there's no mistaking the White Album for anything but an excellent rock LP. The Beatles' playing was tight, their singing strong and the production crisp and innovative. More importantly, the public loved it. Demand for the record was phenomenal. In America alone, the album shipped gold, making it the Beatles' fastest-selling LP to date. After the grandeur of **Sgt. Pepper's Lonely Hearts Club Band** and the still psychedelic **Magical Mystery Tour**, everyone was waiting to see what the Beatles would do next. The wide array of styles seemed to please all.

The White Album's packaging also caught the public's fancy. In sharp contrast to the intricate and colorful **Sgt. Pepper** cover, **The Beatles** was issued in a pure white sleeve with just the word "Beatles" embossed, slightly off-center, in the lower right-hand corner. Accompanying the discs were 8" x 11½" color portrait photos of John, Paul, George and Ringo, and a poster with lyrics to the songs on one side and a collage of Beatles pictures on the other. Each of the first two million copies also bore its own serial number, similar to a limited edition art work.

The album was unique in other ways as well. The two discs were unbanded, with many of the songs linked together. The Beatles experimented with this technique on **Sgt. Pepper's Lonely Hearts Club Band**, but used it to a much greater advantage here. There were also no singles culled from the LP in either Britain or the United States, the two markets the Beatles had some control over. At just under ninety-four minutes, the group clearly intended the music to be taken as a whole.

(EMI did pull two singles for release in other countries. *Ob-La-Di, Ob-La-Da* b/w *While My Guitar Gently Weeps* was issued in Australia, France, Germany and Japan, while *Back In The U.S.S.R.* b/w *Don't Pass Me By* was put out in Sweden.)

The White Album was released at a transitional period in the history of the recording industry. In America, the major labels were pushing to eliminate monaural records entirely and press only in stereo. The companies cited increasing sales of stereo discs and a dramatic drop in price for good stereo components following the introduction of new, solid-state systems from Japan. Now that rock 'n' roll was firmly established as the dominant force in the record business, and young adults, already the largest consumer group in the country, were becoming the primary buyers of new stereo equipment, mono records were looked upon as dinosaurs in the marketplace.

However, with millions of mono turntables still in use, a method had to be found so stereo records could be played on mono systems. The industry certainly could not afford to alienate all those record buyers who were still perfectly happy with their mono equipment. Columbia Records came up with a solution in a new mode of manufacturing it called "Compatible Stereo." Columbia engineers were able to modify stereo pressings so the larger mono stylus would not ruin the twin grooves on a stereo disc. Soon, all the major labels adopted this format.

The White Album was the first Beatles LP to be issued in the United States only in stereo. Other countries were much slower in phasing out mono records. Some never did. In England, mono players continued to outnumber the more expensive stereo units by a sizable margin. The White Album and **Yellow Submarine** were still mixed and pressed in both mono and stereo there. As with most other British records, the first pressing of the White Album was in mono. Several weeks passed before EMI's plants began stamping out the stereo version.

Beatles fans in England were in for a surprise when the stereo copies went on sale. Not only were most of the tracks mixed a little differently, but one song contained an alternate instrumental break while another had been restructured and expanded. Subscribers to *The Beatles Book*, the group's official monthly publication, sent in quite a few letters comparing the two editions.

There has never been any explanation from the Beatles or anyone at EMI/Apple as to why two different versions of the White Album were issued. Both mixes originated from the same basic recordings. On closer examination, it's possible the mono version was nothing more than a rough copy that was never intended for release, yet came out just the same. In June 1966, Capitol Records in the United States received advance mono mixes from EMI of *And Your Bird Can Sing, Dr. Robert* and *I'm Only Sleeping*, which it went ahead and issued on both the mono and stereo pressings of **"Yesterday"** . . . **And Today** (Capitol S/T 2553). Only the later Capitol Record Club edition of this album contained the true stereo versions of these songs, first issued in England in August on **Revolver** (UK: Parlophone PCS 7009).

The overall sound quality of the mono mix also suggests it was nothing more than a rough dub. The sonic range is very limited in comparison to the stereo version, and to the Beatles' previous albums. The bass is booming but hollow, and the top-end treble is non-existent. The cutting crew at EMI had a reputation for delivering clean, clear masters; this wasn't one of them.

The mono mix may almost have been issued in the United States in place of the stereo version. In October-November 1968, George Harrison was in Los Angeles with his Apple Records' protege Jackie Lomax, producing some sessions at Sound Recorders in Hollywood. While there, he received a call from Capitol Records asking if he wanted to check a test pressing of **The Beatles** before it was manufactured. George listened to the two records and found the sound was all wrong. He then borrowed Capitol's master tapes and spent the next two days in the studio remixing the American (stereo only) edition of the White Album (Apple SWBO 101).

Despite having four sides of vinyl to fill, at least two tracks from the White Album were shelved: John's chaotic *What A Shame Mary Jane Had A Pain At The Party* and George's *Not Guilty*, recorded with Eric Clapton. Both tracks were re-recorded in March 1969 at the Apple studios in London. John re-did his song with just George and Yoko, extending the original cut from 6:35 to 7:04. Under a revised title, *What's The New Mary Jane*, it was scheduled for release as a Plastic Ono Band single on December 5, 1969 (UK: Apple 1002), backed with another unissued Beatles number, *You Know My Name*. At the last minute, the single was withdrawn. (In 1981, both versions of *Mary Jane* surfaced, in true stereo, on an excellent quality, albeit bootleg, 12-inch single – A 8028). *You Know My Name (Look Up The Number)*, a satirical piece inspired by the Bonzo Dog Doo Dah Band whom the Beatles worked with in their 1967 television special "Magical Mystery Tour," came out in March 1970 as the B-side of the Beatles' *Let It Be*.

(On September 1, 1983, an original acetate of *What's The New Mary Jane* b/w *You Know My Name* on the Apple Custom Recording label was put up for auction at Sotheby's in London where it sold for £200, or about $320.)

George's *Not Guilty* gained quite a reputation among collectors. So great was the interest in this unreleased track that in 1978, bootleggers included a cut they called *Not Guilty* on **Indian Rope Trick** (Fan Records). Unfortunately, it turned out to be *Frenzy And Distortion*, a Ravi Shankar recording taken from his 1971 **Raga** soundtrack LP on Apple Records. George finally laid to rest the mystery of this number when he updated the arrangement and recorded the song a third time for his 1979 solo album, titled simply **George Harrison**.

DIFFERENCES

Side One

Back In The U.S.S.R. (Lennon-McCartney)
The mono and stereo versions differ in a number of ways. First the jet airplane sounds at the beginning and end of the track come in at different times. Paul's piano also has a solid, more forceful feel in mono.

After the opening jet roar, there's a quick yell just before George's lead guitar enters that can be heard only in the mono version. The three rhythm guitar chords preceding George's solo are not present in the mono mix nor are the shouts and short piano fills in the instrumental break.

Finally, the closing jet sounds that link this song with *Dear Prudence* are two seconds longer in mono. As the track fades out, there's a bass drum beat in the mono version that's inaudible in stereo.

The mono version was also issued as a single in Sweden (Apple SD 6061).

In the spring of 1976, producer George Martin remixed a stereo version of *Back In The U.S.S.R.* at the Capitol Records studio in Hollywood for the double-album compilation **Rock 'N' Roll Music** (US: Capitol SKBO 11537); the U.K. edition (Parlophone PCSP 719) bore the original stereo track.

In Australia, the remixed version was first released as a single (Parlophone R 6016) to help promote EMI's new collection of Beatles rockers. *Back In The U.S.S.R.* was also issued as a single in Britain (Parlophone R 6016), but again, the original stereo mix was used.

In October 1980, the remixed track was finally issued in England (and reissued in the United States) on the single album **Rock 'N' Roll Music — Volume 2**. (See **Rock 'N' Roll Music**, p. 210.)

Dear Prudence (Lennon-McCartney)
A slightly edited version was issued on the American open-reel tape edition of **The Beatles** (Apple Y2WB 101).

Glass Onion (Lennon-McCartney)
During the song's "middle eight," John repeats the words "oh yeah" three times before singing the hook line, "Looking through a glass onion." In the stereo version, John sings the first two "oh yeahs" alone, then on the third one, Paul screams "oh yeah" in the background. In mono, Paul's backup vocal was omitted.

The entire verse that begins, "I told you about the walrus and me - man," including the line "The walrus was Paul," was cut from the American open-reel tape edition of **The Beatles** (Apple Y2WB 101).

Ob-La-Di, Ob-La-Da (Lennon-McCartney)
The opening six handclaps are not present in the mono mix. This version was also issued as a single in Australia (Apple A-8693) and in the West Indies (Parlophone Records).

Wild Honey Pie (Lennon-McCartney)
In the stereo version, Paul's falsetto singing is slightly louder than John's accompanying vocal. In mono, the mix is reversed.

The Continuing Story Of Bungalow Bill (Lennon-McCartney)
This song was reissued on **The Beatles 1967-1970** minus the opening guitar obbligato. (See **"Rarities** ... And Box Sets," p. 83.)

While My Guitar Gently Weeps (Harrison)
In the mono version, Eric Clapton's lead guitar remains mixed forward after his solo rather than blending back into the instrumental track as it does in stereo.

The fade-out in the mono mix is also three seconds longer than in stereo and George's "yeah, yeah, yeah" near the close of the fade-out was omitted. This version was also issued as a single in Australia (Apple A-8693).

Happiness Is A Warm Gun (Lennon-McCartney)
There's some tapping in the background of the mono version that starts at the beginning of the song and continues until the lyric,

"She's well acquainted with the touch . . . ," where Ringo's drums come in. In stereo, the tapping disappears four beats earlier.

Paul's bass is mixed way up in mono, beginning with the words, "I need a fix cause I'm going down . . . "

After the closing line, "Happiness is a warm gun, yeah," but before Ringo's final drum beat, there's some background laughter in the mono mix that's inaudible in stereo.

That final drum beat from Ringo was omitted from the Italian pressing of **The Beatles** (Apple Records).

Side Two

Martha My Dear (Lennon-McCartney)
No differences.

I'm So Tired (Lennon-McCartney)
The first time John sings the line, "You say I'm putting you on," Paul's vocal harmony on the words "You say" is louder in mono than it is in stereo.

Blackbird (Lennon-McCartney)
The bird sounds in the mono version are different from those in stereo and come in at different times. This is most noticeable at the start of the last verse when Paul's acoustic guitar re-enters.

Piggies (Harrison)
The pig sounds in the mono version are not the same as those heard in stereo; they're louder and come in at different times. George's acoustic guitar is also slightly louder in mono, particularly during the first verse.

Rocky Raccoon (Lennon-McCartney)
No differences.

Don't Pass Me By (Starkey)
The stereo version runs 3:52; the mono version was shortened to 3:44 by speeding up the master tape during playback.

The mono and stereo mixes contain different country fiddle breaks in the fade-out. Also, in the mono mix, the fiddle can be heard throughout the track, while in stereo, it comes forward only for the instrumental break and the fade-out.

The mono version was also issued as a single in Sweden (Apple SD 6061). (See "**Rarities** . . . And Box Sets," p. 71.)

The entire verse that begins, "I'm sorry that I doubted you . . ." was omitted from the American open-reel tape edition of **The**

Beatles (Apple Y2WB 101).

Why Don't We Do It In The Road (Lennon-McCartney)
The mono mix has no handclapping in the introduction. A slightly edited version was issued on the American open-reel tape edition of **The Beatles** (Apple Y2WB 101).

I Will (Lennon-McCartney)
In the stereo version, Paul's bass comes in right at the start of the song but stays well in the background. In mono, the bass doesn't enter until Paul first sings the words "I will," but here, it's right in the center of the track, equal in volume to the acoustic guitar.

Julia (Lennon-McCartney)
No differences.

Side Three

Birthday (Lennon-McCartney)
In the spring of 1976, producer George Martin remixed a stereo version of *Birthday* at the Capitol Records studios in Hollywood for the double-album compilation **Rock 'N' Roll Music** (US: Capitol SKBO 11537); the U.K. edition (Parlophone PCSP 719) bore the original stereo track.

In October 1980, the remixed version was finally issued in England (and reissued in the United States) on the single album **Rock 'N' Roll Music – Volume 2** (see p. 210).

An extremely shortened version of this song was put out on the Italian eight-track tape edition of **Rock 'N' Roll Music** (EMI/Parlophone 3C 344-06138).

Yer Blues (Lennon-McCartney)
In the mono version, Ringo's count-off (" . . . two, three . . .") is louder than in stereo; the fade-out is also eleven seconds longer.

An extremely edited version was issued on the American open-reel tape edition of **The Beatles** (Apple Y2WB 101). From the first verse, the song goes straight into the instrumental break, then fades out.

Mother Nature's Son (Lennon-McCartney)
No differences.

Everybody's Got Something To Hide Except For Me And My Monkey (Lennon-McCartney)
No differences.

Sexy Sadie
West Indies: Parlophone Records (45)

Sexy Sadie (Lennon-McCartney)

At the start of the stereo version, there's some rhythmic tapping that's inaudible in mono; there's also an extra beat of tambourine.

In mono, Paul's bass is mixed out of the opening; it doesn't come in until John first sings the words "Sexy Sadie."

The mono version was also issued as a single in the West Indies (Parlophone Records).

Helter Skelter (Lennon-McCartney)

The stereo version runs 4:29; the mono version was shortened to 3:37. As with *Back In The U.S.S.R.*, there are many differences between the two mixes. Paul's lead vocal is stronger in mono, and John and George's backing vocals have more definition. The first time Paul sings "Look out, cause here she comes," there are loud squeaking noises in the mono mix that can't be heard in stereo. Paul's bass is also more prominent throughout the mono track.

The two versions are similar in structure until the song reaches its false ending. After George's slide guitar riff, the mono version contains a completely different finish. John's fuzz guitar continues and Ringo's drums come back in right away. What follows is a unique twenty-nine seconds of music that leads directly into *Long, Long, Long*. There's no second fade-out, thereby eliminating Ringo's anguished, "I've got blisters on my fingers." (See "**Rarities** . . . And Box Sets," p. 69, 71.)

In the spring of 1976, producer George Martin remixed a stereo version of *Helter Skelter* at the Capitol Records studios in Hollywood for the double-album compilation **Rock 'N' Roll Music** (US: Capitol SKBO 11537); the U.K. edition (Parlophone PCSP 719) bore the original stereo track.

In America, the remixed version was first released as a single (Capitol 4274) to help promote EMI's new collection of Beatles rockers.

In October 1980, the remixed track was finally issued in England (and reissued in the United States) on the single album **Rock 'N' Roll Music – Volume 2**. (See **Rock 'N' Roll Music**, p. 210.)

Long, Long, Long (Harrison)

In the opening line of the song, "It's been a *long*, long, *long* time," there's a slight difference in the vocal mix. In the mono version, George's double-tracked harmony begins the first time he sings the word "long." In stereo, George's back-up vocal doesn't start until the third "long."

George's acoustic guitar is noticeably louder in mono, especially on the final chord of the song.

Side Four

Revolution #1 (Lennon-McCartney)
No differences.

Honey Pie (Lennon-McCartney)
The instrumental break in this song is four bars long. However, in the mono version, the lead guitar continues for four more bars of "fills" not included in the stereo mix.

Savoy Truffle (Harrison)
The song's instrumental break is twelve bars long. In the stereo version, the lead guitar plays for just those twelve bars; in mono, the guitar continues for another four bars, right through a repeat of the chorus.

In the mono mix, there are some strange electronic sounds at the start of the instrumental break that are inaudible in stereo. Also, the electric organ that plays throughout the song was mixed out of the final verse in mono.

Cry Baby Cry (Lennon-McCartney)
No differences.

Revolution #9 (Lennon-McCartney)
No differences.

Good Night (Lennon-McCartney)
The stereo version fades in gradually; the mono version opens at full volume.

REISSUES

The joyous feeling exuded by the Beatles' albums took a gruesome turn in the summer of 1969 with the bloody murders in Los Angeles of actress Sharon Tate and others. Charles Manson, the head of the communal family convicted of the crimes, cited many songs on the White Album, particularly *Helter Skelter* and *Piggies*, as signals to him to commit these horrible killings. In 1976, a made-for-TV movie was produced in the United States about the Manson murders based on prosecutor Vincent Bugliosi's best-selling book, *Helter Skelter* (New York: W. W. Norton & Company, 1974). The Beatles would not grant the use of their records in the film, so sound-alike recordings were made. However, a week before the movie was telecast, Capitol Records supplied radio stations with a specially-pressed, one-sided promotional single of the Beatles' *Helter Skelter*

(US: Capitol P-2720). The song received quite a bit of airplay and the exposure from the film pushed the White Album back onto the American charts, eight years after its release.

In May 1976, Capitol Records issued *Helter Skelter* as the B-side of *Got To Get You Into My Life* (Capitol 4274). It was all part of a renewed interest in the Beatles spurred in part by EMI's successful reissuing of the group's singles in Italy, France and Britain, and a world tour by Paul McCartney and Wings. *Helter Skelter* was put on the B-side to avoid suggestions that Capitol was trying to cash in on the sensation created by the Manson movie. This single was also issued in Japan (Odeon 20050) and Germany (Odeon Records).

In England, EMI's Beatles revival was in full swing. All twenty-two of the Beatles' original Parlophone and Apple singles were re-issued in bright picture sleeves and sold well enough to enter Britain's Top 100. EMI answered with a twenty-third and twenty-fourth single, the latter bearing the unusual coupling of *Back In The U.S.S.R.* and *Twist And Shout* (Parlophone R6016). Sales were good for this one, too, and it was also put out in Germany (Odeon 6176).

In November 1976, Capitol followed up the success of *Helter Skelter* with the release of two more White Album tracks, *Ob-La-Di, Ob-La-Da* b/w *Julia* (Capitol 4347). In keeping with tradition, the single was issued in a plain white sleeve with just the word "Beatles" printed on it, slightly off-center, in the lower right-hand corner. Each single also bore its own serial number.

The White Album continued to figure prominently in EMI's worldwide re-release of Beatles product. In 1978, with colored vinyl the latest fad in record merchandising, EMI put out special copies of **The Beatles** on white vinyl. These limited edition pressings were issued in England (Apple PCS 7067/8), France (Apple 2051), Germany (Apple 1C 072-04.173) and the United States (Capitol SEBX 11841).

In January 1980, collectors discoverd a unique packaging of the White Album from Uruguay (Apple 30504/5). It seems EMI had completely redone the inner artwork. Instead of black-and-white portraits of John, Paul, George and Ringo, the inside jacket was covered with pre-1965 photos of the Beatles. The song titles were also printed in both English and Spanish.

In the fall of 1981, EMI in England reissued the Beatles' first ten albums in mono, all except **A Collection Of Beatles Oldies**. This was followed in 1982 by the release of a special, limited edition box set of all ten LPs. Toshiba-EMI then put out the mono albums on red vinyl, as they were first issued in Japan. (See "**Rarities** . . . And Box Sets," p. 87, and "Back To Mono," p. 115.)

The next significant reissue of the White Album came in February 1982 when Mobile Fidelity Sound Lab of Chatsworth,

California put out a special, half-speed mastered edition of **The Beatles** (MFSL 2-072). (See "Audiophile Records," pp. 94-95.)

Finally, in April 1982, Capitol Records in America issued *Rocky Raccoon* and *Why Don't We Do It In The Road* on a seven-inch promotional flexi-disc (Eva-Tone Soundsheet EV-420828-CST). It was one of three such records put out by Capitol in conjunction with major record retailers including Discount Records and Musicland. The one-sided flexis were designed to acquaint newer record buyers with the extensive Beatles catalog and were given away free to customers who purchased a Beatles album. *Rocky Raccoon* and *Why Don't We Do It In The Road* were pressed on clear plastic with each copy bearing its own serial number. The record came attached to a piece of cardboard featuring a black-and-white photo of the Beatles taken from the back cover of **The Beatles Again/Hey Jude** on the front and pictures of the Beatles' entire Capitol catalog on the back, along with the name of the participating record chain.

Rocky Raccoon/Why Don't We Do It In The Road
US: Eva-Tone Soundsheet 420828-CS (promo flexi-disc single)

優れた音づくりに定評のある東芝EMIでは、世界でも数台しかないカッティング・マシン―ノイマンVMS80―を日本で最初に導入使用するなど、レコード界における最高級の音質・品質を誇っております。

"ビートルズの存在と活躍によって、60年代という時代はことさら華やかに彩られた。"また、"未来の人々に20世紀の様相を端的に伝えるには、ビートルズの『サージェント・ペパーズ』のカセットをタイム・カプセルに容れて海に沈めておくことだ。"などと言われます。

ジョン、ポール、ジョージ、リンゴという、イギリスはリバプール出身の若者達が創り出した音楽と風潮は、かくも大きなインパクトを世界規模で人々に与えたのです。

「イエスタデイ」、「ヘイ・ジュード」、「レット・イット・ビー」など全214曲（公式レコード）のレパートリーの中の多くの部分をいわゆる"名曲"の域にまで高めた、ビートルズの集団による独創性は比類ないものですが、彼等の最大の功績といえば実に簡単、"いい音楽は人種・国を越えて受け入れられ、いい歌は時代を飛び越えて歌い継がれていく。"という人類永遠のテーマを実現させたことです。

変動が不可避のポップスの世界でビートルズは今後も、座標の基軸となって次第に音楽スタイルの原点を形成していくことでしょう。それにしても、ビートルズを同時代・同世代で体験できた僕達は、今思えば幸運でした。

東芝EMI／ビートルズ日本盤プロデューサー
　　　　　　　　　　　　　石坂　敬一

**洒落たインテリアの
特製レコードキャビネットもございます。**

Ad for **The Complete Works of The Beatles** box set.

4

"Rarities" . . . And
Box Sets

Beatles fans have long been familiar with boxed record sets. In May 1970, the first British pressing of **Let It Be** (Apple PXS 1) came boxed with a slick, 160-page book that detailed the shooting of the group's planned television special "Get Back" (later retitled "Let It Be" for theatrical release). This limited edition set was also issued in Australia (Apple PXS 1), Canada (Apple SOAL 6351), Germany (Apple Records), Italy (Apple Records), Japan (Apple AP-9009, with the first pressing on red vinyl), the Philippines and Venezuela.

Seven months earlier, John and Yoko had released their **Wedding Album**, a souvenir in sound and pictures of the couple's March 20th marriage in Gilbraltar and honeymoon "Bed-In" at the Amsterdam Hilton Hotel. A single album was just one part of this elaborate package that included a reprint of their marriage license, a photo of a piece of wedding cake enclosed in a plastic bag, a postcard, a booklet of press clippings of the two events, a strip of pictures of the pair taken in a coin-operated photo booth and more. The entire assemblage came in a solid white cardboard box. The same, full-sized packaging was also used to house both the cassette and the eight-track tape editions of the album.

George Harrison's first two major solo efforts were both issued as box sets. **All Things Must Pass** included a large poster of a mystical-looking Harrison, while **The Concert For Bangla Desh** came with a beautiful, full-color scrapbook of the historic Madison Square Garden shows.

In January 1973, two pirated Beatles box sets appeared in the United States, **Alpha Omega Volumes I & II: The Story Of The Beatles** (Audio Tape Inc. ATRBH 3583). These four-LP collections were advertised on TV and radio stations in the Midwest and were sold by mail order. Instead of taking legal action, Capitol Records countered by putting out two official Beatles anthologies, **The Beatles 1962-1966** (US: Apple SKBO 3403) and **The Beatles 1967-1970** (US: Apple SKBO 3404). However, in March, a $15 million lawsuit was filed by manager Allen Klein on behalf of George

Let It Be
UK: Apple PXS 1 (LP box set)

Harrison, along with Capitol and Apple Records, against the manufacturers and distributors of the bootleg package, and against American Broadcasting Companies, Inc., who had been advertising it.

In this chapter, we'll take a close look at the many Beatles boxes issued in the late 1970s and early 1980s. The success of these handsomely decorated collections led many other rock artists to release their own packages. In 1980, record stores were filled with $75-plus boxed compilations by the Rolling Stones, Elvis Presley, Jimi Hendrix, Cream, the Beach Boys and many others.

BOX SETS

In the first week of November 1978, EMI Records announced plans for a "Beatles Gift Box" to be issued simultaneously in England and America. The package would consist of the Beatles' original twelve British studio albums plus an additional record, **Beatles Rarities**, made up of the singles that hadn't yet been included on their LPs. The thirteen discs, plus a composite poster of the group, would come encased in a durable blue cardboard box.

The American set, titled **The Beatles Collection**, was delivered to record stores in mid-December 1978, just in time for Christmas. This release marked the first time Capitol Records had ever marketed the Beatles' recordings in their original British formats. The package was issued in a numbered, limited edition of 3,000 copies and sold out immediately.

The English version did not reach the shops until January 1979 due to problems at EMI's pressing plants. It was also not released in a limited quantity. In fact, the original set is still available today.

Suggested list price for the U.S. collection was $132.98, making it the most expensive commercial Beatles item to date. The British package carried a slightly cheaper price tag and was subsequently exported to America where it sold for as little as $70.

Because of the success of the British and American box sets, EMI subsidiaries in other countries began releasing their own compilations. Toshiba-EMI of Japan issued **The Beatles Collection**, first in a limited edition blue box set, and two months later in a non-limited, cream-colored box.

Australian Parlophone put together a domestic version of **The Beatles Collection** using the Australian editions of **With The Beatles** (Parlophone PCSO 3045) and **Beatles For Sale** (Parlophone PCSO 3062). Both bear cover art unique to Australia. This set also included **Rarities** and, because it was mastered by Australian Parlophone, *She's A Woman, Komm, Gib Mir Deine Hand* and *This Boy* were all pressed in true stereo. Despite a $120 price tag, this set sold over

25,000 units, placing it squarely in Australia's Top 40.

Since early 1979, more than twenty-five Beatles boxes have been issued worldwide, not including at least five pirated ten-LP sets from Taiwan. There have been box sets of Beatles singles, Beatles EPs and the Beatles' mono LPs. **The Beatles E.P.s Collection** consists of the group's original thirteen British extended-play recordings plus a bonus record of Beatles tracks pressed in true stereo, none of which had been available in England in that form before.

Prerecorded cassettes were also put out in boxed compilations. These tapes were sold in miniature plastic boxes, identical in style to the disc sets. In Japan, a full-size folder accompanied the tapes filled with all of the printed enclosures normally packaged with the records.

Toshiba-EMI outdid EMI's other branches with its Christmas 1981 release of **The Complete Works Of The Beatles**. This overwhelming set consisted of eighty LPs by the Beatles, John Lennon, Paul McCartney, George Harrison and Ringo Starr. Many of the Beatles albums were included in their British, American and German formats. The records came in eight cream-colored slip cases that sat on a two-shelf wooden stand, all part of the 190,900 yen price (about $885). In the fall of 1982, this collection was updated to include the Beatles' **Reel Music** and Paul's **Tug Of War**.

At the end of this chapter is a list of all recent Beatles box sets complete with catalog numbers, track differences, packaging variations and release dates.

RARITIES

As noted earlier, **Rarities** was designed to complement the Beatles' original twelve albums by pulling together many of their single releases not available on British LPs. Unlike Capitol Records in America, British Parlophone rarely duplicated songs issued as singles on later albums.

The British **Rarities** (EMI/Parlophone PSLP 261), consists of seventeen tracks, including such obscure B-sides as *The Inner Light* and *You Know My Name (Look Up The Number)*, along with the original version of *Across The Universe* and the first British release of *Sie Liebt Dich* and *Komm, Gib Mir Deine Hand* (*She Loves You* and *I Want To Hold Your Hand* sung in German). Together, these thirteen albums make up most of the Beatles studio output. However, this set is not complete. One glaring omission is *Hey Jude*, the Beatles' biggest selling single.

The U.S. **Rarities** (Capitol SPRO 8969), compiled in Los Angeles, contains two mistakes. For some unknown reason, *Sie Liebt Dich* and *Komm, Gib Mir Deine Hand* were replaced with the not-too-rare

English versions of *She Loves You* and *I Want To Hold Your Hand*. The album became a much sought-after collector's item not only because just 3,000 copies were pressed, but also because it contained the first American release of the original version of *Across The Universe*.

In England, the excessive publicity given the Beatles box sparked a demand for the commercial release of **Rarities**. British fans wanted the convenience of having most of their Beatles collection together on LPs and also of having *Sie Liebt Dich* and *Komm, Gib Mir Deine Hand* available domestically. Due to the pressure exerted by disc jockeys and the music press, EMI decided to issue the album to the general public. The record sold well, resulting in further releases throughout Europe and in Japan (Odeon 63010).

United Kingdom

October 1979   **RARITIES**   (EMI/Parlophone PCM 1001)

A selection of seventeen tracks not included on the Beatles' original twelve British studio albums.

The cover of this commercial release is different from the one included in the box set.

Research for the LP was done by Mike Heatley, track listings were by Colin Miles and the liner notes were by Hugh Fielder of the British pop weekly, *Sounds*.

The album contains:

(Side One) *Across The Universe* (the original version)/*Yes It Is/ This Boy/The Inner Light/I'll Get You/Thank You Girl/Komm, Gib Mir Deine Hand/You Know My Name (Look Up The Number)/Sie Liebt Dich/* (Side Two) *Rain/She's A Woman/ Matchbox/I Call Your Name/Bad Boy/Slow Down/I'm Down/ Long Tall Sally.*

Track Differences

Most of the tracks on **Rarities** had only been available in England on singles or EPs. To guarantee that the sound and feel of these recordings would be the same as when they were first issued, EMI used the original mono masters.

The liner notes claim *You Know My Name (Look Up The Number)* is pressed in stereo when, in fact, it appears in mono.

Bad Boy was included on **Rarities** even though it had already been released in England on **A Collection Of Beatles Oldies**. In fact, it was the only new song on that 1966 "greatest hits" LP. But since eight of the tracks on **A Collection Of Beatles Oldies** were already available on other British albums, this compilation was not included in the box set.

65

Rarities
UK: EMI/Parlophone PCM 1001 (LP)

Because of the success of **Rarities** in Europe, Capitol Records automatically scheduled this "new Beatles record" for a November 1979 U.S. release and went ahead and pressed promotional copies (Capitol SN-12009, green label). Fortunately for American record buyers, this LP was never put out. Production was stopped and Capitol ordered all existing copies destroyed although a few did make their way into the collectors market. The whole intent of **Rarities** was to bring together tracks that had never been issued on albums before. All but four of the **Rarities** titles were already available on U.S. LPs. To issue **Rarities** in the United States in its original form would have been pointless. Capitol Records had already subjected American record buyers to two horrendous Beatles compilations, **Rock 'N' Roll Music** (US: Capitol SKBO 11537) and **Love Songs** (US: Capitol SKBL 11711). Both collections suffered from an apparent random choice of songs, incorrect liner notes and atrocious cover art.

Congratulations go to Randall Davis, then Director of Merchandising and Advertising at Capitol Records in Hollywood, for vehemently protesting the release of **Rarities** in the United States. Davis believed that issuing this collection would be an insult to American Beatles fans. Because of his strong feelings, Davis was given the job of assembling a true Beatles "Rarities" album for the U.S. market made up of various Beatles takes not available in America. With the aid of several eminent Beatles collectors and understanding executives at various EMI subsidiaries, Davis put together a first-class package, **Rarities** (US: Capitol SHAL 12060).

(For a complete report on the research and creation of the American **Rarities**, we recommend a detailed and extremely informative article, "Every Little Thing: The story behind 'Rarities,' the new Beatles LP," by Nicholas Schaffner, published in the June 1980 issue of *Trouser Press*.)

The American **Rarities** was designed for both the average record buyer and the die-hard Beatles fanatic. For the general public, the LP contained several tracks not otherwise available on Capitol Records: *Misery, There's A Place, Sie Liebt Dich* and the George Martin-produced version of *Across The Universe*. For the collector, the album offered the original version of *Love Me Do* with Ringo on drums, *Penny Lane* with the seven-note trumpet ending, and the mono versions of *Don't Pass Me By* and *Helter Skelter*.

The only fault with this collection is that the compilers, in their zeal to include many rare recordings, actually created several new collector's items. On *I Am The Walrus*, Capitol Records engineers John Palladino and George Irwin combined the British stereo version and its two extra beats in the introduction with the American mono recording containing four extra beats of music after the third verse.

THE BEATLES **RARITIES**

Rarities
US: Capitol SHAL 12060 (LP)

And in pressing *Penny Lane*, Palladino and Irwin spliced the seven-note trumpet coda from the mono promotional version onto the true stereo version of this song, which had never been released in the United States before. (The American **Magical Mystery Tour** contains a "reprocessed" stereo mix.) But all in all, the creation of the American **Rarities** was a highly worthwhile endeavor and we can only hope this record will set the standard for future Beatles reissues by Capitol Records.

United States

March 24, 1980 **RARITIES** (Capitol SHAL 12060)

A selection of fifteen tracks that were either 1) never released by Capitol Records before, 2) alternate takes and mixes never available in the United States before, or 3) tracks never issued on an American album until now.

The LP was compiled and annotated by Randall Davis, with research by Ron Furmanek, one of the foremost Beatles collectors in the world, and Walter J. Podrazik, co-author with Harry Castleman of the definitive Beatles discographies, *All Together Now* (Ann Arbor: Pierian Press, 1978), *The Beatles Again* (Ann Arbor: Pierian Press, 1980) and *The End Of The Beatles?* (Ann Arbor; Pierian Press, 1985).

The packaging is completely different from the promotional **Rarities** included in the American box set. Originally, Davis tried to use the uncropped "Butcher Cover" photo for the front of the sleeve but was vetoed by Capitol vice presidents Rupert Perry and Dennis White. However, the photo was included in the inside of the gate-fold jacket along with the unretouched, second **"Yesterday"** . . . **And Today** cover. On the first pressing, there were two errors in the liner notes. The phrase "I've got blisters on my fingers" heard at the end of *Helter Skelter* was credited to John instead of Ringo. Also the words "produced by George Martin" were inadvertently deleted from the back cover. Both mistakes were corrected on the second pressing.

(On September 1, 1983, a proof copy of the **Rarities** artwork, minus George Martin's name, was put up for auction at Sotheby's in London where it sold for £90, or about $144.)

Track Listing

Side One

Love Me Do — (Version 1) with Ringo on drums. It seems the master of this take has disappeared from EMI's vaults, so

Randall Davis had to settle for an excellent quality dub of the original single, supplied by Ron Furmanek.

Misery — the common recording, but this was the first time the song appeared in stereo on a Capitol album. It was previously available just as a single (Capitol Starline 6065).

There's A Place — same circumstances as *Misery*. Issued by Capitol as a single in October 1965 (Capitol Starline 6061).

Sie Liebt Dich — had only been issued in the United States in 1964 as a single on Swan Records (Swan 4182). This marked the first Capitol Records release, and the first stereo release in America. The liner notes on **Rarities** are incorrect. They say "EMI persuaded (the Beatles) to re-cut the *vocal tracks* of . . . 'I Want To Hold Your Hand' and 'She Loves You' - in German. . . ." when the group actually re-recorded the entire songs, both vocals and backing.

And I Love Her — contains Paul's double-tracked vocals and six bars of acoustic guitar in the fade-out.

Help — the mono single version with a slightly different lead vocal track by John.

I'm Only Sleeping — this is the true stereo version, which in America could only be found on the Capitol Record Club edition of **"Yesterday" . . . And Today**. The liner notes on **Rarities** are in error. They claim only two versions of this track exist when, in fact, we have located five so far. They also state that the verses in this version were rearranged. The differences between the various takes are only in the amount of "backwards guitar" included and in the places where it was cued in. The structure of the song is identical in all recordings.

I Am The Walrus — this is a new, composite version created by Capitol engineers John Palladino and George Irwin. They took the British stereo version with the six-beat introduction and spliced in the four extra beats of music heard after the third verse in the mono recording.

Side Two

Penny Lane — another composite track by Palladino and Irwin.

70

This time, they took the true stereo version, which had never been released in the United States before (the version on the American stereo **Magical Mystery Tour** was "reprocessed"), and added the seven piccolo trumpet notes heard at the end of this song on the U.S. and Canadian promotional singles.

Helter Skelter — the mono mix.

Don't Pass Me By — the mono mix.

The Inner Light — the first time this song had ever been issued on an American album. This is the original mono mix.

Across The Universe — (Version 1); the first time this George Martin-produced version had ever been released in the United States.

You Know My Name (Look Up The Number) — the first time this mono track had ever been included on an album in America.

Sgt. Pepper Inner Groove — the first time these four seconds of Beatles sounds had ever been issued in the United States.

Unfortunately, most EMI subsidiaries passed on releasing this compilation, having already put out one "Rarities" album in their market. This LP was not even issued in England, although it was eventually released in Australia (Parlophone PCSO 7581) and Japan (Odeon 81325). In December 1980, EMI's mail-order division, World Records, issued an eight-album box set in Australia, Japan and the U.K., titled **The Beatles Box**. In it, several American **Rarities** tracks were incorporated, including *Love Me Do* with Ringo, the slightly longer *And I Love Her* and the composite versions of *Penny Lane* and *I Am The Walrus.*

An interesting bootleg album, identical in concept to **Rarities**, surfaced on the American collectors market some seven months prior to Capitol's official release. Titled **The Beatles Collectors Items**, it was remarkably similar in content to Randall Davis's compilation. In fact, the LP even bore a fictitious Capitol Records catalog number (Capitol SPRO 9462) and counterfeit Capitol labels.

This limited edition, sixteen-track record gained quite a reputation among collectors for its surprisingly well-conceived sleeve graphics. The front cover had a beautiful, full-color photo of original Beatles memorabilia including Beatles models, Beatles buttons and Beatles dolls, while the back cover offered concise liner notes on the origin of each track along with black-and-white photos of all the Beatles' previous Capitol albums.

According to the credits, **The Beatles Collectors Items** was compiled by "Richard Ian and Steve Thomas Yanovski," but since this was an illegal record, the names are assumed to be phony. A curious point to consider in speculating about where this pirated album actually came from is the fact that both **The Beatles Collectors Items** and **Rarities** contain footnotes regarding the slightly inferior sound quality of the first track, *Love Me Do* (Version 1) and both LPs include composite versions of *Penny Lane* and *I Am The Walrus*. Since **The Beatles Collectors Items** was available months before **Rarities**, it seems fair to assume that the source of this underground album was either someone with access to the project materials or else that Capitol used the bootleg for reference in compiling **Rarities**.

Below is the complete track listing of **The Beatles Collectors Items**:

(Side One) *Love Me Do* (Version 1 with Ringo)/*Thank You Girl* (mono)/*From Me To You* (mono)/*All My Loving* (stereo with "hi-hat" intro)/*This Boy* (true stereo)/*Sie Liebt Dich* ("reprocessed" stereo)/*I Feel Fine* (the reissued stereo version with whispering)/*She's A Woman* (true stereo)/*Help* (the single version)/*I'm Down* (true stereo)/(Side Two) *Penny Lane* (the composite version)/*Baby You're A Rich Man* (true stereo)/*I Am The Walrus* (the composite version)/*The Inner Light* (single)/*Across The Universe* (Version 1 produced by George Martin)/*You Know My Name (Look Up The Number)* (single).

In September 1979, **The Beatles Collectors Items** was reissued as a limited edition, box set. The box featured the same graphics as the original album while the record was packed in a paper sleeve with the LP's front cover printed on both sides. Also included was a small, color badge with the front cover on it. Only fifty copies were made.

In December 1979, a second and easier to locate pressing of **The Beatles Collectors Items** (Capitol SPRO 9463) came out. For some unknown reason, the manufacturers replaced the true stereo version of *I'm Down* with a purportedly unissued stereo mix of *Paperback Writer*. In the introduction of this version, Ringo's drums are echoed using split-second tape delay. After the intro, the track is identical to the common stereo recording. Even though the liner notes claim this to be a "previously unreleased stereo mix," we doubt it. After-all, every one of the other tracks on this album has been commercially released before somewhere in the world. This just sounds like an

The Beatles Collectors Items
US: Capitol SPRO 9462 (bootleg LP)

Casualties
US: Capitol SEAX 11950 (bootleg LP)

unusual effect the album's compilers accidentally created when taping a copy of *Paperback Writer* with a home cassette deck.

In 1982, **The Beatles Collectors Items** (Capitol SPRO 9463) was reissued in a numbered, limited edition of fifty copies, pressed on blue vinyl.

A second bootleg volume of Beatles "rarities" appeared in October 1980, presumably from the same source. Like **The Beatles Collectors Items**, this illegal album was also made up of takes and mixes of common Beatles songs not otherwise available in the United States.

Titled **Casualties**, this record was first issued as a picture disc and like its predecessor, also sported a fictitious Capitol Records catalog number (SEAX 11950). The front of the record featured the full, uncropped "Butcher Cover" photo Randall Davis had wanted to use as the **Rarities** cover. On the back were the track listings with detailed notes about each song, plus rare black-and-white photos of the Beatles, supposedly from Capitol Records' files.

Of special interest to collectors was the long version of *I'll Cry Instead* (2:06) in true stereo, and a version of *Her Majesty* with Paul's final acoustic guitar chord intact. Both of these tracks come from commercial pressings somewhere in the world but we have not, as yet, been able to pinpoint where they were first released. It should also be noted that the left and right channels on the stereo cuts are reversed and that the sound quality of all fifteen songs is very good.

Below is the complete track listing of **Casualties**:

> (Side One) *Please Please Me* (mono)/*I Want To Hold Your Hand* (true stereo)/*Money* (British mono mix)/*A Hard Day's Night* (true stereo)/*I'll Cry Instead* (long version in true stereo)/ *Ticket To Ride* (true stereo)/*Yes It Is* (mono)/*Day Tripper* (British stereo version)/*I'm Only Sleeping* (mono version from a French EP)/(Side Two) *Strawberry Fields Forever* (true stereo)/ *I Am The Walrus* (basic track before overdubbing)/*Only A Northern Song* (mono)/*Revolution* (single)/*Her Majesty* (last note intact)/*Let It Be* (mono mix for Japan).

Following the LP's initial release as a picture disc, it was re-issued in February 1981 as a conventional album (Capitol SPRO 9469), with the graphics from both sides of the record becoming the front and back covers. In 1982, **Casualties** was again re-released, this time in a numbered, limited edition of fifty copies, pressed on blue vinyl.

In early 1982, Randall Davis and Ron Furmanek were involved in putting together a second Beatles compilation for Capitol Records, **Reel Music** (US: Capitol SV 12199). This selection of movie tunes was originally intended to tie-in with the re-release of the motion picture "A Hard Day's Night" (United Artists, 1964) in Dolby stereo. Although David McMacken's cover received mixed reactions, the enclosed twelve-page "souvenir program," which included reprints of rare Beatles movie posters and lobby cards, was a welcome surprise. But for record collectors, the real bonus was Davis's use of true stereo versions of *A Hard Day's Night, I Should Have Known Better, And I Love Her* and *Can't Buy Me Love.* For a nice change Capitol did not use its own Dave Dexter-remixed versions of these songs. There is no echo, reverb or other "re-processed" stereo effects on these tracks, just rich, clean sound. (In the U.S. and Canada, promotional copies of **Reel Music** were pressed on gold vinyl.)

A WORLDWIDE LIST OF BEATLES BOX SETS

Australia

November 1978 **THE BEATLES COLLECTION**
(EMI/Parlophone BC 13)
The same as the U.K. set except: **With The Beatles** and **Beatles For Sale** were issued in their unique Australian covers.
The records were pressed in Australia with their original labels (orange Australian Parlophone and green Apple). **Rarities** was put out on the EMI label and the back cover said "Sampler Album - Not For Sale." The first 2,000 boxes were imported from England.

Track Differences

Komm, Gib Mir Deine Hand - **Rarities** version was in true stereo.

She's A Woman - **Rarities** version was in true stereo.

This Boy - **Rarities** version was in true stereo.

April 1979 **THE BEATLES COLLECTION**
(EMI/Parlophone BC 13)
The same as the first Australian set except: **Rarities** was now issued on the orange Australian Parlophone label.
Both the records and the boxes were manufactured in Australia. The new box had a lift-off top rather than one that turned down.

early 1980 **THE BEATLES COLLECTION**
(EMI/Parlophone BC 13)

The same as the second Australian set except: the individual album titles were now printed on the back of the box.

In early 1981, this compilation was released on tape as a boxed set of thirteen cassettes. This package bore the same catalog number as the record set.

March 1981 **THE BEATLES BOX**
(World Record Club of Australia)
The same as the U.K. set except: the records were pressed on the orange Australian Parlophone label. This set was sold only by mail.

December 6, 1982 **THE BEATLES SINGLES COLLECTION**
(EMI/Parlophone Records)
(See "It Was Twenty Years Ago Today," p. 124.)

Summer 1983 **SIGHT & SOUND** (EMI/Parlophone Records)
A box set that combined **The Essential Beatles** with the book *The Beatles: In Their Own Words* (London: Flash Books, 1976) by Miles.

China (Nationalist)

The Nationalist Republic of China is not a member of the International Copyright Tribunal, so most records manufactured there are pirated releases. These discs usually have inferior sound quality and are sold in thin paper covers. Song titles are written in Chinese on the record labels but in English on the jackets.

early 1970s **THE BEATLES FROM THE BEGINNING**
(HH 7001-10)
A ten-record set.

early 1970s **THE BEST OF THE BEATLES**
(KM 1006-1-10)
A ten-record set.

early 1970s **THE GREATEST HITS OF THE BEATLES**
(LF 2150-59)
A ten-record set.

late 1970s **THE BEATLES GOLDEN ALBUM**
(Yung Feng Records)
A ten-disc set, with no individual album covers.
The box had the **Let It Be** cover on the front.

The set contained:

1 - **Abbey Road**
2 - **Magical Mystery Tour**
3 - **"Yesterday" . . . And Today**
4 - **The Beatles** (White Album)
5 - **Hey Jude**
6 - **Let It Be**
7 - **Please Please Me**
8 - **With The Beatles**
9 - **Meet The Beatles**

late 1970s **THE BEATLES GOLDEN SPECIAL – VOLUME TWO**
A ten-record set.

France

December 1978 **THE BEATLES COLLECTION**
(EMI/Odeon Records)
The same as the U.K. set except: **A Hard Day's Night** was issued in its original French format as **4 Garcons Dans Le Vent.**
The records were pressed in France with their original labels (Odeon and Apple). **Rarities** was put out on EMI.
The box was four inches thick, larger than any other edition, and the individual album titles were printed on the back. **The Beatles** (White Album) was listed as **Back In The U.S.S.R.**

October 1982 **20 ANS COLLECTIONS** (EMI/Odeon Records)
(See "It Was Twenty Years Ago Today," p. 124.)

Germany

November 1978 **THE BEATLES COLLECTION**
(EMI/Odeon Records)
The same as the U.K. set except: **With The Beatles, Yeah, Yeah, Yeah (A Hard Day's Night), Beatles For Sale** and **Rubber Soul** were issued on the Odeon label; the other albums were put out on Apple. For some unknown reason, **Let It Be** was manufactured in Sweden.

Holland

November 1978 **THE BEATLES COLLECTION** (EMI SBC 13)
The same as the U.K. set except: all records were pressed in Holland and were given new catalog numbers (OC 162-53163/

176). Each copy of **The Beatles** (White Album) was individually numbered, the same as when it was first released.

This package is slightly higher in quality than the original U.K. set.

December 1981 **ROCK 'N' ROLL** (Music For Pleasure 54084)
All records were packaged in their reissue sleeves.

The front of the box had a color painting of the Beatles in concert from the finale of the motion picture "A Hard Day's Night" (United Artists, 1964).

The set contained:

1 - The Beatles **Rock 'N' Roll Music — Volume 1**
2 - The Beatles **Rock 'N' Roll Music — Volume 2**
3 - John Lennon **Rock 'N' Roll**

Japan

June 1979 **THE BEATLES COLLECTION** (Apple 50031-44)
The same as the U.K. set except: all albums were issued on the Apple label. Each record was pressed specifically for this package and was given a new catalog number.

Each LP came with a four-page, illustrated lyric book. Two large posters were also part of the set.

The box set was issued in a numbered, limited edition. In July 1979, Capitol Records in America imported 5,000 copies for sale in the United States.

Summer 1980 **THE BEATLES COLLECTION**
(Odeon EAS 50031-44)
The same as the first Japanese set except: this package was not a limited edition nor was it numbered. The box was also cream-colored instead of blue. The first ten copies came with a special set of four, three-inch mirrors with a picture of a different Beatle on each one.

In early 1981, Toshiba-EMI issued this collection on tape in a miniature blue box set of thirteen state-of-the-art cassettes. Each chromium dioxide tape came sealed and packed in foam rubber. A special folder containing the inserts from the record set accompanied the cassettes. Included were many full color photos of long out-of-print Japanese Beatles pressings.

March 1981 **THE BEATLES BOX** (Odeon EAS 77011-18)
The same as the U.K. set except: this package contained a twenty-page lyric booklet (in both Japanese and English) and a

twelve-page chronology of the group.

In 1981, Toshiba-EMI issued this collection on tape in a miniature "wooden packing crate" box set of eight state-of-the-art cassettes (Toshiba-EMI 2R3-57168). Each chromium dioxide tape came sealed and packed in foam rubber. A special folder containing the inserts from the record set accompianed the cassettes.

Winter 1981   **THE COMPLETE WORKS OF THE BEATLES**
(Toshiba-EMI VMS 80)
A set of eighty albums by the Beatles, John Lennon, John Lennon and Yoko Ono, the Plastic Ono Band, Paul McCartney, Paul and Linda McCartney, Paul McCartney and Wings, Wings, George Harrison and Ringo Starr. The eighty records were housed in eight cream-colored slip cases and could be stored on a two-shelf, wooden stand that came as part of the whole package. In the summer of 1982, this collection was updated to include the Beatles' **Reel Music** and Paul's **Tug Of War**.

July 1982   **THE BEATLES E.P.s COLLECTION**
(EMI/Odeon EAS 30013/26)
The same as the U.K. set except: all fifteen records were pressed on red vinyl as they were originally issued in Japan, and the two-record **Magical Mystery Tour** was in mono instead of stereo.

December 1982   **THE BEATLES SINGLES COLLECTION**
(EMI/Odeon EAS 17311/37)
The same as the U.K. set. (See "It Was Twenty Years Ago Today," p. 125.)

March 1983   **THE BEATLES COLLECTION**
(EMI/Odeon EAS 66010/23)
The same as the second Japanese edition, this box set was reissued to commemorate the twentieth anniversary of the release of the Beatles' first album, **Please Please Me.**

Mexico

November 1983   **THE BEATLES EP COLLECTION**
(Capitol de Mexico Records)
A three-volume set. The records were pressed with their original labels (Capitol de Mexico or Apple) but were given new catalog numbers.
The individual discs came in their own wrap-around picture

sleeves and each volume was packed in a glossy, cardboard box with a full-color photo of the group on the front.

It's possible this was a pirated set put together somewhere in the United States.

New Zealand

Winter 1981 **THE BEATLES COLLECTION**
(EMI/Parlophone Records)
The same as the original Australian set except: **Rarities** was the U.S. box set version with *I Want To Hold Your Hand* and *She Loves You*, not the U.K. version with *Komm, Gib Mir Deine Hand* and *Sie Liebt Dich* found in all other packages.

The box was colored light blue instead of the usual royal blue.

Philippines

November 1978 **THE BEATLES COLLECTION**
(EMI/Parlophone Records)
The same as the U.K. set except: **The Beatles** (White Album) was issued on Parlophone instead of Apple and **Yellow Submarine** was replaced by **Hey Jude**.

Accompanying the records was a poster, songbook, and t-shirt.

Spain

Winter 1977 **THE BEATLES SINGLES COLLECTION 1962-1970: PRESENTACION EXCLUSIVA PARA COLECCIONISTAS** (EMI/Odeon 04144)
A complete collection of the Beatles singles from Spain.
All singles were issued on the Odeon label but were given new, consecutive catalog numbers.

All discs were packed in unique, color picture sleeves.

The singles were encased in a cardboard carrying case with full color pictures of the Beatles on the front and back. Also listed on both sides were the titles of the twenty records.

This set was issued in a numbered, limited edition of 500 copies.

United Kingdom

December 1978 **THE BEATLES COLLECTION**
(EMI/Parlophone BC 13)
A set of the Beatles' twelve British studio albums, plus one

additional record, **Rarities**, of selected tracks, many of which had never been issued on any U.K. LP before.

All albums were pressed on their original labels (EMI/Parlophone or Apple) and with their original catalog numbers.

All records were packaged in their original covers and with their original enclosures (**Sgt. Pepper's** cut-out sheet, **The Beatles** four glossies and one poster.)

The LPs were encased in a blue, textured cardboard box with a fold-open top. The set's title and facsimiles of the Beatles' autographs were embossed on the front of the box in gold lettering.

The set contained:

1 - **Please Please Me**
2 - **With The Beatles**
3 - **A Hard Day's Night**
4 - **Beatles For Sale**
5 - **Help**
6 - **Rubber Soul**
7 - **Revolver**
8 - **Sgt. Pepper's Lonely Hearts Club Band**
9 - **The Beatles** (White Album)
10 - **Yellow Submarine**
11 - **Abbey Road**
12 - **Let It Be**
13 - **Rarities**

Rarities was issued on the EMI/Parlophone label and came in a royal blue cover with the words "Sampler Record - Not For Sale" on the back.

In December 1982, EMI put out a cassette edition of this collection (UK: EMI/Parlophone TCBS 13). The fourteen tapes came packed in a blue plastic, hinged carrying case.

mid-1979   **THE BEATLES COLLECTION: THE BEATLES SINGLES 1962-1978** (World Records)

This set of the Beatles' twenty-five British singles was compiled and sold by World Records, EMI's mail order division. It was never commercially released.

The records were pressed on the EMI/Parlophone label and were packaged in their 1976 reissue picture sleeves.

The singles were encased in a blue, textured cardboard box, identical in style to the Beatles album set. Also included was a four-page booklet detailing the history of the group.

December 1980 **THE BEATLES BOX** (World Records SM 701/8)

This eight-album package was compiled and sold by World Records, EMI's mail order division. It was never commercially released in the United Kingdom.

The set consisted of 124 Beatles tracks arranged chronologically from *Love Me Do*, the group's first Parlophone single, to *Her Majesty*, the final cut on **Abbey Road**.

All albums were issued on the EMI/Parlophone label. The eight individual LPs were untitled. Each cover featured a previously unpublished color photo of the Beatles on the front and extensive liner notes detailing their career during the period represented by the album's songs on the back.

The box was designed to look like a wooden shipping crate, carrying the words "From Liverpool" stenciled in black ink across the top, along with a small snapshot of the Beatles pasted across the front of the crate.

Track Differences

Across The Universe - (Version 2) produced by Phil Spector.

All My Loving - begins with five taps on Ringo's "hi-hat" cymbal.

All You Need Is Love - the mono version.

And I Love Her - contains six bars of acoustic guitar in the fade-out instead of the usual four.

Baby You're A Rich Man - the true stereo version, previously found just on the German **Magical Mystery Tour**.

The Continuing Story Of Bungalow Bill - appears as it does on **The Beatles 1967-1970**, minus the opening guitar obbligato.

The End/Her Majesty - the pause between the two songs lasts for only five seconds. On **Abbey Road**, the time between tracks is fifteen seconds.

Get Back - the album version, produced by Phil Spector.

I'm Only Sleeping - the extremely rare version with the slightly delayed guitar solo, previously found just on the U.S. stereo eight-track tape edition of **"Yesterday"... And Today**.

I Am The Walrus - the composite version put together by Capitol

Records engineers John Palladino and George Irwin for the U.S. commercial **Rarities**.

I Feel Fine - the true stereo version that begins with tapping drum sticks, whispering, coughing and Ringo closing his "hi-hat" **cymbal**.

Let It Be - (Version 2) "reproduced for disc" by Phil Spector.

Love Me Do - (Version 1) the rare one with Ringo on drums.

Penny Lane - the composite version from the U.S. commercial **Rarities**.

She's A Woman - the true stereo version previously available just in Australia and in Singapore/Malaysia/Hong Kong.

Strawberry Fields Forever - the true stereo version.

Thank You Girl - the original mono version without John's extra harmonica fills.

This Boy - the mono version.

December 1981 **THE BEATLES E.P.s COLLECTION**
    (EMI BEP 14)
A complete collection of the Beatles' twelve original mono EPs, along with the two-record stereo **Magical Mystery Tour** set and a bonus EP containing four supposedly true stereo tracks.

All EPs were issued on the Parlophone label with their original catalog numbers.

All records were packaged in their original full-color, laminated covers and came complete with any original enclosures (**Magical Mystery Tour**'s twenty-four-page story booklet with lyrics).

The EPs were encased in a blue, textured cardboard box with a fold-open top, identical in style to the Beatles album package. The set's title and facsimiles of the Beatles' autographs were embossed on the front of the box in gold lettering.

The set contained:

1 - **The Beatles' Hits**
2 - **Twist And Shout**
3 - **The Beatles No. 1**
4 - **All My Loving**

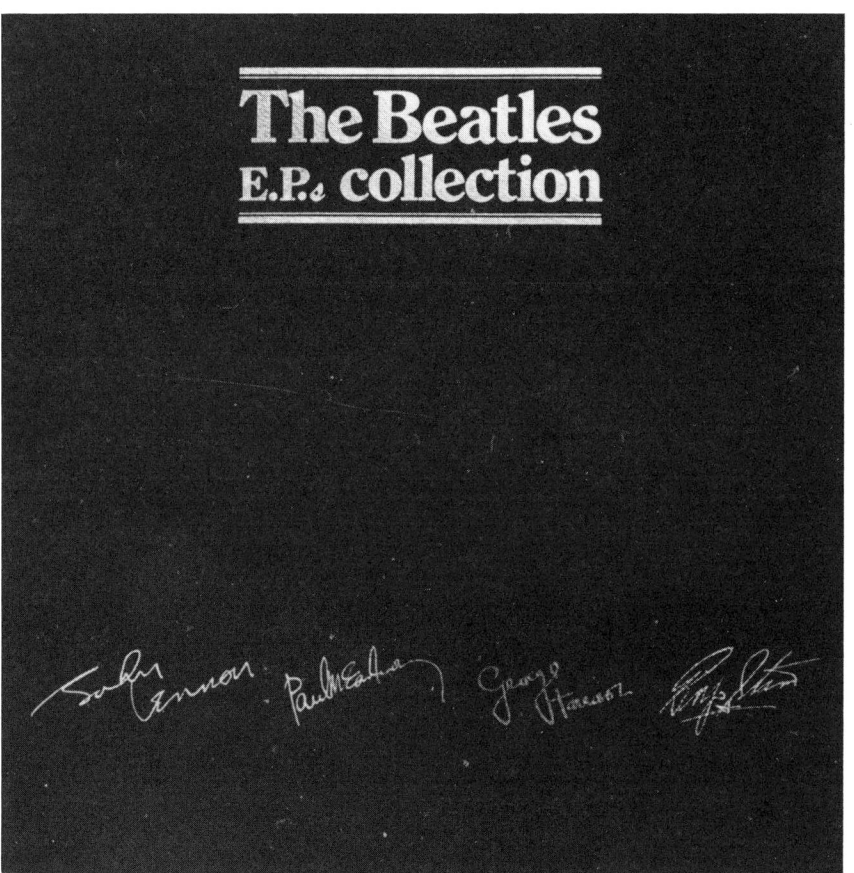

The Beatles E.P.s Collection
UK: EMI BEP 14 (EPs box set)

SGE 1

THE BEATLES

A
THE INNER LIGHT

Originally this was issued as the 'B' side of the single 'Lady Madonna' in 1968. However, this is the first time the track has been released in stereo.

BABY YOU'RE A RICH MAN

Released in mono in 1967 as the 'B' side of 'All you need is Love', this stereo version has only appeared on the UK cassette of 'Magical Mystery Tour' and on the German issue of the 'Magical Mystery Tour' album.

B
SHE'S A WOMAN

This stereo track was originally issued in mono as the 'B' side of 'I feel fine' in 1964. It is only available in stereo on an Australian album and was recently included in the box set compilation 'The Beatles Box' issued by World Records.

THIS BOY

Never before issued in stereo in the UK although it has appeared on releases in both Canada and Australia. It was originally the 'B' side of 'I want to hold your hand' released in 1963.

The Beatles
UK: Parlophone SGE 1 (bonus EP)

5 - **Long Tall Sally**
6 - **Extracts From The Film A Hard Day's Night**
7 - **Extracts From The Album A Hard Day's Night**
8 - **Beatles For Sale**
9 - **Beatles For Sale #2**
10 - **Million Sellers**
11 - **Yesterday**
12 - **Nowhere Man**
13 - **Magical Mystery Tour** (2 EPs)
14 - **The Beatles** (bonus true stereo EP)

Track Differences

The Beatles bonus EP (Parlophone SGE 1):

Baby You're A Rich Man - true stereo version, previously available just on the German **Magical Mystery Tour** and on the U.K. cassette tape edition of **Magical Mystery Tour**.

The Inner Light - the first-ever stereo release of this song.

She's A Woman - true stereo version, previously issued just in Australia/New Zealand and in Singapore/Malaysia/Hong Kong, and most recently included in World Records' **The Beatles Box**. However, this pressing also contained a four-beat count-off by Paul McCartney that can't be found anywhere else.

This Boy - although listed as the true stereo version previously issued in Canada and Australia, this track was actually pressed here in "reprocessed" stereo.

Summer 1982 **THE BEATLES MONO COLLECTION**
(EMI/Parlophone BM 1)
(See "Back To Mono," p. 115.)

December 1982 **THE BEATLES SINGLES COLLECTION**
(EMI/Parlophone BSC 1)
(See "It Was Twenty Years Ago Today," p. 125.)

United States

November 1978 **THE BEATLES COLLECTION**
(Capitol/EMI BC 13)
The same as the U.K. set except: this release was issued in a

numbered, limited edition of 3,000 copies.

Rarities (Capitol SPRO 8969) was packaged in a paper sleeve.

Track Differences

For some unknown reason, *Sie Liebt Dich* and *Komm, Gib Mir Deine Hand* were replaced with *She Loves You* and *I Want To Hold Your Hand* on **Rarities**.

October 1982 **THE BEATLES: THE COLLECTION**
(Mobile Fidelity BC-1)
(See "Audiophile Records," p. 108.)

The success of these various box sets prompted EMI to issue a John Lennon compilation in the summer of 1981 in memory of John. Although released in several countries, the packaging remained uniform. This set was first put out in the United Kingdom and was later sold in Japan (EMI/Odeon EAS 67161/9) and in Germany.

United Kingdom

Summer 1981 **JOHN LENNON** (EMI JLB 8)
A set of eight John Lennon albums recorded with the Plastic Ono Band, Yoko Ono and Elephant's Memory.

All LPs were issued on the Apple label, with their original catalog numbers.

All records were packaged in their original covers. **Imagine** came with its original black-and-white poster.

Also included in the set was a twenty-page, black-and-white booklet, "Liverpool Echo's Tribute To John Lennon," which was loaded with pictures and song lyrics.

The albums were encased in a silver box that had a color photo of John on the front. The set's title and fascimile of John's autograph were also embossed on the front of the box while the LP and song titles were printed on the back.

The set contained:

1 - **Live Peace In Toronto**
2 - **Plastic Ono Band**
3 - **Imagine**
4 - **Sometime In New York City**
5 - **Mind Games**
6 - **Walls And Bridges**
7 - **Rock 'N' Roll**

8 - **Shaved Fish**

EMI in Italy issued its own Lennon compilation, the **John Lennon Anthology**. This set consisted of all the albums in the British edition except for **Shaved Fish**, plus three singles made up of tracks not found on any of the seven LPs. A John Lennon decal was also enclosed. Unlike the other multi-record packages, these discs came in a pizza-style box. The front of the box featured the front cover of **Live Peace In Toronto**. Only 1,000 copies were made.

In the late 1970s, a promotional set of five Paul McCartney and Wings albums was issued to radio stations in New Zealand by EMI/ Parlophone Records. The collection, titled **Take Five**, was made up of **Band On The Run, Venus And Mars, London Town, Wings Greatest** and **Back To The Egg**. The records came in a black box with the Wings logo on the front. Only 100 copies were pressed.

Finally, a pirated thirteen-LP box set appeared in Taiwan around 1975 containing several solo albums each by John, Paul, George and Ringo.

China (Nationalist)

mid-1970s   **THE BEATLES INDIVIDUAL GOLDEN ALBUM** (SB 1009 1/13)

George Harrison:
> 1 - **All Things Must Pass** (3 LPs)
> 2 - **Wonderwall**
> 3 - **Electronic Sound**

John Lennon:
> 4 - **Plastic Ono Band**
> 5 - **Imagine**
> 6 - **Life With The Lions**

Paul McCartney:
> 7 - **Ram**
> 8 - **Wildlife**
> 9 - **Family Way** (Soundtrack)

Ringo Starr:
> 10 - **Sentimental Journey**
> 11 - **Beaucoups Of Blues**

The Beatles: The Collection ad.

5

Audiophile
Records

Since their early successes at EMI, the Beatles, producer George Martin and engineer Geoff Emerick were looked upon by many as leaders in the field of popular recording. In the mid-sixties, they disregarded the formula approach to making pop records in favor of experimentation. The results were often elaborate "aural pictures" achieved by combining sounds that had never been linked on record before. At the time, the full spectrum of these multilayered productions could not be adequately transferred to vinyl.

Because of the advances made in audio technology during the past decade, listeners today can more fully appreciate the richness and inventiveness of the Beatles' sound. The introduction of the half-speed mastered recording, and later the compact disc, now make it possible to hear every nuance and musical shading present on a master tape, and with greater clarity than ever before.

The method of half-speed mastering is easy to understand. Both the master tape and the lacquer disc from which metal stampers are made are rotated at half the normal playing speed, giving the cutting stylus four times as long to accurately etch sound "information" into the grooves.

MOBILE FIDELITY

In December 1979, Mobile Fidelity Sound Lab of Chatsworth, California released a specially-licensed, half-speed mastered edition of the Beatles' final album, **Abbey Road** (US: Mobile Fidelity MFSL 1-023). Mobile Fidelity, pioneers of the half-speed process, specialize in the reissuing of classic rock and jazz LPs using the full range of today's technology to bring out all the subtleties of the original recording.

Mobile Fidelity chose **Abbey Road** to be its first Beatles release for a number of reasons. Besides being the group's best-selling album, it also received critical acclaim as a refined studio effort that showcased the songwriting talents of all four members of the band.

Abbey Road
US: Mobile Fidelity MFSL 1-023 (LP)

But more importantly, **Abbey Road** was the Beatles' best-sounding LP, recorded on eight-track equipment at EMI's No. 2 studio in London. In 1969, **Abbey Road** was voted the "Best Engineered Pop Recording," with a Grammy Award going to Geoff Emerick for his outstanding work at the controls.

In ordinary mastering, loud passages of sound are automatically reduced in volume ("limited") to keep the cutting stylus from jumping out of the grooves in the record. Mobile Fidelity never employs "limiting" or "compression" in the manufacture of its albums. Instead, the output level of the master tape is reduced to where it can be transferred without any equalization yet still be free of distortion. On **Abbey Road**, this is particularly evident in the George Harrison composition *Something*. One can now experience the full crescendo during the song's "middle eight" ("You're asking me will my love grow . . ."). On the standard release, the track seems fuller here but not particularly louder. Listeners should also come away with a new appreciation of George Martin's often overlooked talent as an orchestrator. In *Something*, Martin tastefully blends a full string section with the Beatles' guitars, bass and drums. Producer Richard Perry (**Ringo, Goodnight Vienna**) considers Martin a master at this craft.

During the sixties, Beatles records were always "rush released." Pressing plants worked around the clock to turn out the discs. Metal stampers were often used for too long a time, resulting in inferior and noisy records toward the end of each run. Also, it was not uncommon for EMI affiliates to farm out the pressing of Beatles records to other companies. In early 1964, Capitol Records in the United States had to enlist the services of both Columbia and RCA to meet the overwhelming demand for the single *I Want To Hold Your Hand* (Capitol 5112). Today, Mobile Fidelity spends a minimum of three months on its LPs, beginning with the preparation of a proper lacquer. Also, only 20,000 copies of any one title are pressed. Once an LP is out of print, its availability is limited to the stock on hand.

Mobile Fidelity uses only first-generation master tapes for its releases. In the sixties, Capitol Records employed second- and sometimes third-generation mono dubs for mastering. All of the Beatles early recordings were remixed in Los Angeles under the supervision of Dave Dexter, Jr. In an attempt to compensate for the thin and muddy sound of these copies, Dexter added echo and reverb along with artificial stereo effects for Capitol's "Full Dimensional Stereo" pressings. On early rock 'n' roll records, studio echo and occasional noise were understandable if not expected. In fact, this raw sound provided some of rock's early charm. But on the Beatles later recordings, beginning with **Rubber Soul**, many of the effects the group was trying to convey were lost in these inferior quality pressings.

All Mobile Fidelity albums are pressed on Super Vinyl, a product of the Japanese Victor Company that is harder yet more resilient than any other vinyl formulation. Therefore, the albums have a life-span of four to five times that of an ordinary record.

Each disc is stored in an anti-static "rice paper" sleeve that fits inside a cardboard stiffener. Mobile Fidelity jackets are also made of heavy cardboard, similar to LP sleeves from the fifties and sixties, to provide the best possible protection against warping.

The result of all this state-of-the-art technology is a record that delivers a broader sound spectrum with a richer, fuller bass and better top end than any other conventional vinyl LP on the market today. On **Abbey Road**, George's acoustic guitar playing on *Here Comes The Sun* reproduces so clearly that you can actually hear his pick hitting the strings. Paul was praised for his melodic bass playing on this album. Standout examples can be heard on *Maxwell's Silver Hammer* and *She Came In Through The Bathroom Window*. Surprisingly, Ringo's light-hearted children's tune, *Octopus's Garden*, shows off some of the Beatles' best ensemble playing. John's full-bodied vocals shine through on *Come Together, Mean Mr. Mustard* and *Polythene Pam*. All in all, this special pressing gives listeners the feeling of hearing the Beatles "live" instead of on record.

In early 1981, Mobile Fidelity issued its second Beatles' LP, **Magical Mystery Tour** (US: Mobile Fidelity MFSL 1-047). This half-speed mastered edition garnered excellent reviews for offering a new perspective to an already classic rock album.

The opening trumpet flourish on the title track is crisper and more metallic-sounding than before. The simplicity of *The Fool On The Hill* allows listeners to focus on Paul's superb singing. The back-wards tape loops on George's *Blue Jay Way* take on new definition and John's *I Am The Walrus* has a much cleaner sound than on the original American pressings.

One year later, Mobile Fidelity put out a half-speed mastered copy of **The Beatles** (US: Mobile Fidelity MFSL 2-072). Again, the discs were flawless and the heightened definition brought a new enjoyment to these thirty original Beatles songs.

On the White Album, it's the straight ahead rock 'n' roll tracks that benefit most from the improved sound quality. Paul's pounding piano is rock-steady on *Back In The U.S.S.R.* John's rhythm guitar and Paul's bass jump out of the grooves on *Everybody's Got Some-thing To Hide Except For Me And My Monkey. Helter Skelter* literally screams in all its high energy glory while *Birthday* races along at a manic pace.

In a quieter vein, Paul's *I Will* should be listened to with head-phones in order to fully appreciate the mix. There's just Paul, his acoustic guitar, bass and some light percussion, but he and George Martin created some very imaginative stereo imaging.

Except for the legendary *While My Guitar Gently Weeps*, George's numbers don't fare that well. Both *Savoy Truffle* and *Long Long Long* were compressed so they weren't affected as much by Mobile Fidelity's high quality treatment.

As usual, John's vocals are a high point. From his jagged-edge sound on *Yer Blues* to the bleary-eyed feeling on *I'm So Tired* to the delicacy with which he sings *Julia*, this pressing shows just what a great rock and pop voice John possessed.

In October 1982, Mobile Fidelity released its most ambitious project to date, a limited edition, fourteen-LP box set titled **The Beatles: The Collection** (US: Mobile Fidelity BC-1). Retailing for $325, this overwhelming package featured the Beatles' twelve original British studio albums plus the 1967 American compilation **Magical Mystery Tour**, all manufactured directly from the original master tapes. These audiophile pressings stand as *the* reference recordings of the Beatles.

Unique covers were designed for the LPs. Pictured on each jacket was the original master tape used to manufacture the disc along with the engineer's log sheet from inside the tape box, all of which are stored in EMI's London vaults. (Mobile Fidelity accidentally reversed the covers on **Yellow Submarine**. They printed the Side Two log sheet on the front cover and the sheet for Side One on the back.)

Accompanying the set was a deluxe booklet containing the original full-color artwork for each album along with a narrative by the Mobile Fidelity engineers about the making of this package. Each set also came with a signed, hand-numbered "Certificate of Authenticity."

Finally, Mobile Fidelity included one of its Geo-Discs, a patent-pending method for aligning your cartridge to within an .003 of an inch of its suggested position to insure optimum performance from your stereo system.

All of the albums were housed in a deluxe black presentation case "suitable for coffee table display."

For collectors, the log sheets on the album jackets turned out to be as fascinating as the records themselves. Here one could see exactly what generation tape Mobile Fidelity employed for each LP. **Please Please Me** was pressed from the original stereo master while **With The Beatles** came from a tape "remixed for stereo from twin-track" mono. Beginning with **Beatles For Sale**, most of the other albums were made from "copy tapes ... remixed from 4-track." These, in fact, were first-generation copies made from the original session recordings. However, **Let It Be** was pressed from a "corrected copy," a reference tape made while the lacquer was being cut. This tape bears all of the last-minute adjustments in volume and equalization necessary to transfer the sound to vinyl. As such, the log sheet bore the notation, "for cutting only . . . use original master for tape copies."

The log sheets also showed where the various masters and copy tapes have been sent over the years. France, Spain, Egypt, Holland, Brazil, Sweden, Australia and Guatemala are just some of the countries who received their Beatles records in true stereo. Conspicuous by its absense was the United States. About the only mention of the U.S. appeared on the log sheet for **Help**, which showed that a true stereo sub-master of that LP was supplied to Capitol Records in January 1974. That's surprising. Except for *Ticket To Ride*, the remainder of the tracks have yet to be released in America in anything but "reprocessed" stereo. A notation on **Revolver** also pinpointed when EMI sent a true stereo version of *I'm Only Sleeping* to Randall Davis for inclusion on the U.S. commercial **Rarities** (Capitol SHAL 12060).

One can trace when EMI pulled true stereo versions of certain songs for the anthologies **The Beatles 1962-1966** and **The Beatles 1967-1970** (referred to on the log sheet as "Beatles Package"), as well as for the British **Rock 'N' Roll Music** (listed simply by the matrix number of the album) and **Reel Music** (noted as MV).

The fate of at least one original tape is there to behold. On June 16, 1976, the true stereo version of *Dizzy Miss Lizzy* on the stereo "copy tape" of **Help** was damaged and replaced with a dub from EMI's "safety copy" of the album. Also, even with the outstanding work Geoff Emerick did in mixing, editing and dubbing **Revolver**, a note on the log says that *Tomorrow Never Knows* should be mastered three dbs lower than the rest of the tracks.

While most of the log sheets were taken up with foreign dispatches, the listings also showed that EMI supplied tapes to several companies other than its subsidiaries. On May 15, 1973, a copy of **Sgt. Pepper's Lonely Hearts Club Band** was made for Apple Records in London and on October 4, 1976, a true stereo version of **Magical Mystery Tour** was prepared for Dyna Productions. The most interesting note was on May 21, 1975, when EMI sent McCartney Productions dubs of *Got To Get You Into My Life* and *Here, There And Everywhere*. At the time, Paul McCartney and Wings were sorting through material for their upcoming tour and intended to include a few Beatles numbers. Paul apparently wanted high-quality recordings of these two songs from which to relearn the material if he decided to perform them, instead of settling for an ordinary record.

The most startling discovery was that on April 25, 1973, Phil

McDonald, another of EMI's young, talented engineers (**Abbey Road**), made a "quad remix" of **Sgt. Pepper's Lonely Hearts Club Band**. Unfortunately, the quick demise of four-channel stereo left this monumental recording unreleased. Years ago, producer Richard Perry mentioned in an interview with the late Tom Donahue, one of the originators of underground radio, that he had heard a four-channel copy of **Sgt. Pepper** while in London working on **Ringo**. Not coincidentally, the **Ringo** sessions took place between March and July 1973.

Despite the wealth of information contained in these log sheets, it's still surprising to see the amount of things that are missing. On **Yellow Submarine**, there's a notation that *It's All Too Much* was recorded outside of EMI, although four songs on **The Beatles** (White Album) and at least one number on **Magical Mystery Tour** were also done in different studios but no mention was made of this. Also, some of the timing information varied from what's printed on record labels and even a few song titles were misspelled.

Simultaneous with the release of **The Beatles: The Collection**, Mobile Fidelity issued a UHQR (Ultra High Quality Recording) edition of **Sgt. Pepper's Lonely Hearts Club Band** (Mobile Fidelity MFQR 1-100). In further refining the conventional LP, Mobile Fidelity engineers developed the UHQR series which they described as "beyond the state-of-the-art." These discs even surpassed regular Mobile Fidelity pressings in sonic realism.

Only 5,000 copies of each title chosen for the series are pressed and Mobile Fidelity spends two-and-a-half to three minutes inscribing each disc as opposed to the twelve to twenty seconds alloted for mass-produced LPs. Each record weighs 200 grams, or twice that of a conventional album, resulting in improved stereo imaging and a richer, smoother sound. Each LP comes in its own library presentation box. The disc itself is not only housed in a "rice paper" sleeve but is also packed between two layers of foam rubber. A Technical Specifications Manual is included detailing the manufacture of the record along with a sheet of liner notes about the material. With a $40 price tag, these high-quality editions truly deserve the classification of audiophile pressings.

Because of the extremely limited number of copies produced, **Sgt. Pepper** sold out immediately. The quality of the record was striking considering the album was recorded on only four tracks and with a loss of generations due to dubbing tapes from one machine to another to provide extra channels. On the title song, the crowd noises were suddenly lifelike. The circus effects on *Being For The Benefit Of Mr. Kite* made you almost smell the sawdust and cotton candy. On *When I'm Sixty-Four* you felt as if you could reach out and touch the clarinet and chimes. And for the first time, you could really hear the Abbey Road studios air-conditioning system as Geoff Emerick turned the faders wide-open on the final chord of *A Day In The Life*.

For those who couldn't afford the $325 price for the box set, Mobile Fidelity announced plans to continue issuing the individual Beatles albums at the rate of one a year. With **Abbey Road**, **Magical Mystery Tour** and **The Beatles** already available, the next release came in the summer of 1984 with the British edition of **Rubber Soul** (US: Mobile Fidelity MFSL 1-106).

As noted earlier, **Rubber Soul** was really the first album where the Beatles and George Martin spent a good deal of time on the arrangements and remixing of each song. **Rubber Soul** is beautiful in its simplicity. There was a minimum of overdubbing and production, but with this material it wasn't necessary. The Beatles and Martin made every part count.

Half-speed mastering accentuates the richness of the acoustic guitars and the Beatles' voices. A good example is the introduction of *Norwegian Wood* where you can hear every strum of the guitar. This pristine guitar sound continues even after the other instruments come in and John begins singing.

The Beatles three-part harmonies ring true on *Nowhere Man, The Word* and *Wait*. Although George Harrison's voice was weaker than John and Paul's, his background singing nevertheless added that third harmony part that created the unique Beatles sound. **Rubber Soul** is an excellent album to use for demonstrating the merits of the half-speed mastered process.

Mobile Fidelity also issues select titles on chrome-coated cassette tapes. The same care is taken in manufacturing these cassettes as is with the LPs. Each tape is derived from the original studio master. To insure quality, it's transferred at real time instead of through high-speed duplication. And the blank tape Mobile Fidelity uses is BASF Chromium Dioxide, considered by many to be the best in the business. So far, only two Beatles titles are available in this format, **Magical Mystery Tour** (US: Mobile Fidelity MFSL C-047) and **Rubber Soul** (US: Mobile Fidelity MFSL C-106).

OTHER LABELS

Mobile Fidelity proved that a market did indeed exist for audiophile pressings and in its first year of operation a total of thirty titles were issued. Because of its success, major record companies began eyeing the possibility of entering this new and wide-open field. Columbia Records in America was the first major label to produce its own half-speed mastered records, issuing them on the "CBS Mastersound" series. "CBS Mastersound" titles were also available on chromium cassettes.

The first Beatle record Columbia released was Paul McCartney and Wings' **Band On The Run** (US: CBS HC 46482). Paul had just signed a multi-year contract with Columbia and as part of his agreement, the label would be reissuing all of his previous solo material. With **Band On The Run** being Paul's biggest critical and commercial success, Columbia quickly put out a half-speed mastered edition of the album. **Band On The Run** also won a Grammy Award for its excellent sound (1974: "Best Engineered Pop Recording" — Geoff Emerick).

Since most audiophile records are pressed in Japan, the Beatles' Japanese affiliate, Toshiba-EMI, decided to put out its own selection of half-speed mastered pressings on its "Pro-Use" series. So far, two Beatles albums have been released, **Abbey Road** (Japan: Toshiba-EMI EALF 97001) and **The Beatles Ballads** (Japan: Toshiba-EMI EAS 91006). While **Abbey Road** was already available from Mobile Fidelity, **The Beatles Ballads** gave listeners a chance to hear earlier Beatles material with a new clarity.

Nautilus Records is another California-based label that specializes in re-releasing classic rock records in half-speed editions. In 1981, it acquired the rights to John and Yoko's **Double Fantasy** (US: Nautilus NR-47). The mastering of this album, produced by John, Yoko and Jack Douglas, was first-rate. Again, a chrome cassette version was also put out.

Vitec, Inc., an American research firm, developed a vinyl formulation similar to Japanese Super Vinyl but much cheaper to produce. A&M Records used this patented "Quiex" process to put out affordable half-speed mastered pressings of its more popular albums. Warner Brothers licensed an improved version, "Quiex II," for a promo-only edition of George Harrison's **Gone Troppo** (US: Dark Horse DH 23734) that is far clearer and fuller than any commercial release. In 1982, Geffen Records issued a promo-only "Quiex II" pressing of **The John Lennon Collection** (US: Geffen GHSP 2023) for radio stations and industry personnel. Both LPs were manufactured in limited quantities.

On February 23, 1983, the National Academy of Recording Arts and Sciences celebrated the twenty-fifth anniversary of the Grammy Awards. In honor of the occasion, the Academy issued an official collection of Grammy Award-winning songs titled **The Greatest Recordings Of Our Time** (US: Franklin Mint Record Society). This mammoth 100-LP set was sold by subscription only and was not available in stores.

Featured in the set are George Harrison's *My Sweet Lord* from **The Concert For Bangla Desh** (1972: Album of the Year) and Paul McCartney and Wings' *Live And Let Die* (1973: Best Arrangement

Abbey Road
Japan: Toshiba-EMI EALF 97001 (LP)

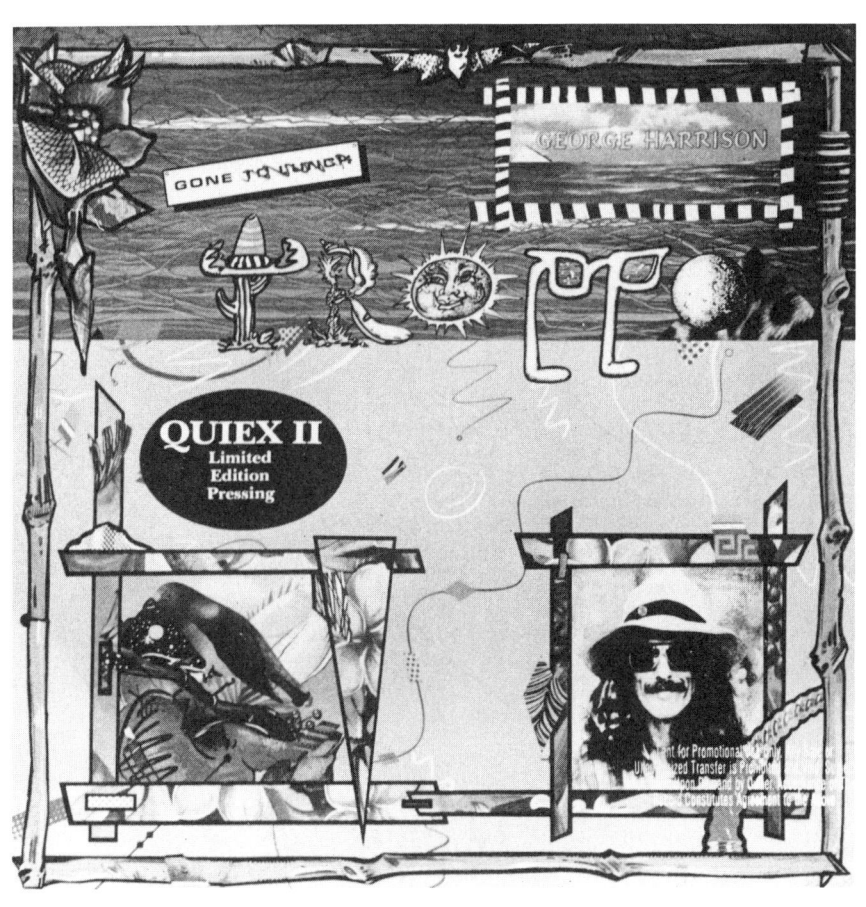

Gone Troppo
US: Dark Horse DH 23734 (promo LP)

Accompanying Vocalists). At least one Beatles track will be included but hadn't been issued at the time of this writing. Candidates are *Eleanor Rigby* (1966: Best Contemporary Pop Vocal Performance, Male-Paul McCartney), *Michelle* (1966: Song of the Year) and *Let It Be* (1970: Best Original Score For Movie Or TV).

The elaborate package is manufactured by the Franklin Mint Record Society of Pennsylvania, a company that specializes in high quality records. The discs are pressed from a special anti-static vinyl compound under "clean room" conditions, resulting in a record that is heavier and more durable than a conventional LP and with a richer, fuller sound. A four-record volume is released every other month. Each set comes with a hardbound booklet containing biographies of the artists, reproductions of the album covers that were nominated for Grammys, and many unpublished photos. The subscription cost is $10.75 per LP, or $11.75 for each Dolby-encoded, chromium dioxide cassette.

COMPACT DISCS

Before Beatles fans had time to fully absorb the beauty and richness of **The Beatles: The Collection**, the era of digital recording arrived and with it, a whole new way to collect and enjoy premium quality Beatles records.

In 1979, producer George Martin wrote of the impending digital revolution in his autobiography *All You Need Is Ears* (London: Macmillian London Limited). Yet to the average record buyer, this new method of recording and playing back sound seemed light years away. Then in October 1982, the first digital audio system was launched in Japan. By May of 1983, players and records (called compact discs) were on sale in Western Europe and in the United States.

The system of digital recording was invented by the Philips Corporation in Germany. However, it was only after Philips exchanged patents with Sony in Japan and embarked on a joint program of research that commercial digital playback became a reality.

Philips and Sony had learned from their pioneering in the field of home video that a worldwide standard for digital audio was needed before any players or discs were manufactured. The video market is still plagued by confusion over Beta vs. VHS and C.E.D. vs LaserVision. This confusion only hurts the growth of the industry. So Philips and Sony, along with Hitachi, Sanyo, Toshiba and Matsushita, came to an agreement on a one-sided, 4.72-inch plastic-coated digital disc that could play up to one hour of sound.

(Beta Hi-Fi is a much-heralded innovation in home video that produces high-quality sound second only to the compact disc. The two channels of audio are encoded across the entire width of the tape right with the video signal instead of being put down separately on a single track like an audio cassette. Beatles titles available in the HiFi format include "A Hard Day's Night" with the new Dolby-stereo soundtrack, "The Concert For Bangla Desh" with the original concert mix and the "Ready, Steady, Go!" volumes culled from the popular English television series.)

Digital audio represents a quantum leap forward for the recording industry. In the past, most advances in audio technology had been merely refinements in the methods of conventional analog recording which dated back to the days of Thomas Edison. But digital recording is an entirely new process of encoding, storing and playing back sound.

The groove of a conventional analog record is, in fact, a reproduction of the original sound waves that were picked up by microphones during recording. When the record is played, the stylus traces the path of the groove and recreates the sound.

In digital recording, every piece of sound is translated into a binary number representing frequency, volume and timbre. These numbers are then encoded as pits beneath the surface of the compact disc. A miniature laser beam "reads" the numbers and turns them back into acoustic energy.

The benefits of CDs are legion. The disc itself is very durable and will not warp. Since the recorded information lies beneath the surface, the sound quality is not affected by minor scratches or finger marks. What the listener gets is a record that gives unparalleled clarity, greater depth and will not wear out.

However, compact discs are not without their faults. Early CDs were often criticized for sounding harsh and metallic. This proved to be more a problem with the original recordings and with early CD mastering than with the digital process itself. Improvements continue to be made in the CD pressing plants and greater care is being taken in choosing quality master tapes for release on CD. Compact discs are only as good as their original sound source.

Beatles recordings were not among the first batch of CDs pressed in Japan nor was there much pop music of any kind. Ninety-percent of the initial titles were classical. The reason was that manufacturers perceived the potential CD audience as male, over forty (due to the $1,000 price tag on CD players) and therefore a lover of the classics. However, in July 1983, Matsushita of Japan surprised the entire industry by introducing a low-priced CD player (about $450) that was well within the reach of the twenty-five to forty-five year-olds. With younger and younger people now purchasing CD units, a demand grew quickly for more pop and rock titles.

Abbey Road
Japan: Toshiba-EMI CD35-3016 (compact disc)

Tug Of War
Japan: Toshiba-EMI CD35-3001 (compact disc)

The first Beatles album to be selected for release on compact disc was **Abbey Road** (Japan: Toshiba-EMI CP35-3016). So far, it's had just a limited pressing in Japan. Although this is the Beatles most technically sophisticated recording, the original master tape is not without a few flaws. The most prominent is a slight tape hiss that runs through most of the songs. Remember, this LP pre-dated Dolby. The noise first came to light on Mobile Fidelity's half-speed mastered edition of **Abbey Road** and is particularly noticeable on *Maxwell's Silver Hammer*. On conventional pressings, the mastering equipment is incapable of relaying such high frequency sound, but on CD there's nothing to mask it.

On the plus side, the CD version of **Abbey Road** offers a crisper, brighter sound than any previous edition, and allows greater depth to Paul's bass. Also, the convenience of the CD player enables listeners to cue up any one of the eight tracks on side two that are linked together in a medley.

In contrast, Paul McCartney's 1981 landmark LP, **Tug Of War**, stands as one of the best-sounding pop CDs around. Part of the album was recorded at George Martin's AIR Studio in Montserrat, an island in the eastern Caribbean. *Pro Sound News*, an industry periodical, voted AIR Montserrat "Studio of the Year" in 1983. It's one of only a handful of studios in the world to offer full digital recording.

All of **Tug Of War** was mixed digitally. The clarity of this record outshines any other work by the Beatles as a group or as solo artists. The ringing of the cymbals, the tightness of the brass and the imaginative placement of the instruments by Martin and McCartney all make this a first-class project. It's hard to believe that Geoff Emerick, chief engineer as usual, was not even nominated for a Grammy Award for this one.

Those without CD players can still get a sample of this incredible sound by listening to the Japanese twelve-inch yellow-vinyl pressing of the *Take It Away* maxi-single (Japan: Toshiba-EMI EPS-10004).

Since Columbia Records in America is one of the pioneers in CD software, the label quickly put out two additional McCartney titles, the record-breaking **Band On The Run** (US: Columbia CK 36482) and **Pipes of Peace** (US: Columbia CK 39149), the second of Paul's LPs to be mixed digitally.

For the McCartney collector, Paul's earlier analog hits were issued in CD form on **Wings Greatest** (Japan: Toshiba-EMI CP35 3114).

1984 saw the release of Paul's first major motion picture, "Give My Regards To Broad Street" (Twentieth Century Fox). The soundtrack was issued simultaneously in three formats: on LP, on high-quality chromium dioxide cassette, and on compact disc. The CD was unique because it contained one extra track, *Goodnight Lonely Princess*, an instrumental Paul wrote as background for Sir Ralph Richardson's brief scene as old Jim.

The music was recorded in London at AIR Studios, Abbey Road Studios, and CTS Studios, Ltd. As with Paul's previous two LPs, the tracks were mixed digitally. Again, the sound is breathtaking. Stewart Elliot's gut-thumping drums on *No More Lonely Nights* can almost be felt, the Philip Jones Brass Ensemble is crisp and rich on *Here, There And Everywhere* and *Wanderlust*, and Dave Edmunds, Chris Spedding and Ringo Starr really rock out on *Not Such A Bad Boy*.

John and Yoko's final album, **Milk and Honey**, was released by Polygram. As one of the world's largest music conglomerates, Polygram was also an early champion of digital audio and wants to see CDs become *the* "universal sound carrier of the future." Needless to say, it soon issued **Milk And Honey** on compact disc (US: Polydor 817 160-2).

Two other albums that are musts are the CD issues of Michael Jackson's **Thriller** (US: Epic EK 38112) and David Bowie's **Young Americans** (US: RCA PCD 1-0998). **Thriller** includes the Jackson-McCartney duet, *The Girl Is Mine*. The Bowie LP contains *Across The Universe* with John on guitar, and *Fame*, the song co-written by John, David Bowie and Carlos Alomar.

The new CD format gives collectors a second chance to pick up many of the albums where one or more of the Beatles made a guest appearance. **Best of Carly Simon** (US: Electra EA 2109) contains *Night Owl*, a James Taylor song on which Paul helped out on background vocals. Paul also can be heard playing guitar on *On The Wings Of A Nightingale*, a song he wrote especially for the Everly Brothers' reunion album, **EB '84**, which is now available on compact disc (US: Mercury 822 431-2). (Paul's original demo is rumored to still be in the vaults at Polygram, Mercury's parent company.)

Many problems can arise in transferring older, analog material to CD. Since CDs bring out all the flaws that may exist in a recording, it's essential to use only the original master tape. Second- or third-generation copies yield nothing but noise, lack of clarity, loss of high end, and muted stereo imaging.

High quality analog tapes will yield high-quality CDs as long as care is taken during the transfer. A case in point is the CD release of Billy Joel's **The Nylon Curtain**, an album that was actually recorded and mixed digitally. Unfortunately, CBS-Sony in Japan was sent a third-generation, equalized analog copy to use as the master for its CD version. The CD was ultimately recalled after numerous complaints and was re-pressed once the original master tape was obtained from the United States.

There are still many benefits to issuing older analog recordings on CD. For one, the new CD master will not deteriorate. In fact, every CD becomes a master since it's simply a list of numbers.

Early proponents predict that CDs will spell the end of the conventional LP by the year 1992. The key will probably lie in whether the bulk of today's albums are indeed transferred to CD or whether there will still be a large amount of titles available only on LPs.

There is an argument against the release of any Beatles material on CD. Remember, the earliest Beatles records were made in twin-track mono, with the instruments purposely mixed down so as not to distort when the two channels were combined. Since a CD is a mirror image of the master tape, early Beatles albums would be unsatisfactory for CD. Capitol Records in America apparently took this into consideration because its first nine pop releases on CD did not include any Beatles material. One can hope that George Martin might be persuaded to remix stereo versions of the early songs, as he did for **Rock 'N' Roll Music**, expressly for CD release. Only time will tell. Gus Dudgeon, Elton John's producer, performed a similar task for a CD-only compilation, **The Superior Sound Of Elton John**. As noted on the jacket, the recordings were "Remixed from the original multi-tracks into a new dimension of sound." The result was clean, practically noise-free music. In contrast, CD pressings of Elton's commercial "greatest hits" albums are full of hiss and suffer from occasional analog drop-outs. With early Elvis Presley and Chuck Berry recordings already available on CD, recordings that are far more primitive than those of the Beatles, it seems inevitable that Beatles compact discs cannot be far behind. Let's hope EMI has the foresight to uphold the quality of any CD issues and doesn't go ahead and put out an inferior product just to get Beatles titles in print in this new format.

George Martin, in his autobiography *All You Need Is Ears*, relates how astounded he was in the beginning when no one but teenagers seemed to hear the Beatles' music "through the noise." It took the success of *Yesterday* for the Beatles to be recognized as accomplished songwriters. Now, with the advent of the half-speed mastered record, and the compact disc, the Beatles can finally be heard as competent rock musicians as well.

AUDIOPHILE RECORDS

All pressings come from the standard version of each album. There are no variations. All are American releases unless otherwise noted.

Half-Speed Mastered Albums

Beatles
>**Abbey Road** Mobile Fidelity MFSL 1-023*
>**Abbey Road** Japan: Toshiba-EMI EALF 97001*
>**The Beatles** (White Album) Mobile Fidelity MFSL 2-072
>**The Beatles Ballads** Japan: Toshiba-EMI EAS 91006
>**Magical Mystery Tour** Mobile Fidelity MFSL 1-047
>**Rubber Soul** Mobile Fidelity MFSL 1-106
>**Sgt. Pepper's Lonely Hearts Club Band** Mobile Fidelity
>   MFQR 1-100 **

Box Sets

United States

October 1982 **THE BEATLES: THE COLLECTION**
>   (Mobile Fidelity BC-1)
>Half-speed mastered editions of the Beatles' twelve British studio albums plus the 1967 compilation **Magical Mystery Tour**, all pressed from the original master tapes.
>All albums were issued on the white Mobile Fidelity Sound Lab label and were given new catalog numbers.
>All records were packaged in new sleeves with photos of the master tape and engineer's log sheets on the front and back. The original artwork was reprinted in a glossy, full-sized booklet that accompanied the discs.
>The LPs were encased in a black presentation box complete with hinged doors and a metal catch. The words "The Beatles: The Collection" were embossed in gold lettering on the front.

>The set contained:

1 - **Please Please Me**
2 - **With The Beatles**
3 - **A Hard Day's Night**
4 - **Beatles For Sale**
5 - **Help**
6 - **Rubber Soul**
7 - **Revolver**

---

* Grammy Award-1969: Best Engineered Pop Recording-Geoff Emerick.
** Grammy Award-1967: Best Engineered Pop Recording-Geoff Emerick.

8 - **Sgt. Pepper's Lonely Hearts Club Band**
9 - **The Beatles** (White Album)
10 - **Yellow Submarine**
11 - **Abbey Road**
12 - **Magical Mystery Tour**
13 - **Let It Be**

George Harrison
    GONE TROPPO (promo-only) Dark Horse DH 23734

John Lennon & Yoko Ono
    DOUBLE FANTASY Nautilus NR-47
    THE JOHN LENNON COLLECTION (promo-only) Geffen
        GHSP 2023

Paul McCartney & Wings
    BAND ON THE RUN Columbia HC 46482*

Various Artists

Michael Jackson
    THRILLER Japan: Epic 303P 431
    Includes the Jackson-McCartney duet *The Girl Is Mine*.

Premium Qualtiy Albums

Various Artists

THE GREATEST RECORDINGS OF OUR TIME
    (Franklin Mint Record Society)
    Includes George Harrison's *My Sweet Lord* and Paul McCartney and Wings' *Live And Let Die*, plus at least one Beatles track.

Chromium Dioxide Cassettes

Beatles
    MAGICAL MYSTERY TOUR Mobile Fidelity MFSL C-047
    RUBBER SOUL Mobile Fidelity MFSL C-106

John Lennon & Yoko Ono
    DOUBLE FANTASY Nautilus NRSC-47

---

* Grammy Award-1974: Best Engineered Pop Recording-Geoff Emerick.

Paul McCartney & Wings
BAND ON THE RUN   Columbia HET 46482

Various Artists
THE GREATEST RECORDINGS OF OUR TIME
Franklin Mint Record Society

Compact Discs

Beatles
ABBEY ROAD   Japan: Toshiba-EMI CP35-3016

John Lennon & Yoko Ono
MILK AND HONEY   Polydor 817 160-2

Paul McCartney (&Wings)
BAND ON THE RUN   Columbia CK 36482
GIVE MY REGARDS TO BROAD STREET   Columbia
CK 39613
PIPES OF PEACE   Columbia CK 39149
TUG OF WAR   Columbia CK 37462
WINGS GREATEST   Japan: Toshiba-EMI CP35-3114

Various Artists

David Bowie
YOUNG AMERICANS   RCA PCD 1-0998
Includes *Across The Universe* with John Lennon on guitar,
and *Fame*, co-written by John, Bowie and Carlos Alomar.

Everly Brothers
EB '84   Mercury 822 431-2
Includes *On The Wings Of A Nightingale*, written by Paul
McCartney, with Paul playing guitar.

Michael Jackson
THRILLER   CBS EK 38112
Includes the Jackson-McCartney duet *The Girl Is Mine.*

Carly Simon
BEST OF CARLY SIMON   Electra EA-2109
Includes *Night Owl* with Paul McCartney helping out on
background vocals.

Ad for Geoff Emerick.

The Beatles
mono collection

B M I

Ad for **The Beatles Mono Collection.**

6

Back To
Mono

In the fall of 1981, EMI Records in England fulfilled the wish of many collectors by re-pressing the mono versions of the Beatles albums, from **Please Please Me** to **Yellow Submarine** (minus **A Collection Of Beatles Oldies**). Actually, the mono editions had always been in EMI's catalog but it had been quite some time since any had been manufactured.

EMI pressed a limited edition of 10,000 copies of each album. The catalog numbers and jackets were identical to the original issues as were the black-and-yellow Parlophone labels on the first eight LPs. The final two records, **The Beatles** (White Album) and **Yellow Submarine**, were both on Apple. Because of the heavy demand by collectors overseas, large quantities were exported to the United States, Australia and Europe, where they sold out quickly.

In the spring of 1982, Toshiba-EMI of Japan reissued the British mono albums. Only 5,000 copies of each title were put out. The ten LPs were also given new, consecutive catalog numbers and were pressed on red vinyl, as they were first issued in Japan.

EMI concluded its mono reissues in the summer of 1982 with the British release of **The Beatles Mono Collection** (UK: EMI/ Parlophone BM1), a limited edition box set of all ten albums. According to EMI, this would be the last time these mono pressings were issued. The box was black with the title and facsimiles of John, Paul, George and Ringo's signatures embossed in silver lettering across the front. Each set was numbered and contained a "Certificate of Authenticity." Only 1,000 copies were made.

A few hundred sets were also put out in red boxes. However, they were not numbered nor did they contain certificates. Today, these sets are quite rare.

The success of these limited mono reissues spurred other labels to put out some of their vintage rock material in its original format. Early mono albums by the Rolling Stones, the Who, and the Yardbirds soon appeared in Britain, Germany, and Japan, and were hailed by collectors. In America, Columbia Records released a compilation of the Byrds' biggest hits in mono.

Interest in the mono Beatles albums stemmed from the fact that each LP had separate mono and stereo mixes. The mono version was not simply a stereo copy with the two channels combined (except **Yellow Submarine**). On the early LPs, producer George Martin spent most of his time on the mono mix while the stereo edition was often relegated to studio engineers such as Norman Smith, Ken Townsend, or Geoff Emerick.

The most sought-after mono LP had been **The Beatles** (White Album) because of the many variations between it and the stereo version. Almost every track was mixed a little differently in mono.

In the early 1960s, mono was still the dominant mode for records in Britain. Stereo was something used for classical music and film soundtracks or for the occasional novelty record, but it hadn't yet established a place in pop or rock 'n' roll. The main reason was expense. The average British family couldn't really afford a big, two-speaker console. Stereo albums also cost about a dollar more than their mono counterparts. In fact, LPs were usually issued first in mono while the stereo pressings were put out anywhere from a week to a month later.

When the Beatles auditioned for Parlophone Records in June 1962, they had no knowledge of studio procedures. However, once they got a little experience, their desire to "make a better record" allowed them to pick up techniques quickly. In the early days, though, EMI policy forbade its artists from even touching the mixing console. That was the job of the engineer.

The Beatles' first two albums, **Please Please Me** and **With The Beatles**, were recorded in twin-track mono, with the vocals on one channel and the backing on the other. This was the best EMI had to offer in 1962 and 1963. George Martin used the two tracks for convenience in making a mono record but never intended for a stereo copy to be put out in this form.

When the Beatles began work on **A Hard Day's Night** in March 1964, EMI had replaced its rather antiquated two-track tape units with brand new four-track equipment. It wasn't until 1965 and the making of **Rubber Soul** that the Beatles were given some control in the post-production of their albums. Still, stereo mixes were pretty much of an afterthought. Even in 1967, the Beatles took three weeks to mix **Sgt. Pepper's Lonely Hearts Club Band** in mono but spent just two-and-a-half days on the stereo version.

The White Album was the first record where the Beatles concentrated on the stereo mix. They spent anywhere from ten to thirty hours on each track, from rehearsal to final master. The results were remarkable. The recording was clean and rich, and the stereo imaging was crisp and innovative.

Abbey Road, which won a Grammy Award as the Best Engineered Pop Recording of 1969, and **Let It Be**, which was "reproduced for disc by Phil Spector," were the only original albums to be issued exclusively in stereo. Mono mixes of both, with the two stereo channels combined, were issued in England in September 1970 on open-reel tape (**Abbey Road** - EMI/Parlophone TA PMC 7088; **Let It Be** - EMI/Parlophone TA PMC 7096).

MONO LPs

	UK	*Japan*
	(Parlophone/Apple)	(Odeon)
Please Please Me	PMC 1202	EAS-70130
With The Beatles	PMC 1206	EAS-70131
A Hard Day's Night	PMC 1230	EAS-70132
Beatles For Sale	PMC 1240	EAS-70133
Help	PMC 1255	EAS-70134
Rubber Soul	PMC 1267	EAS-70135
Revolver	PMC 7009	EAS-70136
Sgt. Pepper's Lonely Hearts Club Band	PMC 7027	EAS-70137
The Beatles (White Album)	PMC 7067/8	EAS-67157/8
Yellow Submarine	PMC 7070	EAS-70138

BOX SET

United Kingdom

Sumer 1982 **THE BEATLES MONO COLLECTION**
(EMI/Parlophone BMI)

A set of the Beatles' ten British mono studio albums.

All LPs were issued on their original labels (Parlophone or Apple) and with their original catalog numbers.

All records were packaged in their original covers and with their original enclosures (**Sgt. Pepper's** cut-out sheet, **The Beatles'** four glossies and one poster).

The albums were encased in a black, textured cardboard box with a fold-open top. The set's title and facsimiles of the Beatles' autographs were embossed on the front of the box in silver lettering.

See above for contents.

From Me To You/Thank You Girl
UK: Parlophone RP 5015 (45 picture disc)

7

It Was
Twenty Years Ago
Today

The year 1982 was a busy one for the ex-Beatles. In April, Paul McCartney released **Tug Of War**, his most critically acclaimed album since **Band On The Run** eight-and-a-half years earlier. It yielded three hit singles (*Ebony And Ivory, Take It Away* and *Tug Of War*), each of which was supported by an inventive promotional videoclip. Paul could also be heard on a duet with Michael Jackson, *The Girl Is Mine*, which Epic Records issued as the first single from Jackson's soon-to-be multi-platinum album **Thriller**. George Harrison put out a new LP, **Gone Troppo**, which was anything but successful, and Ringo Starr began work on a new rock 'n' roll album, **Old Wave**, produced by Joe Walsh. In February, Yoko Ono and Sean attended the Grammy Award ceremonies in Los Angeles to accept the "Album of the Year" award for John and Yoko's **Double Fantasy**.

But 1982 was also a year of nostalgia, marking the twentieth anniversary of the Beatles' first hit record, *Love Me Do*. In September 1963, Tony Barrow, the Beatles' first press officer, predicted quite confidently that ten years later people would still be listening to Beatles music. In the liner notes on the Beatles' second British EP, **The Beatles' Hits** (Parlophone GEP 8880), Barrow even challenged someone to write him a "very nasty letter" in the "middle of 1973" if that were not the case. Although his boast was rooted mostly in record industry hype, he nevertheless must have been a little amused when, twenty years later, the world was still celebrating the musical accomplishments of John, Paul, George and Ringo.

The music the Beatles created in the sixties is certainly still relevant two decades later, but one has to wonder if the group's twentieth anniversary would have stirred up so much excitement, particularly in the media, if it were not for the opening lines of *Sgt. Pepper's Lonely Hearts Club Band* that go, "It was twenty years ago today/Sgt. Pepper taught the band to play." But the question is moot. The many tributes throughout the world sparked a renewed interest in the Beatles, their songs and their time.

The celebration of the Beatles "twentieth anniversary" actually spanned three years. Commemorations were made of the group's first "live" radio appearance (with Pete Best still on drums), the making of their first record in London for Parlophone, and their triumphant first trip to America.

It all began on March 7, 1982 when BBC Radio in England marked the twentieth anniversary of the Beatles' first radio broadcast with a special two-hour program entitled "The Beatles At The Beeb." This exhaustively researched show was put together by producer Jeff Griffin, Kevin Howlett, and disc jockey Andy Peebles. They spotlighted the more than fifty appearances the group made on BBC Radio between March 1962 and June 1965, and in the process unearthed thirty-six songs the band had performed "live" on-the-air but never released on record. The special was so well received it was soon syndicated worldwide by London Wavelength.

October 5, 1962 was the release date of the Beatles' first single on Parlophone Records, *Love Me Do* b/w *P.S. I Love You* (UK: Parlophone R 4949). On October 4, 1982, EMI re-launched the single, still in its catalog, by putting it out for the first time in a full-color picture sleeve. (The only original British Beatles singles that came in picture sleeves were *Penny Lane* and *Let It Be*). The disc also carried a re-creation of the red label Parlophone had employed two decades before. However, EMI continued to use the more common "second version" of *Love Me Do*, which it had been pressing since March 1963, instead of the "first version," which had been available on the original issue back in 1962. The second version features session man Andy White on drums while the first version had Ringo. (See "The Beatles," p.199.)

To further boost sales, EMI also issued the single as a limited edition, 7-inch picture disc (UK: Parlophone RP 4949), with the artwork from the picture sleeve embedded in clear vinyl. Four weeks later, the single peaked at Number 3 on the *New Musical Express* chart, considerably higher than its Number 17 showing twenty years earlier.

On October 5, the airwaves in England were filled with non-stop Beatles music, the Merseyside Tourism Office in Liverpool issued a limited edition, commemorative postcard titled "From the Birthplace of the Beatles," and in the evening, Paul McCartney was interviewed on radio and TV. Asked whether he was sorry the group had never re-formed he replied, "We didn't really want to come back as decrepit old rockers."

A week later, EMI issued **20 Greatest Hits** (UK: Parlophone PCTC 260), a collection of the Beatles' Number One singles in England, including both tracks off their double-A sides (*Day Tripper/ We Can Work It Out* and *Yellow Submarine/Eleanor Rigby*), plus *Love Me Do*. EMI had originally intended to put out a two-record set, **The Beatles Greatest Hits** (UK: EMI EMTV 34) made up of all twenty-two of the group's British singles (with four double-A sides), a total of twenty-six tracks. The double-album was to be sold through television like the highly successful **The Beatles At The Hollywood Bowl** (UK: EMI EMTV 4). One-sided, white label promo copies were pressed, but EMI withdrew the package prior to release. The company felt it would duplicate too much of the material on two other double-LPs, **The Beatles 1962-1966** and **The Beatles 1967-1970**.

20 Greatest Hits contains the common version of *Love Me Do*, along with the stereo take of *From Me To You* (minus the harmonica intro) and the stereo mix of *I Feel Fine* (which begins with whispering). Detailed liner notes give the date each recording began, its release date and the date it hit Number One in England.

In the sixties, EMI's foreign subsidiaries were free to choose what Beatles material to release locally. A survey of overseas record charts reveals that many songs that the Beatles kept as album tracks in England were later put out as singles abroad. Thus, the group's chart toppers in Brazil differ slightly from their "greatest hits" in Italy. In 1982, EMI gave its subsidiaries the option of compiling separate **20 Greatest Hits** compilations to correspond with the band's local successes. Even so, the British edition was still released in many foreign countries, including France (Parlophone 07674) and Japan. In Australia, Parlophone issued a similar twenty-track collection called **The Number Ones**, which came with a bonus three-track maxi-single.

Capitol Records in the United States issued its own version of **20 Greatest Hits** (Capitol SV 12245) on October 11, 1982. The first four cuts were *She Loves You, Love Me Do, I Want To Hold Your Hand* and *Can't Buy Me Love*. Trade ads said the album was made up of the Beatles' American Number One hits, in the order they reached the top of the charts. If that were true, these first four songs would have been arranged as follows: *I Want To Hold Your Hand, She Loves You, Can't Buy Me Love* and *Love Me Do*.

The American compilation also contained six tracks not on the British version: *Eight Days A Week, Yesterday, Penny Lane, Come Together, Let It Be* and *The Long And Winding Road. Eight Days A Week* and *The Long And Winding Road* have yet to be issued as singles in England, while *Yesterday* was not put out until March 1976, when EMI reissued the group's twenty-two original British singles in special picture sleeves.

The one difference in recordings is an abbreviated version of *Hey Jude*, which Capitol shortened from 7:11 to 5:05. (This is not to be confused with the Pocket Disc version authorized by Capitol/Apple in 1968, which ran only 3:56.) (See "The Beatles," pp. 186-187.)

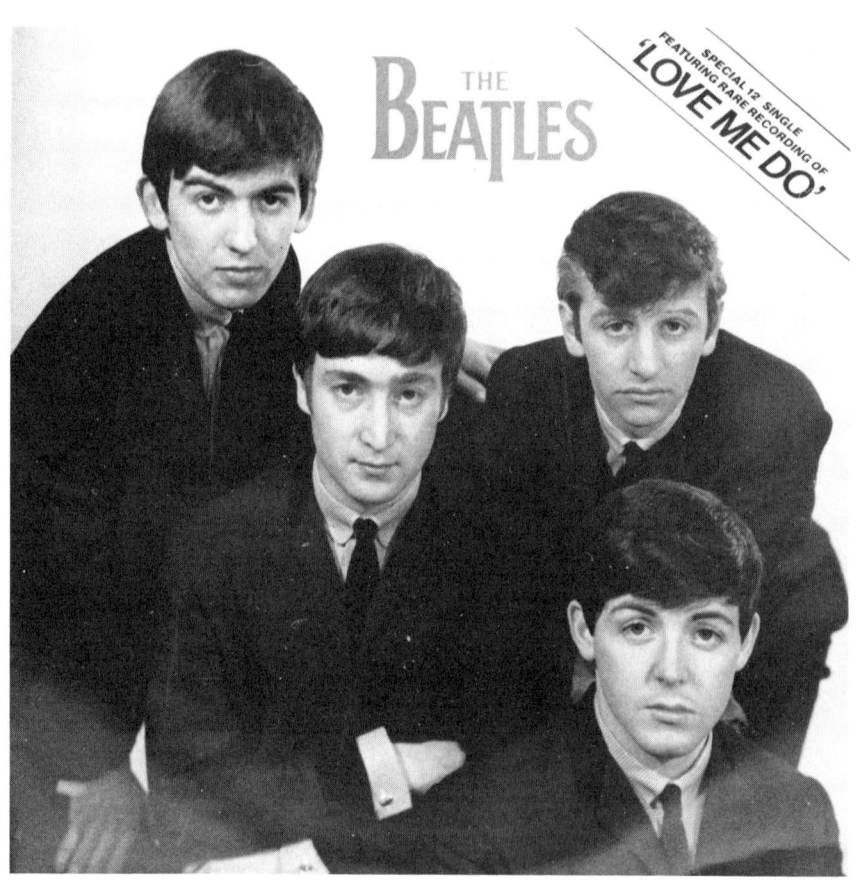

Love Me Do
UK: Parlophone 12R 4949 (12" maxi-single)

On November 1, EMI in England issued a special 12-inch pressing of *Love Me Do* (Parlophone 12R 4949) in an attempt to push the song further up the charts. This was, in fact, a maxi-single with *Love Me Do* and *P.S. I Love You* on one side and the rare, original version of *Love Me Do* with Ringo on drums on the other. A story in the October 30 edition of *New Musical Express* reported that EMI had recently found the long-lost master tape and had decided to issue it now in honor of the group's twentieth anniversary. However, the sound quality shows that this was not true. What EMI actually used was a clean dub made from an original single provided by British collector Mark Cousins, just as Ron Furmanek in America had supplied a copy to Capitol Records for the 1980 LP **Rarities**. Rumor has it that the original 15-ips master tape is in the hands of a private collector in Japan. The 12-inch single bore the same red label as the 7-inch pressing and came with the same picture sleeve. It was also issued in Japan (EMI/Odeon EAS 27005).

Back in the U.S., Capitol Records issued a 7-inch version of *Love Me Do* b/w *P.S. I Love You* (Capitol B-5189) on November 12 to cash in on the American press coverage of the Beatles' twentieth anniversary in England. This was the first time in seventeen years that Capitol had made this single available. (In October 1965, Capitol issued the songs as part of its "Starline" series, having just acquired the recordings from Vee Jay Records, the first label to release them in the United States.) The new single was pressed on Capitol's old orange and yellow swirl label and came in the same picture sleeve as the British release. It was supported by a promotional videoclip put together by Capitol with the help of Ron Furmanek. The clip centered around the Beatles' performance of *Love Me Do* on Granada TV's "People and Places" on December 17, 1962. Unfortunately, Capitol redubbed the soundtrack from the single rather than leaving the original "live" performance.

Beatles fans in England had a nice present to look forward to at Christmas 1982. On December 6, EMI put out **The Beatles Singles Collection** (Parlophone BSC 1), containing all twenty-six British singles. The records were encased in a blue, textured cardboard box, identical in style to the Beatles album set. The set's title and facsimiles of the Beatles' autographs were embossed on the front of the box in gold lettering. Unlike EMI's two previous reissues of the British singles, each disc came in its own unique full-color picture sleeve, with four of the records packaged in their original sleeves (*Penny Lane, Let It Be, Sgt. Pepper's Lonely Hearts Club Band* and *The Beatles' Movie Medley*). Also included was an insert listing the recording and release dates, highest chart position and number of weeks at Number One for each single. *Love Me Do* appeared in its most recent "red label" pressing.

Special export sets (EMI/Parlophone BSCP 1) contained a bonus record, the picture disc of *Love Me Do*. This package was also issued in Japan (EMI/Odeon EAS 17311/37).

EMI in Australia issued its own version of **The Beatles Singles Collection** (Parlophone Records), with thirty-four records housed in a red box. The title was embossed on the front in silver lettering and the discs came in all-new, black-and-white picture sleeves featuring photos from the Beatles' 1964 Australian tour. Also included was a four-page booklet with background information on the records.

In France, EMI reissued the Beatles' LP box set with a new title, **20 Ans Collection**, although it was identical to **The Beatles Collection** first released in 1978. Back in England, EMI put out another Christmas treat, a cassette edition of **The Beatles Collection** (UK: Parlophone TCBS 13) with fourteen prerecorded tapes packed in a blue plastic carrying case. (See "**Rarities** . . . And Box Sets", ·p. 82.)

On January 10, 1983, EMI reissued *Please Please Me* b/w *Ask Me Why*, the Beatles' second single on Parlophone. Again, the record was put out both as a conventional single (UK: Parlophone R 4983) with a red Parlophone label and new picture sleeve, and as a limited edition picture disc (UK: Parlophone RP 4983). Its lack of chart success caused Capitol Records to pass on releasing it in America.

EMI also confirmed that it would continue reissuing each of the Beatles' original twenty-two singles on the twentieth anniversary of its release. The discs would bear original catalog numbers, with the added prefix of RP for picture discs and new picture sleeves would be taken from **The Beatles Singles Collection**.

Two months later, EMI in Japan reissued the thirteen-album box set, **The Beatles Collection** (EMI/Odeon EAS 66010/23) to commemorate the twentieth anniversary of the release of the Beatles' first LP, **Please Please Me**.

In September, Audiofidelity Enterprises (UK) put out two new compilations that no doubt confused many holiday record buyers. **20 Greatest Hits** (UK: AFE P20 623) combined tracks from **The Savage Young Beatles** (reissued in 1982 as **First Movement** by Phoenix Records, a subsidiary of AFE) with much of the material from the group's Decca audition in 1962, while **20 Great Hits** (UK: AFE P20 629) was a random collection of cuts from the Star Club tape.

Atlantic Records jumped the gun on the Beatles' twentieth anniversary in America by reissuing two of the four Hamburg tracks in its vaults, *Ain't She Sweet* b/w *Sweet Georgia Brown* (Atlantic OS13243), on December 19, 1983. The numbers were originally released as the A-sides of two separate singles. Both appear here in mono and in doctored form as they were first issued on the Atco label in the summer of 1964.

In January 1984, Capitol Records started gearing up for its own Beatles bonanza. The planned hoopla was set to coincide with the twentieth anniversary of the group's first trip to America, which began on February 7, 1964. Capitol printed 5,000 copies of a new promotional poster for record stores that spotlighted the Beatles' entire Capitol Records catalog. "Relove the Music, Relive the Memory" was the slogan. Capitol also distributed 2,500 black t-shirts and metal pins with the words "It was twenty years ago today." Somewhat disappointing for collectors was the fact that the t-shirt incorporated the same logo of the group that had appeared on Capitol's tenth anniversary promo items. Capitol also sent out a voluminous press kit made up of reproductions of original 1964 press releases and clippings about the band plus an 8" x 10" glossy photo and a commemorative postcard.

Capitol hired the Howard Bloom Organization, a powerful New York public relations firm, to handle the onslaught of media requests. Cover stories on the Beatles appeared in *Life, People, Rolling Stone* and *Billboard*. Virtually every radio and TV station in the country paused for a look back at those hectic sixteen days in February 1964 when America succumbed to "Beatlemania."

Fortunately, Capitol decided against compiling yet another Beatles "greatest hits" collection and instead opted for reissuing its first Beatles single, *I Want To Hold Your Hand* b/w *I Saw Her Standing There* (US: Capitol B-5112). The record was officially re-released on February 13, 1984 and was pressed with a reproduction of the orange and yellow swirl label, even though the title had been relegated to the Capitol Starline series (Capitol 6278) several years before. Capitol also issued the disc in a black-and-white picture sleeve similar to the original, although two differences were evident. First, Capitol inexplicably airbrushed the cigarette out of Paul's right hand, and second, the sleeve had the A-side title of *I Want To Hold Your Hand* printed in large type on both sides. On the original release, *I Saw Her Standing There* was in large type on the back.

While commercial copies of the single were pressed in mono, the promotional version (Capitol PB-5112) featured *I Want To Hold Your Hand* in both mono and stereo. The stereo side bore the notation " *1rst* time as stereo on U.S. single."

An unexpected bonus from Capitol was the promotional video-clip for *I Want To Hold Your Hand* put together by EMI's video branch, Picture Music International, again with the aid of Ron Furmanek. It was a combination of three different performances of the song intercut with other scenes of the Beatles on tour--a true gem. The full-length clip also included a prologue backed by the opening verse of *Sgt. Pepper's Lonely Hearts Club Band* including, of course, "It was twenty years ago today." (Surprisingly, the shot of the single's picture sleeve seen at the beginning and end of the video was the original 1964 sleeve rather than Capitol's new air-brushed version.)

Other companies benefitted from Capitol's Beatles blitz as well. Maljack Productions reported a surge in sales for its home video edition of "A Hard Day's Night," and MGM/UA released a theatrical version of its home video documentary "The Compleat Beatles" to twenty theaters in the United States.

Overall, the twentieth anniversary tributes to the Beatles were successful and brought back fond memories for those who lived through the sixties. Surprisingly, the Beatles phenomenon has continued well into the eighties and still shows no signs of letting up.

The following is a list of the Beatles special twentieth anniversary releases, 1982-1984:

Australia

October 11, 1982 **THE NUMBER ONES** (Parlophone Records)
The Australian version of **20 Greatest Hits**, which came with a bonus three-track maxi-single.

December 6, 1982 **THE BEATLES SINGLES COLLECTION**
(EMI/Parlophone Records)
A complete collection of the thirty-four Beatles singles issued in Australia.

All records were packed in unique, black-and-white picture sleeves that featured photos from the Beatles' 1964 Australian tour.

The singles were encased in a red cardboard box, with the title embossed in silver lettering on the front. Also included was a four-page booklet detailing the history of each release.

France

October 11, 1982 **20 GREATEST HITS** (Parlophone 07674)
The same as the U.K. issue.

December 1982 **20 ANS COLLECTION** (EMI/Odeon Records)
The same as the first French LP box set, **The Beatles Collection**, issued in December 1978. (See"**Rarities**. . . And Box Sets," p. 78.)

Japan

October 11, 1982 **20 GREATEST HITS** (EMI/Odeon Records)
The same as the U.K. issue.

November 1, 1982 *Love Me Do - P.S. I Love You/Love Me Do*
12-inch pressing (EMI/Odeon EAS 27005)
The same as the U.K. issue.

December 6, 1982 **THE BEATLES SINGLES COLLECTION**
(EMI/Odeon EAS 17311/37)
The same as the U.K. issue.

March 1983 **THE BEATLES COLLECTION**
(EMI/Odeon EAS 66010/23)
The same as the second Japanese LP box set, this edition was put out to commemorate the twentieth anniversary of the release of the Beatles' first album, **Please Please Me.** (See "**Rarities . . .** And Box Sets," p. 80.)

United Kingdom

October 4, 1982 *Love Me Do/P.S. I Love You*
(Parlophone R 4949)

October 4, 1982 *Love Me Do/P.S. I Love You* picture disc
(Parlophone RP 4949)

October 11, 1982 **20 GREATEST HITS**
(Parlophone PCTC 260)
The Beatles' Number One hits in England, including two double-A sides (*Day Tripper/We Can Work It Out* and *Yellow Submarine/Eleanor Rigby*) plus *Love Me Do*.

November 1, 1982 *Love Me Do - P.S. I Love You/Love Me Do*
12-inch pressing (Parlophone 12R 4949)
The B-side contains the rare, first version of *Love Me Do* with Ringo on drums.

December 6, 1982 **THE BEATLES SINGLES COLLECTION**
(Parlophone BSC 1)
A complete collection of the Beatles' twenty-six British singles.
The records were pressed on the EMI/Parlophone and Apple labels with their original catalog numbers.
They were packaged in new, full-color picture sleeves, except

for *Penny Lane, Let It Be, Sgt. Pepper's Lonely Hearts Club Band* and *The Beatles' Movie Medley*, which came in their original sleeves.

The singles were encased in a blue, textured cardboard box similar to **The Beatles E.P.s Collection**. The set's title and facsimiles of the Beatles' autographs were embossed on the front of the box in gold lettering.

Special export-only sets were also manufactured in England (EMI/Parlophone BSCP 1) and contained the *Love Me Do* picture disc.

December 1982   **THE BEATLES COLLECTION** - cassettes
   (Parlophone TCBS 13)
   The Beatles' thirteen British albums, issued for the first time in England on prerecorded cassettes. The tapes came in a blue plastic carrying case.

January 10, 1983 *Please Please Me/Ask Me Why*
   (Parlophone R 4983)

January 10, 1983   *Please Please Me/Ask Me Why* picture disc
   (Parlophone RP 4983)

April 11, 1983 *From Me To You/Thank You Girl*
   (Parlophone R 5015)

April 11, 1983   *From Me To You/Thank You Girl* picture disc
   (Parlophone RP 5015)

August 22, 1983 *She Loves You/I'll Get You*
   (Parlophone R 5055)

August 22, 1983   *She Loves You/I'll Get You* picture disc
   (Parlophone RP 5055)

September 10, 1983 **20 GREATEST HITS**
   (Audiofidelity Enterprises AFE P20 623)
   Tony Sheridan tracks plus Decca audition material.

September 10, 1983 **20 GREAT HITS**
   (Audiofidelity Enterprises AFE P20 629)
   Another Star Club compilation.

November 28, 1983   *I Want To Hold Your Hand/This Boy*
   (Parlophone R 5084)

November 28, 1983   *I Want To Hold Your Hand/This Boy*
  picture disc (Parlophone RP 5084)

March 19, 1984   *Can't Buy Me Love/You Can't Do That*
  (Parlophone R 5114)

March 19, 1984   *Can't Buy Me Love/You Can't Do That*
  picture disc (Parlophone RP 5114)

July 9, 1984   *A Hard Day's Night/Things We Said Today*
  (Parlophone R 5160)

July 9, 1984   *A Hard Day's Night/Things We Said Today*
  picture disc (Parlophone RP 5160)

November 26, 1984   *I Feel Fine/She's A Woman*
  (Parlophone R 5200)

November 26, 1984   *I Feel Fine/She's A Woman* picture disc
  (Parlophone RP 5200)

United States

October 11, 1982   **20 GREATEST HITS** (Capitol SV 12245)
  The American version contained six tracks not found on the
British release: *Eight Days A Week, Yesterday, Penny Lane,
Come Together, Let It Be* and *The Long And Winding Road.*
  Hey Jude appears here in an abbreviated form, shortened
from 7:11 to 5:05.

November 12, 1982   *Love Me Do/P.S. I Love You*
  (Capitol B-5189)

December 19, 1983   *Ain't She Sweet/Sweet Georgia Brown*
  (Atlantic OS 13243)

February 13, 1984   *I Want To Hold Your Hand/I Saw Her
  Standing There* (Capitol B-5112)

Oh! Darling
UK: Apple Custom Recording (45 acetate)

An alternate take of "Oh! Darling," in true stereo, on the Apple Custom Recording label. This is a 7-inch, one-sided acetate.

A belated thanks to Pete and Mike at London's Vintage Record Centre for selling me this disc for the grand total of ƒ5 (then $12) on December 13, 1973 (my birthday) - William McCoy

Beatles Records
Most Collectors
Will Never Own

Over the years hundreds of rare Beatles pressings have disappeared. Publisher's demos, rough mixes, home recordings and alternate takes, all originally cut as reference discs, have either been left forgotten in file cabinets and basement boxes or have been snatched up as souvenirs by greedy assistants, journalists, hangers-on and others who came in contact with the group. Many of these original records have since surfaced in the collectors market while others seem destined never to be seen or heard again. In this chapter, we'll examine the stories behind eight such discs.

> The Quarry Men (1958): *That'll Be The Day* (Jerry Allison-Buddy Holly-Norman Petty) b/w *In Spite Of All Danger* (George Harrison-Paul McCartney)

In 1958, John Lennon spent much of his time playing with the Quarry Men, a skiffle group he'd put together while attending Liverpool's Quarry Bank High School. The band was formed in early 1956, soon after Scottish singer Lonnie Donegan (*Rock Island Line*) had turned "skiffle" into England's newest musical craze. But by 1958, most major skiffle groups had folded. Scratching washboards and thumping tea-chest basses were abandoned in favor of electric guitars, drums, and the more rhythmic sound of rock 'n' roll. The Quarry Men followed suit.

After failing every subject at high school, John was advised to enroll in the Liverpool Art College and pursue a course of study in the only academic subject that seemed to interest him. Once he settled in, John and Bill Harry, a friend and later the founder of *Merseybeat*, persuaded the college to purchase a public address system and a tape recorder to use at school dances. Soon after the equipment arrived, John appropriated it for his group.

After going through many personnel changes, the Quarry Men now consisted of John Lennon, Paul McCartney, George Harrison and, for a short time, a piano player named John Lowe. Lowe, or

"Duff" as he was better known, wasn't too reliable a band member. Paul later told biographer Hunter Davies that " . . . his dad wouldn't let him stay out late."

It wasn't long before the Quarry Men used the new tape recorder to hear what they sounded like. As a lark, they took one of their recordings to a local tape-to-disc transfer service, possibly Welsby Sound Recordings, and came away with their first "single." Once the songs were pressed into vinyl, the original tape was erased.

The A-side of the disc was the Buddy Holly hit *That'll Be The Day* with John singing lead. The B-side was a ballad written by Paul and George (their only known collaboration) titled *In Spite Of All Danger*.

The record was passed around among the band members and was eventually forgotten. After a few years, everyone assumed it had been thrown away. Then, in the summer of 1981, John Lowe announced that he still had the disc and was planning to put it up for sale in Sotheby's second annual auction of rock 'n' roll memorabilia to be held that October in London.

Paul let it be known that he didn't want the record sold. After all, it contained a McCartney-penned composition on the B-side, a song that had never been commercially released, published or copyrighted. And with the murder of John Lennon, the A-side, with John singing lead, would've received considerable attention and would've immediately been bootlegged.

Paul offered Lowe $10,000 for the record and stipulated that he'd donate it to a proposed Beatles museum in England. Sotheby's estimated the disc could command twice that amount. Lowe rejected McCartney's bid.

Nevertheless, Paul was intent on keeping the record out of circulation. On July 23, his attorneys obtained a court order banning the sale of the disc. No explanation was given as to how Paul prevented the record from changing hands. The Beatles weren't under contract to anyone when the disc was made and neither Paul nor George had ever copyrighted their own song. The key probably lies in the fact that Paul's music publishing company, MPL Communications, owns the rights to the record's A-side, *That'll Be The Day*.

When an artist records another person's song, they must first get clearance from the publisher before they can issue their own version of the number. Since publishers earn their money from record royalties and radio play of their songs, it's in their best interest to let as many people as want to record their material. However, publishers also have the option to refuse the release of any record they feel might harm the reputation of their writers.

Since Paul's publishing firm owns the rights to the majority of the Buddy Holly Music catalog, including *That'll Be The Day*, it's most likely that Paul, in the role of the song's publisher, refused permission for this record to be "issued," thereby blocking the sale of the disc. And as the song's copyright holder, Paul could also demand that the disc be turned over to him. The British High Court upheld just such a request and gave John Lowe until October 4 to deliver the record to Paul's attorneys.

> The Beatles mit Wally (1960): *Summertime* (George Gershwin) b/w *Fever* (Johnny Davenport-Eddie Cooley)

In April 1960, the Beatles (John, Paul, George and Pete Best) played their first engagement in Hamburg. They opened at the Indra, a hole-in-the-wall bar on Grosse Freiheit. But after two months as the resident band, and continued complaints by neighbors about the noise they were making, the group was moved next door to the much larger Kaiserkeller. There they alternated with the top Liverpool band of the day, Rory Storm and the Hurricanes.

The Beatles were particularly impressed by one member of the Hurricanes, Lu Walters, who possessed a vocal range that enabled him to sing either falsetto or deep bass with no trouble. During their hour-on, hour-off sets, the Beatles also became drinking buddies with the Hurricanes' bearded drummer, Richard Starkey, better known as Ringo Starr.

In August, the Beatles' manager, Allan Williams, returned to Hamburg to check on his charges and was confronted with a group that very much wanted to make a record with Walters, or "Wally." John, Paul and George also asked that Ringo, and not Pete Best, play drums on the session since he already knew all of Walters's material.

Williams took the Beatles to the only recording facility he could afford, Akustik Studio, a glorified vocal booth located behind Hamburg's Central Railway Station. Here, for a nominal fee, tourists could cut short messages to send back home to their loved ones.

After setting up their equipment, the Beatles and Walters ran through one of the singer's favorite numbers, *Summertime*. Halfway into the song, Walters panicked and forgot the words. The second time, though, he got them right and the Beatles had half of their record finished.

For the B-side they performed *Fever*, this time without a hitch. Unfortunately, Akustik Studio wasn't accustomed to recording musical groups and therefore didn't have any baffles to isolate Ringo's booming drums. Allan Williams described Ringo's drum sound on this record as similar in tone to "two coconuts being clapped together."

The Akustik engineer also wasn't equipped to press the Beatles' disc as a standard single. It came out at 78rpm. And the studio apparently had run out of vinyl, because they put the Beatles' two tracks on the back of a promotional record advertising a local leather goods store. Allan Williams paid the engineer £10 ($24) for the session. In the end, four copies of *Summertime* b/w *Fever* by "The Beatles mit Wally" were pressed on the Akustik Studio label. Williams kept a copy for himself, one copy each went to Wally and to Ringo, and one copy was given to their group leader, Rory Storm.

The Beatles were excited after hearing their sounds on vinyl and wanted to stay and cut a disc of their own, but Allan Williams said no. He was worried they might miss the start of that night's Kaiserkeller performance and he didn't want to get on the wrong side of the club's owner, Bruno Koschmider. It would be another two years before John, Paul, George and Ringo recorded together again.

After returning to England, Williams reportedly took the Beatles' disc to London and played it for representatives of the Lew Grade Organization, the most powerful booking agency in Britain. But no one took the least bit of interest in the record because of its horrendous sound quality. Williams held onto his copy until 1976, then lost it during a long evening of carousing when someone lifted it from his briefcase.

The Beatles and Gerry Marsden (1961): *There's A Shanty In Old Shanty Town*

In 1961, the Beatles were close friends with Gerry Marsden, the lead singer of another popular Liverpool beat group, the Pacemakers. The two bands often shared the same bill, going back at least a year when Gerry and his boys were the opening act for the "Silver Beatles." In July 1961, the groups even joined forces for a night and played to a jam-packed crowd at Liverpool's Litherland Town Hall as the "Beatmakers."

Sometimes, Gerry and the Beatles practiced together and occasionally they'd tape their rehearsals. This record probably comes from one such session. It features Gerry singing lead with John, Paul, George and Pete Best playing back-up. Gerry was undoubtedly the one to take this particular track and have it transferred to disc. There was apparently only one copy made.

The location of the recording is not known although it was probably done "after-hours" at the Cavern, where the two bands frequently alternated sets. There's a photo in Billy Shepherd's *The True Story Of The Beatles* (US: Bantam Books, 1964) of the Beatles "taping 'Misery' at the Cavern" along with a picture of George listening to a playback.

The Beatles (August 1962): *Some Other Guy* (Jerry Leiber-Mike Stoller-Richard Barrett)

In late August 1962, the Beatles were filmed "live" at the Cavern by England's Granada Television Limited. This was the Beatles' first involvement with TV and stands as the first commercial sound film of the group in concert. Although the band was already signed to Parlophone Records, it would be several weeks before they traveled to London to cut their first single. Granada had agreed to send a camera crew to the Cavern as the result of a letter-writing campaign spearheaded by Mrs. Mona Best, Pete Best's mother. Ironically, this film was made just days after Ringo Starr replaced Pete on drums.

Granada TV director Dick Fontaine captured the sights and sounds of the Cavern and the Beatles during a lunchtime session. The highlight was a clip of John and Paul singing lead on *Some Other Guy*. The original Cavern film also featured several other songs (including John belting out *Money*) as well as a glimpse of the young, mostly female audience as they danced and tried to get close to their heroes. However, since 1963, the "Some Other Guy" segment is all that has ever been rebroadcast.

When Granada televised its film, Brian Epstein made an off-the-air recording of *Some Other Guy* and had the tape transferred to disc. Several acetate copies were pressed for Brian and for the Beatles. The records had *Some Other Guy* on both sides, complete with an introduction by the Cavern's resident deejay Bob Wooler, but bore no labels.

Soon after the Cavern piece was shown, bootleg copies of *Some Other Guy* appeared in Liverpool. Brian acted quickly to remove them from circulation.

On December 22, 1982, one of the original acetates was put up for auction at Sotheby's in London. According to the catalog, the record had been purchased at Brian's NEMS record store in Liverpool "for half a crown." Sotheby's appraised the value of this unreleased disc at £2500/5000 ($6,000-$12,000).

The record sold for £1100 ($2,640), an incredible sum but far short of its estimated worth. Part of the reason for this relatively low figure may have been because the track itself was not all that rare.

On April 2, 1971, a fifty-second segment of the *Some Other Guy* clip was broadcast in the United States for the first time during "The Record Makers," the original Guinness Book of Records television special. Bootleg tapes and kinescopes began circulating in America shortly after.

An excellent-quality version of *Some Other Guy* was included on the late 1970s European bootleg, **Beatlemania** (Zakatecas ST 57

The Compleat Beatles
US: MGM/UA Home Video MB 700166 (videocassette)

633XU). All U.S. bootleg versions, including the one on **Some Other Guy** (CBM 3813), were of average quality at best and were usually abbreviated recordings.

On December 8, 1980, ITV in England aired an excellent quality print of "Some Other Guy" in its entirety, in memory of the slain John Lennon.

In October 1982, a 1:15 portion of the film clip was released in re-edited form on the home videocassette "The Compleat Beatles" (Delilah Films). The print quality was excellent. This independently compiled "rockumentary" also included some of the other Cavern footage. Unfortunately, the producers chose to omit the original soundtrack. In its place they dubbed in a commercial "live" recording of *Hippy Hippy Shake* taken from the Star Club album.

The Beatles (1963): *Bad To Me* (Lennon-McCartney)

This primitive recording is a publisher's demonstration disc (Dick James Music Limited TEM 1687/8). John sings lead on this Lennon-McCartney song the Beatles chose not to issue themselves. Instead, the number was given to Billy J. Kramer and the Dakotas, another group managed by Brian Epstein. Their single, produced by George Martin, went to Number One on the British charts the week of August 24, 1963.

On December 22, 1981, the Beatles' original demo was put up for auction at Sotheby's in London along with Paul McCartney's demo of *Goodbye*. Together, the two discs sold for £308 ($739.20).

The Beatles (January 1964): *One And One Is Two* (Lennon-McCartney)

Also a publisher's demonstration record (Dick James Music Limited TEM 1687/8 1610/1035), this is another one of "the songs Lennon and McCartney gave away." Paul sings lead and plays guitar while John plays piano. The recording was made in the Beatles' suite at the George V hotel in Paris following one of their performances at the Olympia theatre, where they shared the bill with French singer Sylvie Vartan and Trini Lopez.

The song was written by Paul and John for Billy J. Kramer. The original tape began with John saying, "Billy J. is finished when he gets this song." As it turned out, Kramer never did release this number. It was ultimately covered by Mike Shannon and the Strangers and was issued in England (Philips BF 1135) in May 1964, but was never put out in America. The Strangers weren't in Brian Epstein's stable of acts and therefore didn't receive the customary publicity blitz given to all NEMS artists. The group was obviously counting on the names Lennon-McCartney to lift this record into the charts, but that wasn't to be. This composition didn't even make it into the British Top 50.

On September 1, 1983, the Beatles' original demonstration disc was put up for auction at Sotheby's in London where it sold for £600 ($1440).

Paul McCartney (1965): *Christmas Record* (McCartney)

On October 20, 1963, the Beatles gathered at EMI's Number Two studio in London's Abbey Road and recorded a special Christmas greeting for all the members of their official fan club. The idea came from the Beatles' publicist, Tony Barrow. During the five-minute message, each of the Beatles stepped forward and thanked the fans for their tremendous support. The recording was issued on December 6 on a 7-inch flexi-disc and was mailed, free of charge, to all fan club members as a year-end bonus. The disc was so well received it started a tradition that lasted until the group disbanded.

In 1965, Paul took this idea one step further and recorded his own Christmas message just for his fellow Beatles. Using a home tape machine, Paul put together a short Christmas record in which he was heard as announcer, singer and comedian. In keeping with his original intent, only four copies were pressed.

Paul McCartney (1969): *Goodbye* (Lennon-McCartney)

One more publisher's demo. Paul sings and plays acoustic guitar on a song he wrote and gave to Apple recording artist Mary Hopkin. Although composed entirely by Paul, the tune was still credited to Lennon-McCartney.

Paul produced Mary's recording. The single (UK: Apple 10) peaked at Number Two on the British charts the week of May 3, 1969.

On December 22, 1982, Paul's original demonstration disc was put up for auction at Sotheby's in London, along with the Beatles' demo of *Bad To Me*. Together, the two records sold for £308 ($739.20).

Cover of Sotheby's 1983 catalog.

John Lennon Sings The Great Rock & Roll Hits/Roots
US: Adam VIII A8018 (LP)

9

The Roots
Of
Rock 'N' Roll

"It started in '73 with Phil and fell apart. I ended up as part of mad, drunk scenes in Los Angeles and I finally finished it off on me own. I can't begin to say, it's just *barmy*, there's a jinx on that album."   John Lennon*

On September 26, 1969, Apple Records issued **Abbey Road**, the last and most popular album the Beatles recorded. It eventually sold over five million copies in the United States alone.

The LP opens with *Come Together*, a Lennon-McCartney composition that was actually written entirely by John. The first line, "Here come old flat top, he come grooving up slowly" is suspiciously close to, "Here come old flat top, he was grooving up with me," a lyric from the 1956 Chuck Berry single, *You Can't Catch Me*. John admitted being influenced by Berry while writing *Come Together* but denied plagiarizing his work. Nevertheless, Morris Levy, president of Roulette Records and the head of Big Seven Music Corporation (publishers of *You Can't Catch Me*), filed suit against John for copyright infringement. As with most legal action, the case took years to come to trial and months to settle.

YOU SHOULD HAVE BEEN THERE

In the fall of 1973, John and Yoko were living in New York City at the Dakota, a Gothic-styled apartment building on West 72nd Street across from Central Park. John had entered the United States with Yoko in August 1971 on a non-immigrant visa. He soon found he liked being in the country so much that he wanted to stay. Unfortunately, his visa expired on February 29, 1972 and couldn't be renewed. John petitioned the U.S. Immigration and Naturalization Service to obtain a "green card," which would enable him to enter and leave the country as he pleased, but all of his requests

---

*Pete Hamill, "Long Night's Journey Into Day," *Rolling Stone*, June 5, 1975.

139

were denied. The official reason given was that he was ineligible for such status due to his November 28, 1968 conviction in London for possession of one ounce of cannabis resin. However, years later it was revealed that the Nixon administration had illegally intervened in John's case after members of the Committee to Re-elect the President became worried that John would participate in a massive peace demonstration outside the 1972 National Republican Convention that was then scheduled to be held in San Diego.

Nineteen months of legal maneuvering and court appearances caused friction between John and Yoko. John's unrelenting desire to live in America coupled with Yoko's wish to locate Kyoko, a daughter by a previous marriage who had disappeared with her father, Anthony Cox, all took its toll on their personal life. Then, one afternoon in early October 1973, John walked out of their seventh-floor apartment to buy some cigarettes and a newspaper and didn't return. Instead, he caught a plane to Los Angeles and began his fifteen month "lost weekend."

To avoid dwelling on his separation from Yoko, whom he still loved and needed, John tried to bury himself in his work. He moved into a Santa Monica beach house and talked to producer Phil Spector about working on an album of rock 'n' roll "oldies." The idea dated back to the days of **Let It Be** when the Beatles toyed with the notion of doing a similar project.

John spent three weeks trying to convince Spector he'd be given complete control of the album. He promised not to come into the booth between takes and co-produce as he'd done on **John Lennon/ Plastic Ono Band**, **Imagine** and **Sometime In New York City**.

John wasn't lacking for material. His just-completed **Mind Games** had yet to be released. John just wanted to have some fun in the studio singing some of the rock 'n' roll songs he'd performed as a teenager. He didn't want to be bothered with arranging the tunes, hiring the musicians or mixing the tapes.

Work on the album finally commenced in mid-October 1973. John sang and played rhythm guitar while Phil dictated orders from the control room. The sessions took place in Los Angeles at A&M Studios and Record Plant West. They quickly gained legendary status among the city's top session men as Phil was using up to twenty-eight musicians on a single track, all playing "live" (and often out-of-tune).

Although not credited on the album, those participating in the sessions included Hal Blaine, Larry Carlton, David Cohen, Steve Cropper, Jesse Ed Davis, Jose Feliciano, Jim Gordon, Nicky Hopkins, Jim Horn, Jim Keltner, Bobby Keys, Barry Mann, Harry Nilsson, Dan Phillips, Mac Rebennack (alias Dr. John), Leon Russell, David Scott, Phil Spector, Nino Tempo, Klaus Voorman and Charlie Watts.

Shortly after the sessions began, the copyright infringement suit between Morris Levy and John came to an end. Levy was victorious although John still maintained he hadn't plagiarized anything.

According to the first part of the settlement, John agreed to record three Big Seven Music songs on his next LP. The Big Seven catalog consists primarily of rock and pop tunes from the late fifties and early sixties. Since John was already working on an "oldies" collection, it would be easy to include several Big Seven numbers without it being obvious that he was bound to record them.

The second part of the agreement called for John, as part owner of Apple Music Publishing Company, Inc. (U.S.) to let Big Seven license any three of the following seven Apple Music titles: *Those Were The Days* and *Goodbye* (Lennon-McCartney), the first two international hits by Mary Hopkin; *Carolina In My Mind* and *Something's Wrong*, both sides of James Taylor's 1970 Apple single; *Come And Get It* (McCartney) and *No Matter What*, the first two Top Ten hits by Badfinger, plus their final A-side, *Apple Of My Eye*.

On October 29, Apple Records released *Mind Games* b/w *Meat City* in America (Apple 1868), followed on November 2 by **Mind Games** (Apple SW 3414). Both records sold quite well and showed a marked lyrical change from John's political sloganizing on **Sometime In New York City**. To the public, it was ex-Beatle John Lennon playing straight ahead rock music for the seventies.

Back in Los Angeles, rumors were running rampant in the music trade about the wild goings-on at the Spector sessions. According to drummer Jim Keltner, Phil had fired a gun inside Record Plant West although studio representatives denied it. *Rolling Stone* reported that Spector had drawn two guns on Stevie Wonder, a guest one evening, in protest of Wonder supposedly hiring away an engineer Spector wanted to use. John later told BBC Radio's Andy Peebles that he once heard a loud noise, possibly gunfire, coming from the men's room of the Record Plant. Harry Nilsson also recounted how Spector had John tied to a chair during one session and then left him in the studio at the end of the night. Fortunately, John managed to free himself and called a friend to come get him out of the building. According to Anthony Fawcett, John's personal assistant, much of this lunatic behavior was caused by those in the studio consuming considerable amounts of brandy while they worked.

By late December 1973, Spector had eight tracks "in the can," including three that satisfied John's settlement with Morris Levy*. Below is the list of songs along with the performers who made them famous:

Bony Moronie (Larry Williams)
Sweet Little Sixteen (Chuck Berry)

My Baby Left Me   (Arthur Cruddup/Elvis Presley)

Just Because   (Lloyd Price/Larry Williams)

Be My Baby   (The Ronettes)

Angel Baby   (Rosie and the Originals; John's all-time favorite single and a Big Seven song)

You Can't Catch Me   (the Chuck Berry hit that caused the lawsuit)

Ya Ya   (Lee Dorsey; not actually a Big Seven title but it was co-written by Levy)

(The changing credits to *Ya Ya* is a story in itself. In the sixties, the songwriter was listed as Morris Robinson. By the early seventies, the credits expanded to Morris Robinson/Clarence Lewis/Lee Dorsey. Then in the late seventies, they changed again to Morris Levy/Clarence Lewis.)

After these eight tracks were completed, Spector quit coming to the sessions. One evening, he called John and told him not to bother driving into the studio because it had burned down. A little skeptical, John had one of his companions phone the Record Plant where they found business as usual.

A few days later, Spector disappeared altogether and, as John soon learned, he'd taken the master tapes with him. It was standard procedure for EMI Records to pay all the production costs for any Beatles or solo Beatles project. Expenses for these marathon sessions were now over $200,000. Apple Records discovered that Phil had been paying for the sessions himself through his Warner-Spector affiliation and therefore had been taking the tapes home with him each night.

With the Watergate scandal front page news, Phil called John a week later and told him he had "the John Dean tapes." Phil said he was the only one who could tell if they'd been tampered with. What he was actually saying was that he had John's "oldies" tapes and there was no way John was going to get them back.

Knowing Spector's eccentric habits, John decided to wait around Los Angeles for Phil to turn up but months passed and no one could locate him.

By January 1974, John's mental state was anything but healthy. After the sessions broke down, he became increasingly depressed over his separation from Yoko. It was the first time he'd been without her since 1968. He phoned her constantly and tried to get her to take him back but she refused, saying he wasn't ready to move in with her yet. Then there was the loss of the Spector tapes. John needed them to fulfill his agreement with Morris Levy. He'd never left an album unfinished before and had certainly never had anyone walk off with his work. John's immigration status was also shaky at best, with the possibility of him being deported at any time. And in England, legal proceedings were in full swing to dissolve the Beatles' partnership.

WHATEVER GETS YOU THROUGH THE NIGHT

In November 1973, John started hanging out with an old friend, singer Harry Nilsson. Harry had wandered into A&M Studios one night not knowing who was recording and ended up working on John's album for the next month. The two of them soon became drinking buddies and together they started putting away Brandy Alexanders "like milkshakes."

By March 1974, John was fed up waiting around for the Spector tapes so he decided to produce a Harry Nilsson album for RCA Records, **Pussy Cats** (US: RCA CLP 1-0570). John figured the best way to pull this project together in a hurry was to have everyone involved move into his Santa Monica beach house. Living under one roof were John, Harry, Harry's fiancee Una, Ringo Starr, Klaus Voorman and Keith Moon.

Reports of John and Harry's drunken antics became a staple of the Hollywood gossip columns. In March, the two of them were thrown out of the Troubador club in Los Angeles for heckling during a reunion performance by the Smothers Brothers. John finally had to lock himself in his bedroom for several days to give up booze so he could settle down to some serious recording with Harry and friends at Record Plant West.

About a month before the sessions started, Harry's voice became hoarse. Most of his friends attributed it to hard living and figured it would clear up in time. Others thought the problem was psychological. It turned out he was actually suffering from a ruptured vocal chord that was bleeding everytime he sang.

During the sessions, rumors started to circulate about what had happened to Phil Spector. In April, Spector's secretary, Judy Sakawye, issued a statement that said Phil had been in a serious automobile accident somewhere between Los Angeles and Phoenix around February 10 and had received numerous head and body injuries. Sakawye said she got her information by phone from Spector's personal aide and bodyguard, George, but that no one she knew had actually seen Phil. (Phil's New York attorney, Martin Machat, later told *Rolling Stone* that the accident happened just outside of Phoenix.)

Then on March 31, Spector was supposedly involved in a second accident, this time definitely in Los Angeles. Phil himself said he was thrown through the armor-plated front window of his car and suffered multiple facial cuts and severe burns when the automobile caught fire. According to Phil, he was almost pronounced dead on the way to the emergency hospital.

Spector later told Roy Carr of *New Musical Express* that he received 380 stiches in his face and 480 stiches on the back of his head, that his nose had to be sewed back on after it was completely torn off the bridge and that his hair turned white overnight from shock. Phil also said that after being on the critical list for seventy-two hours, he underwent complete plastic surgery on his face.

Whatever the circumstances, Spector was released from the hospital the week of July 8. His first public appearance was in a Santa Monica courthouse where he was trying to keep ex-wife Veronica Bennett (Ronnie Spector of the Ronettes) from getting visitation rights to see the youngest of their three adopted children, five-year-old Dante. The Spectors divorced earlier in 1974 and Phil was awarded custody of all three kids.

In August 1974, John finally gave up waiting to hear from Spector even though Phil was back in the studio producing an album for Dion. John flew back to New York to finish remixing **Pussy Cats.** He'd also written a new song, *Nobody Loves You (When You're Down And Out)*, and was anxious to record a new album of his own.

John had a court appointment to keep in New York as well. As of July 17, the U.S. Justice Department had given him sixty days to leave the country voluntarily or face deportation. John appealed the ruling.

Before leaving Los Angeles, John wrote the title track for Ringo's next album, **Goodnight Vienna**, and joined Ringo, producer Richard Perry and a host of familiar session men, including Jim Keltner, Jesse Ed Davis and Bobby Keys, at Sunset Sound studios to play piano on the cut.

SURPRISE, SURPRISE

Back in New York, John moved into the Hotel Pierre on Fifth Avenue, where he wrote ten more songs. In late August, he booked the tenth-floor studio of New York's Record Plant East, on 44th Street, and started work on a new album, **Walls And Bridges**. From Los Angeles, John flew in Ken Asher (keyboards), Jesse Ed Davis (guitar), Nicky Hopkins (piano), Jim Keltner (drums), Bobby Keys (sax) and Klaus Voorman (bass), all of whom played on the Spector sessions. From New York, John hired Arthur Jenkins (percussion) and Eddie Mottau (acoustic guitar) plus additional horn players and back-up singers.

One night, John got quite a surprise when Elton John dropped by the sessions. Tony King of Apple Records had introduced the two giants of the music industry during the Spector sessions and Elton later participated on both **Pussy Cats** and **Goodnight Vienna.** In

New York, he ended up singing and playing piano on the up-tempo *Whatever Gets You Through The Night*. (John returned the favor by singing back-up and playing rhythm guitar on the A-side of Elton's next single, a cover version of the Beatles' *Lucy In The Sky With Diamonds*, and by playing guitar on the B-side, *One Day (At A Time)*, a Lennon song off of **Mind Games**.)

Two days before the sessions began, John regained possession of the Phil Spector material. Rather than using studio time to sort through the ten boxes of tape, John decided to go ahead and record his new album and put the Spector tracks aside for the time being. To get the tapes back, John had to have Capitol Records sue Phil, yet in the final settlement, it was Capitol president Al Coury who paid Spector $90,000 in cash for their return.

On September 23, Apple Records released *Whatever Gets You Through The Night* b/w *Beef Jerky* in America (Apple 1874), followed on September 26 by **Walls And Bridges** (Apple SW 3416). John's friends thought the album might sound negative, since the songs dealth with his L.A. ' lost weekend," but the record turned out to be refreshing and alive and marked the return of some of the magic that surrounded John when he was a Beatle.

STEEL AND GLASS

Unfortunately, the release of **Walls And Bridges** before the "oldies" album posed a serious problem. All the songs were John Lennon originals. (*Old Dirt Road* was co-written by John and Harry Nilsson). The only acknowledgement to Morris Levy was the inclusion at the end of Side Two of a snippet of *Ya Ya* recorded during a break by John, with John's eleven-year-old son Julian playing drums. John's settlement with Levy called for three complete Big Seven Music songs to appear on his "next" album.

Levy phoned Lennon's attorney, Harold Seider, and insisted on talking to John face-to-face. On October 8 the three met for lunch at New York's Club Cavallero on 58th Street. John explained what had happened to the Spector tapes and that he had indeed recorded three Big Seven songs for what he thought would be his "next" LP.

At the end of the **Walls And Bridges** sessions, John listened to the eight Spector tracks but found that only four were suitable for release. He debated what to do with them. He thought of issuing the four cuts on an EP but American record companies weren't pressing EPs in 1974. He also considered putting them out as successive singles but didn't feel the individual tracks were strong enough for that. Finally, he decided to go back to the Record Plant and re-record enough material to make a full album using many of the same musicians who played on **Walls And Bridges.**

During lunch, John also told Levy he was considering marketing his "oldies" album through television. John figured the public might have lost interest in the nostalgia craze that swept the entertainment industry following the 1973 release of George Lucas's blockbuster motion picture, "American Graffiti." Putting out an "oldies" collection seemed like a good idea in 1973, but after a year of problems it now sounded stale. And the hard-core rock community's expectations of what John and Phil would produce together had now eclipsed anything John could hope to salvage from the already finished tracks.

After John explained that he was going back into the studio to re-record most of the cuts, Levy let John spend a weekend rehearsing at his upstate New York farm. Levy later claimed that while there, John gave him permission to sell the finished "oldies" album through TV on his Adam VIII Ltd. mail-order label.

Before going back into the studio, John also spent some time with Mick Jagger at Mick's summer home in Montauk, Long Island. One afternoon, the two of them went out on a sailboat with their guitars and played through all of the old rock 'n' roll classics they could think of. According to Jagger, John was trying to "pick (his) brains" over what material to record for his "oldies" album, which John now referred to as "Old Hat."

Eventually, John typed a list of the songs he intended to put on tape*:

Be-Bop-A-Lula   (Gene Vincent)
Peggy Sue   (Buddy Holly)
That'll Be The Day   (Buddy Holly)
Breathless   (Jerry Lee Lewis)
Slipping And A Sliding (sic)   (Little Richard and Buddy Holly)
Come On Everybody   (Eddie Cochran)
Rip It Up   (Little Richard)
Reddy Teddy (sic)   (Little Richard)
Do You Wanna Dance (sic)   (Bobby Freeman)
Bring It On Home To Me   (Sam Cooke and Carla Thomas)
Send Me Some Loving (sic)   (Little Richard, Buddy Holly and
    Sam Cooke)
Stand By Me   (Ben E. King)
Also included, but crossed out, were:
(30) 40 Days   (Chuck Berry and Ronnie Hawkins)
Ain't That A Shame   (Fats Domino)
Summertime Blues   (Eddie Cochran)

---

*The Editors of Rolling Stone, *The Ballad Of John And Yoko* (New York: Rolling Stone, 1982).

Between October 21 and October 25, John and his crew of seven studio musicians recorded nine new tracks at Record Plant East:

Be-Bop-A-Lula
Stand By Me
Ready Teddy/Rip It Up
Ain't That A Shame
Do You Want To Dance
Slippin' And Slidin'
Peggy Sue
Bring It On Home To Me/Send Me Some Lovin'
Ya Ya

John re-recorded *Ya Ya*, the Morris Levy number, despite having a finished version "in the can" from the Spector sessions. He probably wanted to make sure he had a clean take for release since he'd angered Levy by using a one-minute practice tape of the tune on **Walls And Bridges**.

It's possible that John also re-recorded *Bony Moronie*. Tom Panunzio, an assistant engineer at Record Plant East who started working there only a few weeks before John's "oldies" sessions began, said he "stretched a finished tape" of the song one evening, thereby destroying it. Since the commercially released version came from the Spector sessions, the tape Panunzio ruined must have been a second recording of the number made in New York.

The last track to be completed was *Just Because*, a Lloyd Price song that Phil had suggested John record. Phil produced the basic track in Los Angeles but John redubbed his lead vocals in New York. As the track fades out, you can hear John saying: "This is Doctor Winston O'Boogie saying goodnight from Record Plant East, New York. We hope you had a swell time. Everybody here says 'hi,' goodbye." Several years later, John wondered whether saying "goodbye" at the end of the number was his unconscious farewell to the recording industry, since that word turned out to be the last thing he put on tape for five years.

During the making of the "oldies" album, John, George and Paul were involved in a lawsuit against Apple Corps Limited manager Allen Klein. It's ironic that John then went ahead and recorded Sam Cooke's *Bring It On Home To Me*. Although John described it as "one of my all-time favorite songs," the publishing rights were held by Kags Music Corporation, a company owned in part by Klein. By releasing the track, John was actually putting money back into Allen Klein's pocket.

In a similar situation, John was also earning money for Paul McCartney. As a teenager, John had been a die-hard Buddy Holly fan and later said he'd performed everything Holly released. When it came time to pick a particular Buddy Holly song for his "oldies" collection, John chose *Peggy Sue*. Prior to the release of the album, Paul McCartney purchased the Buddy Holly Music publishing company. That meant the publisher's royalties for John's recording of *Peggy Sue* went to McCartney Music.

In mid-November 1974, Morris Levy persuaded John to send him a rough mix of the "oldies" album. Since Levy controlled three of the songs and since John's recordings of those three titles served as the final settlement between them, John gave Levy a 7½-ips stereo dub of the fifteen tracks.

On November 28, 1974, John made his first public appearance in two years when he turned up as a surprise guest with the Elton John Band at Madison Square Garden. John had promised Elton that if *Whatever Gets You Through The Night* became a Number One hit in America, he'd join him onstage in New York to sing it. John remained true to his word and together the two of them romped through a rousing version of the song before an ecstatic, sold-out crowd. They also performed Elton's current single, *Lucy In The Sky With Diamonds* and delighted everyone by closing with another Beatles' number, *I Saw Her Standing There*, which John had never sung lead on before.

(A "live" recording of *I Saw Her Standing There* was issued as the B-side of Elton's next single, *Philadelphia Freedom*. Shortly after John's murder, Elton's record company, DJM, released all three "live" cuts, both on a 7-inch and 12-inch maxi-single, and as part of a "live" album of highlights from Elton's highly-acclaimed New York performance).

As time passed, John began to have his doubts about the "oldies" album. The initial tracks that Spector produced sounded lethargic and overblown and the nine additional cuts he'd recorded in New York had been churned out at the rate of two-a-day with little time spent on arranging or overdubbing. The idea of an "oldies" album seemed good in 1973, but now it would be at least spring of 1975 before the record could be in the stores. John thought about shelving the whole project but he'd never left an entire LP "in the can" before and had no desire to start now.

He played some of the tracks for his friends and for executives at Capitol Records. They all said they liked them so eventually he decided to go ahead and release the album.

At the end of December, John took his son Julian and secretary May Pang to Florida for a combination vacation and business trip. While there, they shared an apartment with Morris Levy and spent much of their time relaxing in Disney World.

A few days after arriving in Florida, John met with his attorney,

Harold Seider, to sign the necessary papers for the final dissolution of the Beatles' partnership. John found it more than a little amusing that the tangled business affairs of the group should finally be settled amid Disney World's fantasy atmosphere.

Before leaving Florida, Morris Levy tried to persuade Seider to speak to Capitol Records about getting him the necessary clearances to sell John's "oldies" album via television on his own Adam VIII Limited label. According to John, Levy expected to earn between one and two dollars profit per album. This would net John and EMI Records only twenty-three cents per LP after expenses.

When Capitol learned that Levy might indeed get John's tapes, tapes which they'd spent $90,000 to recover, they were furious. Afterall, neither Capitol Records nor John Lennon had given Levy the right to market John's recordings, his name or his likeness. Several weeks later, Seider, acting on behalf of Capitol and John, told Levy he would not be able to issue any John Lennon records.

January 1975 was a good month for the Lennons. Most important was John's reconciliation with Yoko. The two had met backstage at Madison Square Garden after John's appearance with Elton John and found they were still very much in love. With the start of the new year, John moved back in with Yoko at the Dakota.

Another relief was the announcement in London on January 9 that the Beatles partnership was now officially dissolved. It brought to an end four unpleasant years of court battles.

Even John's immigration fight was starting to go his way. On January 2, John and his attorneys won the right to inspect his U.S. Immigration and Naturalization Service files in an attempt to prove that the Nixon administration had interfered in John's case.

John also spent several days in the studio with David Bowie, where he played guitar on Bowie's cover version of the Beatles' *Across The Universe* and co-wrote the A-side of Bowie's next single, *Fame*, with Bowie and Carlos Alomar.

With everthing else in John's life improving, his problems with Morris Levy were far from over. In early February 1975, Levy took the rough tape John had given him and pressed it into an album, **John Lennon Sings The Great Rock & Roll Hits/Roots** (US: Adam VIII A8018). The jacket and record labels said, "Produced from master recordings owned by and with permission of John Lennon and Apple Records, Inc.," even though the LP had been transferred from a 7½-ips dub. Naturally, the sound quality was inferior.

The album's front cover featured a cheaply reproduced cut-out photo of John taken by Ethan Russell during the **Let It Be** sessions. It bore little resemblance to the way John looked in 1975. The back cover had the list of song titles plus illustrations of two other Adam VIII TV compilations.

The running order of **Roots** is as follows:

(Side One) *Be-Bop-A-Lula/Ain't That A Shame/Stand By Me/ Sweet Little Sixteen/Rip It Up/Angel Baby/Do You Want To Dance/You Can't Catch Me/*(Side Two)*Bony Moronie/Peggy Sue/ Bring It On Home To Me/Slippin' & Slidin'* (sic)*/Be My Baby/ Ya Ya/Just Because.*

Levy left himself vulnerable to a lawsuit from Venice Music, Incorporated for failing to credit two of its songs on the album. On Side One, *Rip It Up* is actually a medley of *Ready Teddy* and *Rip It Up*. Here there's no real problem since both numbers were written by Robert Blackwell and John Marascalco and published by Venice Music. But on side Two, *Bring It On Home To Me* turns out to be a combination of that song and *Send Me Some Lovin'*. Levy made no mention on the cover or label of the latter tune, its writers (Lloyd Price and John Marascalco) or Venice Music.

As soon as Capitol Records learned that Levy was getting ready to release **Roots**, it rush-released an authorized version of John's "oldies" album, **Rock 'N' Roll** (US: Apple Records SK-3419). Besides being pressed from the original master tapes, **Rock 'N' Roll** also featured cover art selected and approved by John. The front of the jacket bears a striking black-and-white photo of a young John Lennon leaning against a doorway in downtown Hamburg. This shot was taken by Jurgen Vollmer, one of the Beatles' few close German friends, during their second trip to Hamburg in the spring of 1961.

John also re-sequenced the songs and eliminated two of the rougher tracks, *Angel Baby* and *Be My Baby*, both from the Spector sessions.

Angel Baby was a Big Seven Music song and was one of three numbers John recorded as a settlement to Morris Levy's copyright infringement suit. By omitting it, John was openly disregarding the terms he'd agreed to and was leaving himself wide-open for further legal action.

Below is the running order of **Rock 'N' Roll**:

(Side One) *Be-Bop-A-Lula/Stand By Me/Medley: Rip It Up-Ready Teddy/You Can't Catch Me/Ain't That A Shame/Do You Want To Dance/Sweet Little Sixteen/*(Side Two) *Slippin' And Slidin'/Peggy Sue/Medley: Bring It On Home To Me-Send Me Some Lovin'/Bony Moronie/Ya Ya/Just Because.*

On February 7, Capitol Records shipped out the first copies of **Rock 'N' Roll**. The album featured thirteen tracks and carried a list price of $5.98. On February 8, Adam VIII television ads for

Wall And Bridges ad.

Roots appeared on many independent stations in the eastern United States. **Roots** had fifteen cuts and was selling for $4.98.

Capitol immediately informed TV and radio stations that **Roots** was not an "official" John Lennon album and that anyone who continued to advertise and sell it would be liable for criminal prosecution. Capitol was able to force Adam VIII to stop production on **Roots** but not until after 3,000 copies had been pressed. John later said he'd ordered several copies for himself and waited over three weeks for the records to arrive.

Capitol's initial pressing of **Rock 'N' Roll** was 2,444 LPs and 500 eight-track tapes, but after its first month in the stores only 1,270 LPs and 175 eight-track tapes had actually been purchased. In overall sales, **Rock 'N' Roll** ranks as the second-worst-selling music album by John Lennon, just ahead of **Sometime In New York City**, John and Yoko's strongly political LP, which to date has sold less than 175,000 copies in the United States.

Once Capitol removed all copies of the Adam VIII album from the market, Morris Levy sued John for breach of an oral agreement and asked for $42 million in damages. Surprisingly, Levy made no mention of John's failure to comply with their original settlement.

John promptly filed a countersuit against Levy for his unauthorized use of John's recordings, his name and his likeness. John also asked for damages, claiming his reputation as a recording artist had been harmed due to the "shoddiness" of the **Roots** packaging.

On October 7, 1975, the U.S. Court of Appeals overturned the Immigration and Naturalization Service's order to deport John. In September, the INS had given John temporary non-priority status due to Yoko's pregnancy but his attorneys told him not to expect a decision in the case for at least two months. The INS had officially denied John the right to live in America because of his 1968 marijuana conviction in London, but the Court of Appeals determined that under U.S. law John's guilty plea to possession of one ounce of cannabis resin couldn't be used as grounds to prevent him from obtaining permanent residency, and therefore John had been prosecuted unjustly. In its thirty-page decision, the court called "Lennon's four-year battle to remain in our country . . . a testimony to his faith in this American dream."

Then on October 9 (John's thirty-fifth birthday), an even more joyful event occurred in John and Yoko's lives: the birth of their son Sean. Since Yoko had already suffered three miscarriages, both were concerned about the well-being of their child, but Sean, delivered by cesarean section, turned out to be a healthy, eight-pound, ten-ounce baby boy. An elated John told reporters, "I feel higher than the Empire State Building."

WHAT YOU GOT

In January 1976, the Morris Levy suit finally came to trial in U.S. District Court in Manhattan with Judge Thomas Griesa presiding. John had excellent legal counsel and was prepared to fight to the end. Ultimately, John may owe thanks to Levy's attorney, William Schurtman, for the direction the case took.

John contended that the tape Levy had used to manufacture **Roots** was only a 7½-ips dub (and a rough mix at that) and therefore, the resulting records could only be of substandard quality. Schurtman attempted to disprove this by showing that if both **Roots** and **Rock 'N' Roll** were played on an ordinary record player, no one could hear any difference between the two. To demonstrate this, he brought his daughter's portable stereo into the courtroom along with copies of both LPs. He first put on **Roots** and played the opening cut, *Be-Bop-A-Lula*, but he'd neglected to check the speed of the turntable and the record played back at 45rpm. After a quick adjustment, he tried to play *Be-Bop-A-Lula* again, but something else went wrong. Finally, Judge Griesa volunteered to take the two LPs to the nearby apartment of his law clerk and compare them at a later time.

John also argued that the cover photo on **Roots**, an early 1969 shot of him in shoulder-length hair, could damage his credibility as a recording artist because it neither reflected how he looked when the record was made nor was it a conceptual design, as on **Rock 'N' Roll**, created to evoke the spirit of the material on the album. Prior to the trial, John had gotten his hair cut quite short and now looked nothing like the photo in question. Schurtman put John on the stand and tried to intimidate him by maintaining that he'd had his hair cut just for the trial.

"Rubbish," John replied. "I cut it every 18 months."

Everyone in the court, including Judge Griesa, broke into laughter.

Schurtman eventually caused a mistrial. It happened one afternoon when, for no apparent reason, he began examining the front cover of John and Yoko's **Two Virgins** (with both of them nude) in full view of the jury. To top it off, once Judge Griesa ended the proceedings, Schurtman walked over to John and asked him to autograph the album.

Following the mistrial, both parties again presented their case to Judge Griesa but this time without a jury. The second trial lasted until February 5.

On February 20, Judge Griesa issued his twenty-nine-page opinion. He said he had no doubt that John had made a "tentative verbal agreement" with Morris Levy concerning Levy's right to issue John's "oldies" album on Adam VIII Records, but pointed out that John was never in a legal position to negotiate any deal related to his recordings because he was under an exclusive contract to EMI Records.

In March 1976, John's counterclaim against Levy went to trial. John Lennon, Capitol Records and EMI Records were asking for reimbursement of lost income due to the release and sale of **Roots**. John was also asking for punitive damages for any harm to his career suffered because of the poor quality of Adam VIII's packaging.

On July 13, Judge Griesa set the damages in Levy's original suit, awarding Big Seven Music Corporation $6,795 for John's breach of an oral agreement. But in John's countersuit, Judge Griesa ruled that John, Capitol Records and EMI Records should receive $109,700 to compensate for lost income from the sale of **Roots**. John was also awarded an additional $35,000 in punitive damages.

Levy appealed but John was victorious again. However, the second judge reduced the amounts of the damages. In the opening of his opinion, the judge chose several lines from John's *Nobody Loves You (When You're Down And Out)* to comment on the circumstances of the case: "Everybody's hustlin' for a buck and a dime/I'll scratch your back and you scratch mine . . ./All I can tell you is it's all show biz."

After the trial was over, John told *Rolling Stone's* Chet Flippo, "The reason I fought this was to discourage ridiculous suits like this. They didn't think I'd show or that I'd fight. They thought I'd just settle, but I won't."

Concerning unreleased songs, the only finished track that's known to exist is *My Baby Left Me*, produced in Los Angeles by Phil Spector. There's also an alternate take of *Ya Ya*, produced by Spector, that's still "in the can"; the version on **Rock 'N' Roll** comes from the New York sessions.

Angel Baby and *Be My Baby* were available for a short time on **Roots**, although they were omitted from **Rock 'N' Roll**. Today, these two numbers can be found on many John Lennon bootlegs, including **Angel Baby** (US: Wizardo 362), **The Toy Boy** (US: Bag 5069) and **Working Class Hero** (US: Chet Mar CMR-75).

Collectors should also be aware that about six months after Capitol Records stopped Adam VIII from distributing **Roots**, excellent-quality counterfeit copies surfaced in the United States and were later available in Canada, Great Britain, and Europe. While the color printing and quality of the vinyl were quite good, the lettering on the record label was below-par compared to genuine

Adam VIII albums.

A bootleg pressing of **Roots** was also put out by King Kong Records but no attempt was made to reproduce the original cover graphics or label.

In March 1975, Apple Records issued a single from **Rock 'N' Roll**, *Stand By Me* b/w *Move Over Ms. L* (US: Apple 1881). The B-side was a previously unreleased John Lennon song recorded October 23, 1974, in New York during the **Rock 'N' Roll** sessions. In 1980, Capitol Records in America deleted the original Apple pressing and re-released *Stand By Me* as a double A-sided single b/w *Woman Is The Nigger Of The World* (US: Capitol Starline 6244), leaving *Move Over Ms. L* out-of-print. However, the track is currently available in most other countries, including Australia, England, Germany, and Japan.

Apple had also planned to put out a second **Rock 'N' Roll** single in America. At the last minute the record was withdrawn, but not before many major radio stations received special mono/stereo promotional copies of both titles: *Ain't That A Shame* m/s (Apple P-1883) and *Slippin' And Slidin'* m/s (Apple P-1883).

DIFFERENCES

As we've already pointed out, the covers of these two albums are completely different. **Roots** features a color cut-out photo of John taken during the **Let It Be** sessions. **Rock 'N' Roll** offers one of Jurgen Vollmer's black-and-white portraits of a young John Lennon in Hamburg, Germany, circa 1961. The running order of the two LPs is also slightly different and **Roots** contains two more tracks (*Angel Baby* and *Be My Baby*) than **Rock 'N' Roll**.

Ain't That A Shame   (Antoine Domino-Dave Bartholomew)
The original version on **John Lennon Sings The Great Rock & Roll Hits/Roots** (US: Adam VIII A8018) runs 2:34; on **Rock 'N' Roll** the track is only 2:31. The difference is in the length of the fade-out.

Do You Want To Dance   (Bobby Freeman)
The original version on **Roots** (US: Adam VIII A8018) runs 3:02; on **Rock 'N' Roll** the cut is only 2:53. Again, the difference is in the fade-out.

Slippin' And Slidin'   (Richard Penniman-Edwin J. Bocage-Albert Collins-James Smith)
The original version on **Roots** (US: Adam VIII A8018) runs 2:20; on **Rock 'N' Roll** the track is only 2:16. In the latter version,

155

John ends the song by saying, "I won't be your fool no more, honey"; on **Roots**, he continues with, " . . . you done got hip to your jive."

Stand By Me (Ben E. King-Elmo Glick)
The American single (Apple 1881) has strings added to the introduction and the entire track is mixed a little differently from other pressings.

You Can't Catch Me (Chuck Berry)
The original version on **Roots** (US: Adam VIII A8018) runs 4:03; on **Rock 'N' Roll** the cut was artificially lengthened to 4:51 by editing the first verse back into the middle of the song.

Rock'N'Roll
US: Apple SK-3419 (LP)

156

Every
Little
Thing

Beatles catalog/Capitol Records ad.

10

The
Beatles

The Beatles will long be remembered for their music, particularly for the songs of John Lennon and Paul McCartney. Their lyrics and melodies struck a chord with an entire generation. Many of their numbers have become standards. But it should not be forgotten that the Beatles made *records*.

John once said that as a teenager he preferred listening to the single of *Be-Bop-A-Lula* to actually seeing Gene Vincent and the Bluecaps "in person" when they came to Liverpool. Why? Because the sound was in the grooves.

Rock 'n' roll was the first form of popular music to embrace and broaden the realm of studio production. Tape echo was an integral part of the early rockabilly classics of Elvis, Carl Perkins and Jerry Lee Lewis. The "girl group" era was dominated by Phil Spector's "Wall of Sound." Likewise, a thumping bass and stinging horns were key ingredients in the early Motown hits.

From the Beatles' first recording session at EMI's Abbey Road studios in London, George Martin began instructing them in the ways of studio production. On their first LP, **Please Please Me**, Martin double-tracked Paul's lead vocal on *A Taste Of Honey* to get a more "pop" oriented feel. Soon the Beatles were bringing their favorite American rock records to the studio and asking Martin and engineer Norman Smith how they could duplicate certain sounds on their own discs.

When the Beatles stopped touring in 1966, the recording studio became their creative retreat. No longer was the studio used just to put new songs on tape. It now was also a place to experiment and come up with new sounds. Beginning with **Revolver**, more and more of the Beatles' material originated in the studio as the band discovered Indian instruments, tape loops and the many uses of the Mellotron, predecessor of the Moog synthesizer.

As everyone knows, the Beatles possessed no formal musical training. They played and wrote by ear. Unlike commercial songwriters, they usually thought in terms of a finished record. Arrangements were often built around studio techniques such as "double-tracking" and ' phasing." Tape was the Beatles' medium. Their true legacy is their recordings, not just their words and music.

Unfortunately, the Beatles, like other artists at the time, were not in control of their recordings. Major record companies traditionally owned all of the recordings of their artists. EMI forever holds the rights to its entire Beatles catalog, including all of the unissued tracks and raw session tapes. In England, Parlophone Records gave the group the final say in compiling their albums, allowing them to choose the title, the running order of the songs, the single to be released and the final mix. But the band's sphere of influence stopped there. Outside the U.K., EMI subsidiaries were free to handle the Beatles' material as they saw fit.

Each time the Beatles went to America, they were dismayed at the way Capitol Records dealt with their work. A few tracks were withheld from each LP to create more product for the U.S. fans to buy. Also, many of the cuts were electronically "reprocessed" for stereo through the use of echo, not always with the best results.

George Martin worked hard recording the Beatles. Their sound was rich, clean and flat. The early numbers were heavily compressed to convey the power the band delivered on stage but they were hardly ever echoed. Yet millions of Americans grew up listening to Capitol's altered tracks. In all fairness, most times the sound was not all that bad, it just wasn't what the Beatles and George Martin created.

INDUSTRY

During their eight years in the studio, the Beatles brought about several significant changes in the recording industry. As artists they gradually loosened the company policy of having to finish both sides of a single record in one, three-hour session. More importantly, they redefined the commercial approach to making rock albums.

In the early sixties, the record companies generally did not give rock acts the opportunity to record an album until after they had a hit single. Then, to ensure sales, the LP would feature the single as its title track and would often be rounded out with hastily recorded filler material. EMI was no different. In February 1963, the Beatles were alloted just one day to record their debut LP, **Please Please Me**, which had been approved to "cash-in" on the sales of the group's first Number One hit. Fortunately, the Beatles and George Martin viewed the making of an album differently. Because of the group's large repertoire of rock and pop hits, which had been honed in Germany, George Martin was able to choose the best from the Beatles' stage act to come up with an LP that contained fourteen spirited performances. To EMI's surprise, **Please Please Me** rose quickly to the top of the charts, where it stayed for a record twenty-nine weeks.

With each successive album, the Beatles pushed for more creative control. By early 1964, they were allowed six or so sessions to finish **A Hard Day's Night**. A year later, they spent several weeks perfecting **Rubber Soul**. Everything culminated in 1967 with the recording of **Sgt. Pepper's Lonely Hearts Club Band**. The Beatles planned this album to be something different. Instead of another collection of songs, the LP was designed to be listened to as a whole. There were recurring themes and several tracks were linked together. Paul's original idea was to have the Beatles pretend they were another band (Sgt. Pepper's) while they recorded. Sessions were spread over four months at a cost of £25,000 (much to EMI's dismay). But the result was a milestone in recording history about which the music press coined a new phrase, the "concept album." **Sgt. Pepper** also became Britain's biggest-selling LP to date.

RECORDING

When the Beatles recorded **Please Please Me** on February 11, 1963, they did so on a two-track tape machine, standard equipment at the time. Since George Martin had only one day to put the album together, he used the same recording techniques he had on the group's first two Parlophone singles. This meant putting the instruments on one channel and overdubbing the vocals on the other. In mono, **Please Please Me** featured the two channels compressed, while the stereo edition offered "direct stereo."

With The Beatles, the group's second LP taped in July, was recorded the same way. However, the stereo version was "remixed from twin-track to stereo" by dubbing the master onto a second tape machine and spreading the instruments across both channels.

A Hard Day's Night was the first Beatles album recorded in four-track, and with noticeably different mono and stereo mixes. Mono copies were relatively flat, while stereo issues had a high degree of double-tracking. This was also the first LP available in "true stereo," with some instruments on the right, others on the left and the voices in the "middle."

Four-track recording continued as the norm at EMI until the summer of 1968, when an eight-track machine was installed in Number Two studio at Abbey Road. *Helter Skelter* from **The Beatles** ("White Album") was the band's first venture into this new mode of recording. Work continued in this form on **Abbey Road** and **Let It Be**, although it's possible that Phil Spector did his remixing of **Let It Be** on sixteen-track equipment.

161

MIXING

Until 1969 and the release of **Abbey Road**, all of the Beatles' British LPs were issued in both mono and stereo. (Mono mixes of **Abbey Road** and **Let It Be** were put out in England in September 1970 on prerecorded, open-reel tapes). Theoretically, mono and stereo editions of the same album should have been identical except that the mono copy had the two stereo channels combined. But as collectors soon discovered, that was far from the case with the Beatles' recordings. In fact, **Yellow Submarine**, the last LP put out in both formats, was the only album not to contain any differences.

On the early albums, some of the variations turned out to be slightly different takes of the same song. *Money* on **With The Beatles** features different piano intros in mono and stereo. Likewise, the stereo version of *I Should Have Known Better* bears a different harmonica intro than the mono version. *Help* has entirely different lead and backing vocals in mono and stereo plus slightly different percussion.

More often, though, the differences were in the mix. One recording technique George Martin employed with the Beatles was double-tracking the vocals. Double-tracking meant recording the original vocal track and then having the singer go back and match his voice to the prerecorded tape. In 1964, Ken Townsend, a young engineer at EMI, discovered a way to double-track electronically and thus eliminate the need for re-recording. The first album to benefit from the new approach was **A Hard Day's Night**. The Beatles and George Martin tried it out on the stereo mix, using it quite liberally on *If I Fell, And I Love Her* and *Tell Me Why*. In mono, the voices were left flat.

By 1966, mixing differences also involved the inclusion or exclusion of various layers of tape loops. *I'm Only Sleeping* is available in five different mixes worldwide, each containing a different amount of "backwards" guitar. In 1967, *Blue Jay Way* from the soundtrack of "Magical Mystery Tour" also differed in the amount of tape loops heard in mono and stereo.

George Martin was aware that certain production techniques were not equally effective in both formats. Hence the variations to several elaborate cuts on **Revolver** and **Sgt. Pepper**. Rather than merely combining the stereo channels for mono, separate and distinct mono and stereo mixes were made.

Then in 1968 came the mono and stereo copies of **The Beatles** ("White Album"), in which nearly all of the thirty tracks contained variations.

The Beatle's Greatest
Holland: Odeon OHMS 3001 (LP)

The true stereo version of "I Want To Hold Your Hand " first surfaced
in 1965 on this European compilation, along with a 'direct stereo' copy
of "From Me To You."

OVERSEAS

Besides differences between the British mono and stereo records, confusion really set in when EMI began supplying Beatles tapes overseas. In the early days of Beatlemania, foreign subsidiaries chose to make their own compilations rather than simply releasing **Please Please Me** and **With The Beatles** as they had appeared in England. Such was the practice in France, Germany, Australia, Canada, the United States, Mexico and many other countries. Problems arose when the foreign companies began asking for stereo tapes of tracks that had only been released in England as singles. Although all the early cuts were done in twin-track, stereo masters were not readily available. It appears EMI kept on file only the finished masters it had issued in England and left what stereo versions of singles it had put away with the Beatles' uncataloged session tape.

Most often, EMI sent out mono tapes and dubs, which the affiliates would "reprocess" for stereo. But in mid-1965, Odeon Records in Germany issued **The Beatles' Greatest**, a European compilation that included a clean true stereo version of *I Want To Hold You Hand* plus a "direct stereo" copy of *From Me To You*.

It wasn't until December 1966 that Parlophone in England issued a similar compilation, **A Collection of Beatles Oldies**. This Christmas release featured thirteen British single tracks plus one cut previously unavailable in the U.K., *Bad Boy*. The mono edition contained the original singles while the stereo copy featured some true stereo versions, including several variations.

Years later, true stereo tracks began to appear overseas. In 1976, a true stereo version of *This Boy*, the original B-side of *I Want To Hold Your Hand*, surfaced in Canada and Australia on a reissue single. *She's A Woman* was also available in true stereo, but only in Australia and New Zealand on **The Beatles' Greatest Hits Volume 2.**

MISSING MASTERS

As the years passed and EMI began to track down the true stereo tapes, certain masters were discovered missing. The first version of *Love Me Do* with Ringo on drums can no longer be located. Rumor has it that the original 15½-ips master tape is now in the hands of a private collector in Japan. Likewise, the true stereo version of *She's A Woman* has disappeared from Australian Parlophone's vaults. Finally, the true stereo album master for **Magical Mystery Tour**, first used in Germany, is supposedly in the possession of a collector in Texas.

UNITED STATES

The tracks on the Beatles' first British album, **Please Please Me**, reached American record buyers untouched. In July 1963, EMI sent a mono dub to VeeJay Records in Chicago, which it used for both the mono and stereo pressings of **Introducing The Beatles**. (There were no real stereo Beatles albums on VeeJay, even though the material was recorded in twin-track). The mono recording was transferred to a stereo tape without any electronic rechanneling.

Such was not the case at Capitol Records. Although the Beatles' tracks were not significantly altered for mono, Capitol chose to "reprocess" them for stereo by changing the equalization and adding a fair amount of echo. From 1964 to 1967, Dave Dexter, Jr., and later Bill Miller, supervised the remixing at the ground floor studios of the Capitol Records Tower in Hollywood. (Dexter performed similar chores on Capitol's other transatlantic releases of the day, including those by Peter and Gordon.)

The credits on **Something New, Beatles '65** and **Help** read "Produced by George Martin (and Dave Dexter, Jr. in the U.S.)." Over the years, Dexter was criticized quite a bit for his heavy-handed work on the first two albums. Bill Miller used a lighter touch on the Beatles' 1966 recordings. It was Miller who sequenced and remixed the infamous American compilation, **"Yesterday". . . And Today**.

Capitol Records was a pioneer in stereo recording since its introduction in the summer of 1958. Early stereo albums by Frank Sinatra, Dean Martin, Peggy Lee, and Nat King Cole were quite successful, both critically and commercially. The LPs featured the vocalist backed by a lush orchestra. These "Full Dimensional Stereo" albums, as Capitol called them, were recorded in a large studio to create a "concert hall" effect. The orchestra was spread across both channels but mixed slightly into the background while the singer was placed front and center. Often the vocal track was given a bit of reverb to simulate "concert hall" ambience.

Capitol intended to continue with this style of sound for its stereo Beatles albums but didn't have true stereo master tapes to work with. In early 1964, EMI had supplied only mono tapes for *I Want To Hold Your Hand, This Boy* (two songs that had originated as a single in England) and *I Saw Her Standing There*, and twin-track dubs for the rest of the cuts off **With The Beatles**. Capitol had to settle for "reprocessing" the tracks.

After the introduction of stereo sound some six years earlier, engineers at RCA Records came up with several methods for taking a mono master tape and simulating stereo sound through the use of equalizers, filters, echo and reverb devices. These techniques were devised not so much for artistic reasons but as a way for record companies to continue to sell older recordings to a new stereo market. Since record labels also charged a dollar more for stereo releases, they would be able to realize extra revenue by "reprocessing" their mono catalog.

RCA will forever hold a place in the annals of rock 'n' roll for "reprocessing" its first four Elvis Presley albums and then destroying the original masters. Not until 1984 were mono copy tapes discovered. As one story goes, RCA set up a speaker at the top of a stairwell. Then, with two microphones at the bottom, the sound playing through the speaker was taped as it filtered downstairs. To anyone who has heard these atrocious stereo versions, this explanation does not seem farfetched. There is absolutely no bass on any of the recordings and the mid-range and treble swirl around as if bouncing off steel.

Capitol was less drastic in its approach to the Beatles tracks, but the end result was still a far cry from the originals. With the mono dubs of *I Want To Hold Your Hand, This Boy* and *I Saw Her Standing There*, Capitol used an equalizer to divide the frequency spectrum, panning the bass frequencies to the left and the treble to the right, and then echoed the entire track. For the **With The Beatles** cuts in twin-track, they re-balanced the voices in relation to the instruments by changing the levels of the two channels and again echoed everything slightly.

Prior to the Beatles, Capitol usually labeled recordings that were electronically rechanneled from mono as "Duophonic," while material that was derived from multi-track tapes was said to be in "New Improved Full Dimensional Stereo." Tracks on Capitol's other albums, whether pop, classical, or jazz were so designated. But Capitol refrained from making this distinction on any Beatles LP.

To hear just how distorted the American stereo versions can sound, compare mono and stereo copies of both *You Can't Do That* and *She's A Woman*. Again, Capitol Records received mono dubs of these songs when they were first issued in England as singles. On *You Can't Do That*, John sounds as if he were singing inside a cardboard box. While Paul's bass, Ringo's drums and John's rhythm guitar come crashing out of the record, John's vocal and George's opening lead guitar were mixed back into the track. On the original British mix, all the instruments remain flat, with no echo or reverb, and John's voice is dead center. (A true stereo version of *You Can't Do That* was released in England on **A Hard Day's Night** but Capitol Records never bothered to secure it).

She's A Woman was a song that John and Paul finished writing in the studio just before they were set to record. Again, all the instruments were mixed flat on the original British version, with Paul's soulful singing right on top. In America, both the mono and stereo copies were drastically remixed, although again the stereo copies suffered far worse. Here, both the vocals and instruments were

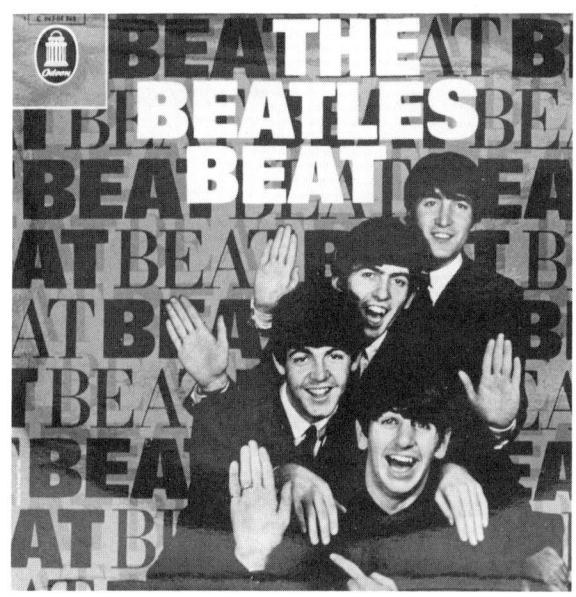

The Beatles Beat
Germany: Odeon C062-04 363 (LP)

And Now: The Beatles
Germany: S*R International 73 735 (LP)

These two identical German compilations contained five
tracks in "reprocessed" stereo from the American collection,
The Beatles' Second Album.

set back into the track, creating a new spaciousness to the recording. Then everything was echoed and the track was re-equalized with a severe amount of treble put on Ringo's "hi-hat" cymbal. While the cymbal is relatively quiet on the British mix, it overshadows the rest of the track at times on the American copies.

For the most part, Capitol's "reprocessed" stereo mixes were unique to Capitol Records releases in America and Mexico. (Capitol of Canada received its own twin-track and true stereo tapes directly from EMI in England, and in fact began releasing Beatles records as early as February 1963.) However, in 1964, several American "reprocessed" tapes made their way to Odeon Records in Germany where they were included on a German-only compilation **The Beatles Beat** (later reissued on a subsidary, S*R International, as **And Now: The Beatles**). The five "reprocessed" tracks (*She Loves You, Thank You Girl, I'll Get You, You Can't Do That*, and *Roll Over Beethoven*) all came from **The Beatles' Second Album**. (Soon after, Odeon put out domestic editions of two of Dave Dexter, Jr.'s American compilations, **Something New** and **Beatles '65**, in addition to its own releases and the regular British LPs.)

In the mid-seventies, Odeon Records in Japan issued the Beatles' entire Capitol Records catalog side-by-side with the original British releases and the special Japanese compilations, making Capitol's "reprocessed" stereo mixes available for the first time in Japan. And in November 1977, the American double-album **Love Songs** was put out in Australia, using the American "reprocessed" stereo tapes as the source.

TRUE STEREO

The first Beatles album to be issued in America in true stereo was **"Yesterday"** . . . **And Today**, put out in the summer of 1966. However, it was only the specially-pressed Capitol Record Club edition that was actually derived from the British true stereo master tapes. The commercial copies were still in "reprocessed" form.

The first Beatles LP to make it across the Atlantic unaltered in any way was **Sgt. Pepper's Lonely Hearts Club Band**, released June 2, 1967, although there were still several differences between the original mono and stereo masters.

Millions of Beatles fans in America grew up hearing nothing but the Capitol Records releases. Those who later had a chance to listen to the British issues were in for quite a shock. Beginning with the group's third album, **A Hard Day's Night**, the British LPs were all put out in true stereo. More importantly, the tracks had a much wider frequency spectrum than the American counterparts. While top-end sounds such as Ringo's drumsticks hitting his cymbals or

George's guitar pick strumming an acoustic guitar were lost in the echo or simply cancelled out when the tracks were re-equalized in America, they came through crisp and clear on the British pressings. Also, the only use of reverb or echo was where it was originally intended by George Martin.

RUSH RELEASED

One of the reasons for so many differences between the British and American Beatles records is that Capitol always pushed to get the latest Beatles tapes as soon as it could. This often meant receiving advance mono dubs and unfinished stereo mixes.

In 1964, Capitol got ahold of the tapes from the Beatles' first releases even though the material was licensed to VeeJay Records. Capitol went ahead and issued *I Saw Her Standing There*, the opening cut on VeeJay's **Introducing The Beatles**, as the B-side of its debut Beatles single, *I Want To Hold Your Hand*, and then included the song on its first Beatles LP, **Meet The Beatles**. Similarly, Capitol put *Thank You Girl*, the B-side of VeeJay's *From Me To You*, on **The Beatles' Second Album**, Here, the track contained an extra harmonica part at the end of the song that wasn't found on the original British release or on VeeJay's American pressing. After several lawsuits, Capitol gained the American rights to this material. It soon released the numbers on an album, **The Early Beatles**, and also reissued the VeeJay singles on its own "Starline" series. As with the other early Capitol releases, **The Early Beatles** was also " re-processed" for stereo.

Long Tall Sally and *I Call Your Name* were two tracks that were actually released in America two months before they came out in England. In April 1964, Capitol put these two numbers on **The Beatles' Second Album**. Again, differences occured. The American stereo version of *I Call Your Name* had an alternate twelve-string guitar introduction spliced onto the beginning. This intro was not available in mono, and because the song was issued in England on an EP, did not appear there in stereo until 1976 when it was included in the compilation **Rock 'N' Roll Music**, a set that originated in the United States. Also, *Long Tall Sally* appeared in America in mono with a flat mix while the American stereo and British EP issues carried a slightly echoed lead vocal by Paul McCartney.

In 1965, *You Like Me Too Much, Tell Me What You See* and *Dizzy Miss Lizzy* came out in America on **Beatles VI** two months before they were released in England. A fourth cut on the album, *Bad Boy*, was forgotten by EMI and not issued in Britain for another eighteen months, as the only new track on **A Collection Of Beatles Oldies**.

169

One year later, *I'm Only Sleeping, And Your Bird Can Sing* and *Dr. Robert* were put out by Capitol in America on **"Yesterday"** . . . **And Today** two months before they were issued in England on **Revolver**. *I'm Only Sleeping* appeared in the U.S. minus most of the famous "backwards" guitar parts as the Beatles apparently had not done the final mix when EMI sent out the mono dubs.

REISSUES

Problems with the quality of the Beatles recordings didn't disappear after the group split up. In fact, they multiplied. In early 1973, two pirated four-record sets, titled **Alpha Omega Volumes I & II**, surfaced in the United States. The packages were sold by mail-order and were heavily advertised on radio and TV stations in the Midwest. Rather than stopping the sales by legal means, Allen Klein, then manager of Apple Corps, had Apple Records issue its own "official" Beatles compilations, **The Beatles 1962-1966** and **The Beatles 1967-1970**. The contents were made up of the A-sides of the group's British singles along with the more popular B-sides and a representative selection of album cuts.

EMI contacted each of the Beatles to get their approval on the project and to see if they had any suggestions. Only John took an interest. He told EMI to make sure George Martin supervised the transfer of the tapes. John was worried that if someone else was assigned the task, they might go ahead and use second generation dubs rather than taking the time to hunt up the correct masters. (John also helped design the jackets, combining an outtake photo from the Beatles' first album cover, **Please Please Me**, with a matching shot of the group taken six years later by Linda McCartney for the front of the unreleased **Get Back**.) All in all, the package turned out quite well. On April 13, 1973, Gold Discs were awarded in the U.S. for each of the double albums. But one had to wonder just how the LPs would have materialized if John had not gotten involved.

The answer came three years later when Capitol Records put out **Rock 'N' Roll Music**, a collection of the Beatles' best hard rockers. In the early days, the Beatles had told EMI that if their records were ever reissued, they had to go out exactly as recorded. What they meant was that the songs could not be augmented with strings, voices, or other instruments, nor could they be edited in any way. The Beatles had seen this happen to many of the early rock 'n' roll stars they idolized, including Buddy Holly and Chuck Berry, and were determined it would never happen to them. But EMI also took this to mean that their tapes could not even be filtered or equalized, if only to improve their sound. So Capitol was prepared to reissue these early numbers, many of them primitive twin-track recordings,

The Beatles 1962-1966
UK: Apple PCSP 717 (LP)

without any sort of modern equilization. Fortunately, George Martin got wind of what was up and demanded a chance to re-work the tapes before they went out. Since Bhaskar Menon, the president of Capitol Records, was a personal friend, he got his wish. However, EMI in England was furious with Martin for going against company policy and went ahead and issued the unequalized tapes on the U.K. edition of **Rock 'N' Roll Music**. (Two years later, the material was re-released on EMI's budget label, Music For Pleasure, on two single LPs. By this time, EMI recognized its mistake and used George Martin's remixes.)

* * *

Variations between different pressings of the same Beatles song began with the group's first commercial recordings in Hamburg, Germany. Long before EMI released **Rarities** in 1978, bootleggers began compiling the rarer tracks. The first such collection was **EMI Outtakes** (US: Phonygraf 1115), which included the stereo version of *All My Loving* with the "hi-hat" count-off, the promotional version of *Penny Lane* with the seven-note trumpet coda, and the mono mix of *Blue Jay Way* minus the backwards vocals. **Dr. Robert** (US: Wizardo WRMB 378) featured *Blue Jay Way* and *Penny Lane* plus the original British stereo versions of *I'm Only Sleeping, And Your Bird Can Sing* and *Dr. Robert*. **Strawberry Fields Forever** (US: Nems Clue 9) offered the true stereo version of *The Inner Light*, while **Recovered Tracks** (US: Barnaby Records FF-9) carried the mono version of *Tomorrow Never Knows* plus mono mixes of *Savoy Truffle* and *Back In The U.S.S.R.* from **The Beatles** ("White Album").

DIFFERENCES

The following is a worldwide list of variations to the Beatles recordings. Included is information about alternate takes, alternate mixes, different instrumental passages, edited promotional discs and more, with the original British versions used as a point of reference. Differences between mono, "reprocessed" stereo, true stereo and quadraphonic pressings are noted. There are also several references to prerecorded tapes and to film soundtrack material.

Citations are arranged alphabetically by song title. Album titles are capitalized and catalog numbers are given whenever possible.

This listing covers primarily original releases and original pressings. Beginning in 1979, about two dozen hard-to-find or out-of-print Beatles takes (including the first version of *Love Me Do* with Ringo on drums and *Penny Lane* with the seven-note trumpet coda) have been reissued on various compilations, all of which are covered in detail in Chapter 4. Such songs bear the notation: See "**Rarities** . . . And Box Sets," followed by the appropriate page number(s).

A similar notation appears for tracks that EMI reissued as part of its Beatles twentieth anniversary celebration, referring the reader back to Chapter 7, "It Was Twenty Years Ago Today."

For material recorded in Hamburg with Tony Sheridan or taped "live" at the Star Club, see Chapters 1 and 2. A complete rundown on the "White Album" is found in Chapter 3.

As outlined earlier, Dave Dexter, Jr. and Bill Miller at Capitol Records remixed many of the Beatles tracks issued in America before 1967 (and a few after) by "reprocessing" them for stereo. To avoid repetition, all entries have been omitted for songs where this was the only difference.

All references have also been eliminated to pressings where the right and left channels of the original recording were reversed. In June 1976, Capitol Records issued its **Rock 'N' Roll Music** compilation with the two channels switched. The same thing happened to five tracks (*Yesterday, Norwegian Wood, You've Got To Hide Your Love Away, She's Leaving Home* and *Here, There And Everywhere*) on EMI's October 1980 set, **The Beatles Ballads.**

Across The Universe (Lennon-McCartney)

(Version 1) - Recorded February 4-8, 1968 and produced by George Martin, this version was released on EMI's **No One's Gonna Change Our World** (UK: Star Line SRS 5013), a benefit compilation for the World Wildlife Fund. In October 1980, it was also included on **The Beatles Ballads** (UK: Parlophone PCS 7214). (See "**Rarities** . . . And Box Sets," pp. 65, 71, 72.)

(Version 2) - In March 1970, producer Phil Spector took the "Version 1" master tape, slowed it down, omitted the bird sounds, the backing vocals, and the organ, then overdubbed strings to create this second version for **Let It Be.** In April 1973, this recording was reissued on **The Beatles 1967-1970.** (See "**Rarities** . . . And Box Sets," p. 83.)

Ain't She Sweet (Jack Yellen-Milton Ager)
(See "Tony Sheridan And The 'Beat Brothers'." p. 13.)

All My Loving (Lennon-McCartney) - studio

Paul sings lead on this popular track off the group's second British LP, **With The Beatles.** On the master tape, the song begins with five taps on Ringo's "hi-hat" cymbal. This short count-off was included on the original German single (Odeon O 22 679), the

German **With The Beatles** (Odeon SMO 73 568) and on **The Beatles' Greatest** released in Germany (Odeon SMO 73 991), Holland (Parlophone OHMS 3001), and later issued in Japan (Apple EAS-81056) and Israel (Portrait PHMS 3001). The count-off was omitted from most other pressings. (See "**Rarities** . . .And Box Sets," pp. 72, 83.)

A "live" version, taped August 23, 1964, is available on **The Beatles At The Hollywood Bowl**.

All You Need Is Love   (Lennon-McCartney)

Performed "live" June 25, 1967 on "Our World," the first international satellite television broadcast, which was seen by an estimated 400 million people. Two weeks later, a polished version was released worldwide as a single.

The recording begins with a brass section playing the opening bars of "La Marseillaise" accompanied by a snare drum roll. In mono, the horns are front and center while the snare drum is in the background; in stereo, the mix is reversed.

The mono version runs 3:57 and can be found on all original singles, on the U.S. mono **Magical Mystery Tour** (Capitol MAL 2835) and in "reprocessed" stereo on the U.S. stereo **Magical Mystery Tour** (Capitol SMAL 2835), later issued in England (Parlophone PCTC 255). In February 1978, the "reprocessed" version appeared in England as the title track on **All You Need Is Love - A Story Of Popular Music** (Theatre Projects Records 9199 995), a "tie-in" LP with director Tony Palmer's British television documentary. (See "**Rarities** . . . And Box Sets," p. 83.)

The true stereo version, first issued in January 1969 on **Yellow Submarine**, was shortened to 3:48 by eliminating the second strain of *Greensleeves* in the fade-out. Mono pressings of **Yellow Submarine** also contain the same track, as the mono LP was created by combining the two stereo channels rather than making unique mono mixes.

In the fade-out, the backing vocals and hand claps remain upfront in mono; in stereo, they fade evenly with the other voices and instruments.

A :34 excerpt of *All You Need Is Love* was included in *The Beatles' Movie Medley*, edited by John Palladino of Capitol Records in America and first issued in March 1982.

And I Love Her   (Lennon-McCartney)

One of seven songs written specifically for the Beatles' first motion picture, "A Hard Day's Night" (United Artists, 1964). Separate and distinct mono and stereo mixes were made. In mono, Artificial Double Tracking (see "Glossary") was added to Paul McCartney's lead vocal on the line "(And) I love her" at the end of each verse, and on the bridge of the song, which begins "A love like ours/could never die . . ." The rest of Paul's vocal remained flat.

In contrast, the stereo mix has Paul's vocal double-tracked throughout the song, except for the first two lines of the third verse, "Bright are the stars that shine/dark is the sky . . ."

The Beatles and George Martin apparently preferred the stereo mix because it was issued in England on both the mono and stereo pressings of **A Hard Day's Night** (Parlophone PMC 1230/PCS 3058), and on the mono-only EP **Extracts From The Film A Hard Day's Night** (Parlophone GEP 8920).

The mono mix, which is heard in the movie soundtrack, was only released in the United States. It appeared on the soundtrack album **A Hard Day's Night** (United Artists UAL 3366/UAS 6366), on a single (Capitol 5235), and on the mono edition of **Something New** (Capitol T 2108). (Stereo pressings of **A Hard Day's Night** had the Beatles' film songs "reprocessed" from mono, while the background music arranged by George Martin turned out to be in true stereo.)

A second variation to this track concerns George Harrison's acoustic guitar riff in the coda. On the German **Something New** (Odeon SMO 830 756), the riff is repeated six times instead of the usual four heard on other pressings. (See "**Rarities** . . . And Box Sets," pp. 70, 83.)

Two short excerpts from *And I Love Her* were used by Capitol Records in America in its 1964 documentary release, **The Beatles' Story** (Capitol S/TBO 2222), produced by Gary Usher and Roger Christian.

And Your Bird Can Sing (Lennon-McCartney)

John sings lead on this track off the Beatles' seventh British LP, **Revolver**. In America, it appeared on **"Yesterday" . . . And Today**.

The only pressings of **"Yesterday" . . . And Today** that contain the true stereo version of this song are the Capitol Record Club edition (Capitol ST-8 2553) and the regular Japanese issue (Apple AP-80061).

Anytime At All (Lennon-McCartney)

One of four songs recorded June 1-3, 1964 to round out the British **A Hard Day's Night**, although it was not part of the movie.

In the spring of 1976, George Martin remixed a stereo version of *Anytime At All* in Los Angeles for **Rock 'N' Roll Music**. (See **Rock 'N' Roll Music**, p. 210.)

Baby You're A Rich Man (Lennon-McCartney)

The B-side of *All You Need Is Love*, released in July 1967.

The mono version runs 3:07; the true stereo version was faded out early, shortening the track to 2:58.

175

The true stereo version is available only on the German **Magical Mystery Tour** (Horzu SHZE 327), and on the British **Magical Mystery Tour** cassette (EMI TC-PCS 3077) and eight-track cartridge (EMI 8X-PCS 3077), both issued in December 1973. (See "**Rarities** . . . And Box Sets," pp. 72, 83, 87.)

(The U.S. and British copies of **Magical Mystery Tour** contain a "reprocessed" stereo version of this song.)

On **Por Siempre Beatles** (Spain: Odeon J 060-04.973), *Baby You're A Rich Man* fades in quickly.

Back In The U.S.S.R. (Lennon-McCartney)
(See "The White Album," p. 51.)

Bad Boy (Larry Williams)
John sings lead on this classic rocker, issued in June 1965 in the United States and Europe on **Beatles VI**. However, the track remained "in the can" in England for another eighteen months, when it surfaced on **A Collection Of Beatles Oldies** as the only new cut on this "greatest hits" collection.

The mono version was heavily compressed, with the bass and drums mixed way up. The true stereo version, first put out on **A Collection Of Beatles Oldies** (UK: Parlophone PCS 7016), had the rhythm section mixed softer in relation to John's vocal and George's lead guitar. (See "**Rarities** . . . And Box Sets," p. 65.)

In the spring of 1976, George Martin remixed a stereo version of *Bad Boy* in Los Angeles for **Rock 'N' Roll Music**. (See **Rock 'N' Roll Music**, p. 210.)

Ballad Of John and Yoko, The (Lennon-McCartney)
Released as a single in June 1969, this record was actually made by just John (guitars and vocal) and Paul (bass, drums, piano and vocal).

The track ends with a final drum beat. On the single, this is heard at full volume. However, when the cut was reissued on **The Beatles Again/Hey Jude** and later on **The Beatles 1967-1970**, it fades out during the final beat.

The *Ballad Of John And Yoko* b/w *Old Brown Shoe* (UK: Apple R 5786) was the first Beatles single to be issued in stereo in England. In America, Capitol/Apple had switched over to stereo a month earlier with the release of *Get Back* b/w *Don't Let Me Down* (US: Apple 2490).

Odeon Records in Spain deleted *The Ballad Of John And Yoko* from **The Beatles Again/Hey Jude** because of the lyric "Christ! You know it ain't easy." On **The Beatles 1967-1970**, Odeon replaced the song with *One After 909*.

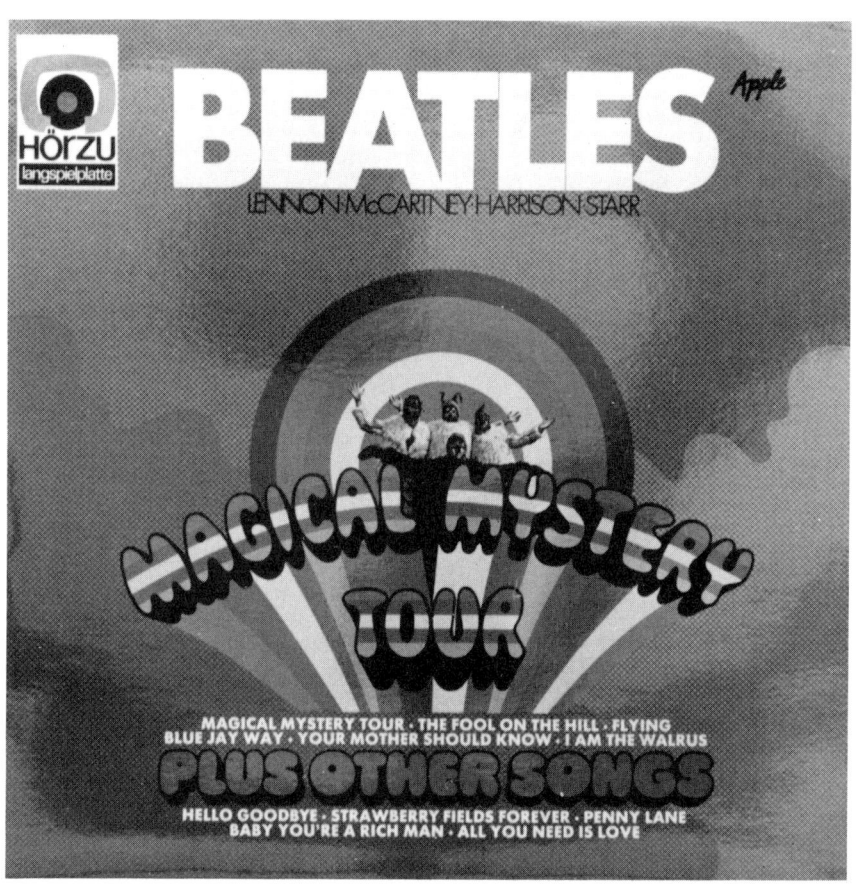

Magical Mystery Tour
Germany: Horzu SHZE 327 (LP)

The German pressing of this American compilation, with its slightly
different cover design, was the first to offer all eleven tracks in true
stereo including "Baby You're A Rich Man," "Penny Lane" and
"Strawberry Fields Forever."

Being For The Benefit Of Mr. Kite (Lennon-McCartney)
Written in February 1967 for **Sgt. Pepper's Lonely Hearts Club Band**, John got most of the words for this song off a Victorian circus poster.

George Martin's background circus effects create more of a swirling sensation in stereo than in mono. However, the mono version contains more tape loops after the line "and of course Henry The Horse dances the waltz!"

Birthday (Lennon-McCartney)
(See "The White Album," p. 54.)

Blackbird (Lennon-McCartney)
(See "The White Album," p. 53.)

Blue Jay Way (Harrison)
George's contribution to the Beatles' ill-fated 1967 Christmas television special, "Magical Mystery Tour."

An extra layer of "backwards" voices was added to the true stereo mix of this song. The original mono version, minus some of the tape loops, can be found on the British mono **Magical Mystery Tour** EP (Parlophone MMT 1/2), the U.S. mono **Magical Mystery Tour** (Capitol MAL 2835), and in "reprocessed" stereo on **Por Siempre Beatles** (Spain: Odeon J 060-04.973).

Boys (Luther Dixon-Wes Farrell) - studio
Ringo sings lead on this cover version of a Shirelles song, recorded February 11, 1963 for the Beatles' first British LP, **Please Please Me**.

A 1:54 excerpt from *Boys* was used by Capitol Records in America in its documentary set, **The Beatles' Story** (Capitol S/TBO 2222), issued on November 23, 1964. In fact, this was Capitol's first release of this song in any form. VeeJay Records had previously held the American rights to the Beatles' first British album, which it repackaged three different times (the last being as **Songs, Pictures And Stories Of The Fabulous Beatles**, put out on October 12, 1964). After much litigation, Capitol eventually gained control of these tracks. Capitol first issued *Boys* in its entirety, along with much of the other material, in March 1965 on **The Early Beatles** (Capitol S/T 2309).

In the spring of 1976, George Martin remixed a stereo version of *Boys* in Los Angeles for **Rock 'N' Roll Music**. (See **Rock 'N' Roll Music**, p. 210.)

A "live" version, taped August 23, 1964, is available on **The

Beatles At The Hollywood Bowl.

Can't Buy Me Love   (Lennon-McCartney) - studio

First released as a single in March 1964, this recording is truly international. The backing track was taped January 29 at the Pathé Marconi studios in Paris, the lyrics were written in February while the Beatles were in Miami, and the vocals and lead guitar were over-dubbed back at EMI in London on February 25, George Harrison's twenty-first birthday.

Different mono and stereo mixes were made. The mono version, which is heard twice in the motion picture "A Hard Day's Night" (United Artists, 1964), is heavily compressed, with Ringo's drums mixed way up. In the true stereo version, first issued in England on the stereo edition of **A Hard Day's Night** (Parlophone PCS 3058), the drums are much softer.

(The true stereo version was not released in the United States until February 1970, when it appeared as the opening cut on **The Beatles Again/Hey Jude** (Apple SO 385/SW 385). Earlier American stereo issues were "reprocessed" from mono.)

The instrumental break features two simultaneous lead guitar solos, both played by George on his new Rickenbacker twelve-string. The main solo was mixed forward while the second one was mixed way down to echo the first. However, in stereo, there's one more note in the middle of the main solo than there is in mono.

A "live" version, taped August 30, 1965, is available on **The Beatles At The Hollywood Bowl.**

Christmas Time (Is Here Again)

The Beatles' fifth annual holiday gift for members of their official fan club, this 7-inch flexi-disc runs 6:10 and was issued on December 15, 1967.

In 1968, the American branch of the fan club mounted a membership drive. In March, the first pressing of *Lady Madonna* came with a fan club flyer inside the picture sleeve. Then, in December, a promo-only Christmas record was sent to Top 40 radio stations across the country. Also titled *Christmas Time (Is Here Again)*, it featured highlights from the four earlier discs, all edited around the 1967 title song. The record runs approximately four minutes and today is extremely rare.

Come Together   (Lennon-McCartney)

John sings lead on the opening cut on the Beatles' final LP, **Abbey Road**.

The first "sshh . . ." in the introduction was omitted from the French pressing of **Abbey Road** (Apple PCS 7088).

Come Together was shortened slightly on a Mexican EP (Apple EPEM 10457) by fading it out early. (See **The Roots Of Rock 'N' Roll**, p. 139.)

Continuing Story Of Bungalow Bill, The   (Lennon-McCartney)
(See "The White Album," p. 52.)

Cry For A Shadow   (Harrison-Lennon)
(See "Tony Sheridan And The 'Beat Brothers'," pp. 12,15.)

Day In The Life, A   (Lennon-McCartney)
The finale to the Beatles' 1967 landmark LP, **Sgt. Pepper's Lonely Hearts Club Band**.

On a later Japanese edition of **Sgt. Pepper** (Apple EAS-80558), the *Sgt. Pepper Inner Groove*, an unlisted four seconds of tape loops that had been omitted from most reissues, was spliced back onto the end of *A Day In The Life*. The running time of the song was listed here as 5:13 instead of the usual 5:03. (See *Sgt. Pepper Inner Groove*, p. 215.)

In the fall of 1978, EMI issued a Beatles single of *Sgt. Pepper's Lonely Hearts Club Band/With A Little Help From My Friends* b/w *A Day In The Life*. The single was put out to "cash-in" on the non-Beatles motion picture "Sgt. Pepper's Lonely Hearts Club Band," produced by Robert Stigwood and based on characters in the Beatles' songs.

A Day In The Life appears in its entirety on the British pressing (Parlophone R 6022). However, the Australian pressing (Parlophone A 12000) is missing the first four beats of the song, while the Japanese single (Odeon EAS-17335) begins when the piano enters, eight beats in.

Day Tripper   (Lennon-McCartney)
Released worldwide as a single in December 1965.

The British stereo **A Collection Of Beatles Oldies** (Parlophone PCS 7016) contains a unique stereo mix of *Day Tripper*. Here, George's opening guitar riff is double-tracked, appearing on both the right and left channels and sounding like two guitars. Other pressings, whether mono or stereo, have only one guitar in the intro.

The British stereo mix is also available on the Japanese **"Yesterday". . . And Today** (Apple AP-80061). (See **"Rarities** . . . And Box Sets," p. 75.)

Dear Prudence   (Lennon-McCartney)
(See "The White Album," p. 52.)

Devil In Her Heart (Richard Drapkin)

George sings lead on this cover version of a Donays song, recorded in mid-July 1963 for the group's second British LP, **With The Beatles**.

The final line of the song, "She's an angel sent to me," was omitted from the Mexican release, called **The Beatles Volume III** (Capitol SLEM 045).

Dizzy Miss Lizzy (Larry Williams) - studio

John sings lead on this cover version of a Larry Williams song, recorded May 10-11, 1965.

The stereo version runs 2:51 while the mono version was faded out early, shortening the track to 2:42.

In the spring of 1976, George Martin remixed a stereo version of *Dizzy Miss Lizzy* in Los Angeles for **Rock 'N' Roll Music**. (See **Rock 'N' Roll Music**, p. 210.)

A "live" version, taped August 30, 1965, is available on **The Beatles At The Hollywood Bowl**.

Dr. Robert (Lennon-McCartney)

Recorded in the spring of 1966 for the Beatles' August release, **Revolver** (UK), this track actually surfaced in America two months earlier on **"Yesterday"**. . . **And Today**.

On the U.S. mono **"Yesterday"**. . . **And Today** (Capitol T 2553), John can be heard mumbling "O.K. Herb" right after the song ends.

The only pressings of **"Yesterday"**. . . **And Today** that contain the true stereo version of *Dr. Robert* are the Capitol Record Club edition (Capitol ST-8 2553) and the regular Japanese issue (Apple AP-80061).

Don't Let Me Down (Lennon-McCartney)

The B-side of *Get Back*, released worldwide in the spring of 1969.

Get Back b/w *Don't Let Me Down* (US: Apple 2490) was the first Beatles single to be issued in stereo in America. In England, it was still pressed in mono. British fans had to wait until April 1973 and the release of **The Beatles 1967-1970** (Apple PCSP 718) for the stereo version of *Don't Let Me Down*.

This song was shortened slightly on a Mexican EP (Apple EPEM 10458) by fading it out early.

Don't Pass Me By (Starkey)

(See "The White Album," p. 53, and **"Rarities** . . . And Box Sets," p. 71.)

Drive My Car   (Lennon-McCartney)

Recorded in the winter of 1965 for the Beatles' sixth British LP, **Rubber Soul**, this track wasn't issued in the United States for another six months when it came out on **"Yesterday". . . And Today**.

The mono mix on the British EP **Nowhere Man** (Parlophone GEP 8952) contains less piano than other pressings, mono or stereo.

In the spring of 1976, George Martin remixed a stereo version of *Drive My Car* in Los Angeles for **Rock 'N' Roll Music**. (See **Rock 'N' Roll Music**, p. 210.)

Eleanor Rigby   (Lennon-McCartney)

Released worldwide in August 1966 as a single and on **Revolver**, this recording features Paul backed by a string octet.

The stereo version contains a mixing error at the beginning of the first verse. In mono, Paul's voice is flat. But whoever remixed *Eleanor Rigby* for stereo started to double-track Paul's vocal here. The result is that the first half of the first word ("Elean . . .") is heard through both channels before Paul's voice shifts to the right side.

The End   (Lennon-McCartney)

The closing track on the Beatles' last LP, **Abbey Road,** released in the fall of 1969.

The penultimate piano chord is longer on the original acetate of **Abbey Road** than on any commericial pressing. (See **"Rarities** . . . And Box Sets,"** p. 83.)

Everybody's Trying To Be My Baby   (Carl Perkins) - studio

George sings lead on this cover version of a Carl Perkins tune, first released in December 1964 on the group's fourth British LP, **Beatles For Sale**.

In the spring of 1976, George Martin remixed a stereo version of this song in Los Angeles for **Rock 'N' Roll Music**. (See **Rock 'N' Roll Music**, p. 210.)

A "live" version was taped in December 1962 at the Star Club in Hamburg, Germany. (See "The Star Club Tape," p. 32.)

Fixing A Hole   (Lennon-McCartney)

Paul sings lead on this cut off the Beatles' 1967 landmark LP, **Sgt. Pepper's Lonely Hearts Club Band**.

Although the running time is listed as 2:33, the stereo version is actually 2:35 while the mono version plays for 2:37.

Flying   (Harrison-Lennon-McCartney-Starkey)

An instrumental from the Beatles' 1967 Christmas TV special, "Magical Mystery Tour," and the first number to credit all four members of the group as writers.

The running time is listed as 2:16. However, the mono version fades out early, shortening the tack to 2:10. The stereo version runs 2:13.

The ending was also mixed differently in mono and stereo. In mono, the "backwards" tape loops come in sooner than in stereo and an extra guitar is also present.

Fool On The Hill, The   (Lennon-McCartney)

Another song from the Beatles' self-produced television special, "Magical Mystery Tour."

The running time is listed as 3:00. However, the stereo version was faded early, shortening the track to 2:55. The mono version actually runs 2:58 but has a slightly different vocal mix. At the end of the song, just after the last chorus, Paul begins ad-lib singing "round, round, round, round." In stereo, this is still mixed forward, but in mono the vocal track is faded here, making these words almost inaudible.

For You Blue   (Harrison)

One of two George Harrison tracks from the 1970 LP, **Let It Be**.

"Queen says no to pot-smoking FBI members," John's off-the-cuff remark that precedes this song on **Let It Be** and **The Best Of George Harrison**, was omitted from the original single (US: Apple 2832), shortening the cut from 2:33 to 2:25.

From Me To You   (Lennon-McCartney)

The Beatles' third British single, issued on April 11, 1963.

The mono version features John's overdubbed harmonica in the introduction; in stereo, the harmonica is missing. The harmonica "fills" in the rest of the song are the same.

The stereo version comes from the original twin-track master tape before the overdub was made. (See "**Rarities** . . . And Box Sets," p. 72.)

Get Back   (Lennon-McCartney)

(Version 1) – Produced by George Martin and first issued as a single in April 1969, this is a complete studio recording of the song with a clean ending and fade-out. In America, *Get Back* b/w *Don't Let Me Down* (Apple 2490) was the first Beatles single issued in stereo. In England, it would be another month before EMI began pressing singles in stereo. In fact, *Get Back* wasn't available in Britain in stereo until April 1973, when it was reissued on **The Beatles 1967-1970** (Apple PCSP 718).

(Version 2) - Comes from the same basic recording as "Version 1," but was "reproduced for disc" by Phil Spector in March 1970 for **Let It Be**. This version opens with a few seconds of "chit-chat" before the song actually starts, and is missing its original ending. In its place, Spector spliced on John's closing remark from the Beatles' January 30, 1969 concert on the roof of their No. 3 Savile Row offices in London, "I'd like to say 'thank you' on behalf of the group and ourselves and I hope we pass the audition." A :36 excerpt of this version of *Get Back* was included in *The Beatles' Movie Medley*, edited by John Palladino of Capitol Records in America and first issued in March 1982. The same month, the song appeared in its entirety on **Reel Music**. (See "Rarities . . . And Box Sets," p. 83.)

(Version 3) - In the spring of 1976, George Martin remixed Spector's stereo version of *Get Back* in Los Angeles for **Rock 'N' Roll Music**. (See **Rock 'N' Roll Music**, p. 210.)

Glass Onion   (Lennon-McCartney)
(See "The White Album," p. 52.)

Good Day Sunshine   (Lennon-McCartney)
Paul sings lead on this song, the opening cut on Side Two of **Revolver**, released in August 1966.

In the fade-out, the percussion differs slightly between the mono and stereo versions. As the fade-out begins, John, Paul and George sing the words "good day sunshine" unaccompanied. Then, in the mono version, Ringo's snare and bass drum re-enter; in stereo, only the snare drum comes back in.

Good Morning, Good Morning   (Lennon-McCartney)
Written in February 1967 by John for **Sgt. Pepper's Lonely Hearts Club Band**, this song was inspired by a Kellogg's Corn Flakes commercial.

Paul McCartney provides the lead guitar work in the instrumental break. In fact, his playing continues on into the bridge of the song. In stereo, Paul's guitar remains mixed up while John sings "People running round it's five o'clock/Everywhere in town it's getting dark." In mono, these extra guitar "fills" are audible but mixed well below John's vocal.

The stereo version is also slightly longer than the mono version. In stereo, the closing vocal refrain ("Good morning, good morning, girl") is repeated ten times before it fades out completely. In mono, it repeats only nine times, shortening the track by four seconds.

Good Night (Lennon-McCartney)
(See "The White Album," p. 57.)

Got To Get You Into My Life (Lennon-McCartney)
Paul sings lead on this Motown-inspired track, released in August 1966 on **Revolver.**

The mono version runs 2:31, while the stereo version is 2:27. In the fade-out, Paul's ad-lib vocal differs slightly between the two mixes. In mono, Paul sings ". . . every single day of my life"; in stereo, he phrases it "every single day . . . of (fade)."

In the spring of 1976, George Martin remixed a stereo version of *Got To Get You Into My Life* in Los Angeles for **Rock 'N' Roll Music.** In America, this version was first released as a single (Capitol 4274) to help promote Capitol's new Beatles' two-record set. (See **Rock 'N' Roll Music,** p. 210.)

Happiness Is A Warm Gun (Lennon-McCartney)
(See "The White Album," p. 52.)

Hard Day's Night, A (Lennon-McCartney) - studio
The title song from the Beatles' first motion picture, recorded on April 16, 1964.

The song is three seconds longer in stereo than it is in mono. The difference is in the length of the fade-out with George's repeated twelve-string guitar riff. The true stereo version wasn't put out in the United States until March 1982 on **Reel Music** (Capitol SV-12199). Earlier stereo issues were "reprocessed" from mono.

In America, all United Artists prerecorded tape issues of **A Hard Day's Night** (open-reel, eight-track cartridge, and cassette) had the lyric "You know I feel alright" repeated five times at the end of the song; every other release finishes with this line sung just three times.

A 1:04 excerpt from *A Hard Day's Night* was used by Capitol Records in its 1964 documentary release, **The Beatles' Story** (Capitol S/TBO 2222), produced by Gary Usher and Roger Christian. Almost two decades later, a :22 clip was also included in *The Beatles' Movie Medley*, edited by Capitol's John Palladino and first issued in March 1982.

A "live" version of *A Hard Day's Night*, taped August 30, 1965, is available on **The Beatles At The Hollywood Bowl.**

Help (Lennon-McCartney) - studio
The title song from the Beatles' second movie, recorded April 13, 1965.

The mono and stereo versions turned out to be different takes, with different lead vocals by John Lennon. Several passages in the first verse distinguish the two. In mono, John sings the third line as "(now) *and* now these days are gone I'm not so self assured," while in stereo he changes a word to "(now) *but* now these days are gone . . . ." Also in mono, John phrases each word in the line "now I find I've changed my mind" evenly. In stereo, he runs the last three words together, "now I find I've *changed-my-mind* . . . ."

In the repeat of the first verse, "I *never needed* anybody's help in any way" comes out in a raspy voice in mono. In stereo, it's sung clearly.

Finally, a tambourine is heard throughout the song in stereo, particularly in the repeat of the first verse. No tambourine was used in mono.

The mono version, heard twice in the soundtrack of the motion picture "Help" (United Artists, 1965), was issued on all original singles, EPs and mono LPs, including compilations, except in the U.S., where the mono edition of **Help** (Capitol MAS 2368) contained the stereo mix with the two channels combined. Dave Dexter, Jr. also spliced a short rendition of the James Bond theme as performed by George Martin and his orchestra onto the beginning of *Help* on the U.S. soundtrack LP. This coupling was also issued on the Japanese pressing of the same album (Odeon EAS 80567) and on the American **The Beatles 1962-1966** (Apple SKBO 3403). (See "**Rarities** . . . And Box Sets," pp. 70, 72.)

A "live" version of *Help*, taped August 30, 1965, is available on **The Beatles At The Hollywood Bowl**.

Helter Skelter (Lennon-McCartney)
(See "The White Album," p. 56.)

Her Majesty (Lennon-McCartney)
(See "**Rarities** . . .And Box Sets," pp. 75, 83.)

Hey Bulldog (Lennon-McCartney)
One of four songs recorded for the feature-length, animated cartoon, "Yellow Submarine" (United Artists, 1968), although it was edited out of the film following its premiere in London.

In the spring of 1976, George Martin remixed a stereo version of *Hey Bulldog* in Los Angeles for **Rock 'N' Roll Music**. (See **Rock 'N' Roll Music**, p. 210.)

Hey Jude (Lennon-McCartney)
At the time of its release in August 1968, *Hey Jude* stood as the longest-running pop single ever released. At 7:11 this rock anthem became the Beatles' most successful single ever, selling over five million copies by the end of the year. More than half of the track is

the epic sing-a-long ("na na na na-na-na na") performed by the Beatles and by members of the forty-piece orchestra George Martin had on hand in the studio.

Since Top Forty radio stations in America were geared to play three-minute songs, Capitol Records sought to head off any possible resistance to *Hey Jude* by supplying each station with an edited promotional copy of the number. This one-sided, 7-inch disc was pressed with an orange Capitol label, although it bore the standard Apple catalog number and was still listed as being 7:11. However, the recording had actually been faded just after the start of the sing-a-long, bringing the running time down to 3:56.

This specially edited version (master number: APP CUS 7 EDIT 2276 45-X-46434 F3 #2) had a limited commercial release in America in the fall of 1968 when Capitol/Apple licensed it to Americom to manufacture in its short-lived "Pocket Disc" format. Pocket discs were 4-inch, 33 1/3 rpm records that retailed for forty-nine cents and were aimed at teenagers with the idea that they could take these records anywhere because they would fit in their pockets. Two other Apple titles that were also put out as Pocket Discs before the venture went bankrupt were the Beatles' *Get Back* b/w *Don't Let Me Down* and Mary Hopkin's first hit, *Those Were The Days* b/w *Turn, Turn, Turn*. Today, these hard-to-find singles are valued in excess of $100 each.

In October 1982, Capitol issued a second, edited version of *Hey Jude* on The Beatles' **20 Greatest Hits** (Capitol SV-12245). Here, a little more than two minutes was cut from the track, shortening it to 5:05. (Non-U.S. pressings of this album contained the complete commercial recording.) (See "It Was Twenty Years Ago Today," pp. 119, 127.)

As mentioned earlier, the original single (mono) runs 7:11; the album track (in true stereo), first issued in America on **The Beatles Again/Hey Jude**, is 7:06. On **The Beatles 1967-1970**, the song was shortened further to 6:54.

Ringo's drums were mixed further forward in stereo than in mono.

Hold Me Tight (Lennon-McCartney)

Paul sings lead on this song, recorded in July 1963 for the Beatles' second British LP, **With The Beatles**.

In the mono version, Paul sings the final words of the song ("you you you") alone. In stereo, his voice is double-tracked here.

Honey Pie (Lennon-McCartney)
(See "The White Album," p. 57.)

I Am The Walrus   (Lennon-McCartney)

The B-side of *Hello Goodbye* and a featured song in the Beatles' ill-fated 1967 Christmas TV special, "Magical Mystery Tour" (Apple Films).

This intricate track, with its many overdubs and electronic effects, was subjected to a fair amount of editing, even after it was first issued. In fact, there are three differences between the mono and stereo versions: the length of the introduction, the existence of a drum "fill" in stereo only, and the four beats of music found only on the American single. As mentioned in the liner notes of the commercially released American **Rarities** (Capitol SHAL 12060), the true stereo version switches to "reprocessed" stereo approximately two minutes into the track. This occurs at the start of the bridge of the song which begins with the ringing of an alarm clock.

The introduction of *I Am The Walrus* consists of John repeating two notes on a Mellotron. The mono version, which was used in the soundtrack of the television special, opens with a four-beat intro. This version is available worldwide as a single, in England on the original mono **Magical Mystery Tour** EP (Parlophone MMT 1/2), and in America on the mono edition of **Magical Mystery Tour** (Capitol MAL 2835).

The stereo version, first issued in England on the stereo **Magical Mystery Tour** EP (Parlophone SMMT 1/2) and later reissued on **The Beatles 1967-1970** (Apple PCSP 718), has a six-beat introduction. However, in America, Capitol Records trimmed the intro back to four beats on the stereo edition of **Magical Mystery Tour** (Capitol SMAL 2835) to match the mono version. It wasn't until March 1982 and the release of **Reel Music** (US: Capitol SV-12199) that Capitol finally issued the correct stereo version of *I Am The Walrus* with the six-beat intro.

(In August 1972, EMI's mail order division, World Records, made available a foreign pressing of the American **Magical Mystery Tour** compilation in Australia (World Record Club S-4574) that was derived from the American master tape, thereby leaving just a four-beat intro to *I Am The Walrus* in stereo. In November 1976, EMI in England put out a commercial edition of this American LP (Parlophone PCTC 255) even though it had long been available as an import. Again, the American master tape was used.)

The second variation occurs between the first and second verses of the song. In mono, Ringo's drums drop out completely for four beats. However, in stereo, there's a two-beat pause followed by a two-beat "fill" on cymbal and snare drum that leads straight into the second verse.

Finally, the American single of *I Am The Walrus* (Capitol 2056) contains a unique four bars of music between the third and fourth

Long Tall Sally
UK: Parlophone GEP 8913 (EP)

The four cuts on this EP (*Long Tall Sally, Slow Down, I Call Your Name,*
and *Matchbox*) were not available in England in stereo until 1976 when they were
included on **Rock 'N' Roll Music**. Differences between the mono and
stereo versions exist for each of the four tracks.

verses that can't be found on any other pressing. (See "**Rarities . . . And Box Sets**," pp. 70, 72, 83.)

I Call Your Name (Lennon-McCartney)

John sings lead on this song, first issued in July 1963 as a cover version by another of Brian Epstein's groups, Billy J. Kramer and the Dakotas. The Beatles' finished rendition was not recorded until February 1964 and was first put out in April on the American compilation **The Beatles' Second Album**.

The track begins with a twelve-string guitar introduction by George Harrison. The original version was mixed in mono and was released in England in June 1964 on the **Long Tall Sally** EP (Parlophone GEP 8913). The stereo version features a noticeably different guitar intro spliced onto the front of the mono recording; it was put out in America on the stereo edition of **The Beatles' Second Album** (Capitol ST 2080), but was not issued in England until June 1976 when it was included on **Rock 'N' Roll Music** (Parlophone PCSP 719). Prior to that, British collectors had to seek out the U.S. import or a Japanese reissue of the **Long Tall Sally** EP (Apple AP-4572), which was pressed in stereo.

The percussion in this record includes a cowbell that was overdubbed for the final mix. In mono, the cowbell starts in the introduction. In stereo, since the alternate guitar intro was spliced on, the cowbell doesn't come in until after the splice occurs, which is just as John starts singing the first line of the song, "I call your name . . . ."

In the spring of 1976, George Martin remixed a stereo version of *I Call You Name* in Los Angeles for **Rock 'N' Roll Music**. Here, the cowbell enters eight beats later as John finishes the opening line, ". . .*but* you're not there." (See **Rock 'N' Roll Music**, p. 210.)

I Don't Want To Spoil The Party (Lennon-McCartney)

Recorded in the fall of 1964 for the Beatles' fourth British LP, **Beatles For Sale**, and issued in America on **Beatles VI** and as the B-side of *Eight Days A Week*.

In stereo, one of the Beatles shouts "woo" just before the instrumental break; in mono, this yell is omitted.

I Feel Fine (Lennon-McCartney)

Recorded in October 1964, this song became the Beatles' eighth Parlophone single in England.

On the true stereo version, first issued in Europe in 1965 on **The Beatles' Greatest** (Germany: Odeon SMO 73-991) but not put out in Britain until December 1966 on **A Collection Of Beatles Oldies** (Parlophone PCS 7016), Ringo can be heard closing his "hi-hat" cymbal five seconds into the track, before the drums come in.

The reissued stereo version begins with a few seconds of tapping drum sticks and whispering before John's "feedback" guitar intro starts. Ringo also coughs before he closes his "hi-hat." This version was first released in April 1973 on the British **The Beatles 1962-1966** (Apple PCSP 717).

Additional pressings that contain this elongated track include the Japanese (Apple EAP-9032B) and Israeli (Parlophone PCSP 717) editions of **The Beatles 1962-1966**. Colored vinyl releases that bear this version include the gold vinyl pressing of **The Beatles' Greatest** from Holland (Parlophone/Odeon 5C 062-04.207), and the red vinyl copy of **The Beatles 1962-1966** from France (Apple 309). Finally, this version is available on a Japanese single (Apple EAR-20228). (See "**Rarities** . . . And Box Sets," pp. 72, 84.)

The fade-out to *I Feel Fine* is slightly longer on stereo editions of **The Beatles' Greatest**. On most pressings, the track disappears when John starts barking in the background. Here, it continues for a few more seconds into a repeated guitar riff.

If I Fell (Lennon-McCartney)

One of the seven songs written especially for the Beatles' first motion picture, "A Hard Day's Night" (United Artists, 1964).

Separate and distinct mono and stereo mixes were made. In stereo, Artificial Double Tracking (see "Glossary") was added to John Lennon's vocal in the song's introduction. In contrast, John's voice remains flat here in mono. The telltale line in differentiating between the two mixes is ". . .'cos I've been in love before, *and I* found that love was more." In mono, John phrases the lyric with a slight pause between the words "before" and "and." But in stereo, the ADT throws John's vocals out-of-sync. The result is that this lyric is heard as ". . .'cos I've been in love before, *(and) and I* found that love was more."

A second variation concerns Paul's vocal in the final verse. In stereo, when Paul harmonizes with John on the line "And I would be sad if our new love was in *vain*," Paul's voice disappears for a moment during the word "vain." However, in mono, engineer Norman Smith edited out this mistake by replacing this fluff with the identical words from earlier in the song.

It's the mono version of *If I Fell* that is heard twice in the soundtrack of the movie "A Hard Day's Night."

A :36 excerpt from *If I Fell* was used by Capitol Records in its 1964 documentary release, **The Beatles' Story** (Capitol S/TBO 2222), produced by Gary Usher and Roger Christian.

If I Needed Someone (Harrison)

Recorded in the winter of 1965 for the Beatles' sixth British LP,

Rubber Soul, this track wasn't issued in the United States for another six months when it came out on **"Yesterday"**. . . **And Today**.

The only pressings of **"Yesterday"** . . . **And Today** that contain the true stereo version of *If I Needed Someone* are the Capitol Record Club edition (Capitol ST-8 2553) and the regular Japanese issue (Apple AP-80061).

If You Love Me Baby   (Charles Singleton-Waldenese Hall)
(See "Tony Sheridan And The 'Beat Brothers'," p. 15.)

I'll Cry Instead   (Lennon-McCartney)
Although written especially for the Beatles' first motion picture, "A Hard Day's Night" (United Artists, 1964), director Richard Lester vetoed its use in favor of repeating *Can't Buy Me Love* later in the film.

The mono version of *I'll Cry Instead* that was issued in the United States had been artificially lengthened for the movie from its original 1:44 to 2:06 by splicing the first verse back onto the latter part of the song. That made it approximately the same length as *Can't Buy Me Love*, which was used again in its place. This version was released in America as a single (Capitol 5234) and was included on **A Hard Day's Night** (United Artists UAL 3366-mono, UAS 6366-stereo) and on the mono pressing of **Something New** (Capitol T2108).

In the summer of 1981, EMI in Australia issued a domestic version of the American **A Hard Day's Night** soundtrack album (Parlophone PCSO 7584), pressed from the original United Artists master tape. This marked the first non-U.S. release of the long version of *I'll Cry Instead*. (See "**Rarities** . . .And Box Sets," p. 75.)

I'll Get You   (Lennon-McCartney)
The B-side of *She Loves You*, the Beatles' first million-selling record.

To date, no true stereo version of this song has been released.

I'm Down   (Lennon-McCartney)
The B-side of *Help*, recorded in late May 1965.

The true stereo version, first issued on a Japanese EP (Apple AP 4110) and later made available on a reissued Japanese single (Apple EAR-20230), features two lead guitars in the instrumental break. In mono, there's only one. (See "**Rarities** . . . And Box Sets," p. 72.)

In the spring of 1976, George Martin remixed a stereo version of *I'm Down* in Los Angeles for **Rock 'N' Roll Music**. (See "Rock 'N' Roll Music," p. 210.)

I'm Happy Just To Dance With You (Lennon-McCartney)

One of seven songs written especially for the Beatles' first motion picture, "A Hard Day's Night" (United Artists, 1964).

A :31 excerpt from *I'm Happy Just To Dance With You* was included in the five-song *Beatle Medley* created in America in 1964 by Capitol Records for its documentary release, **The Beatles' Story** (Capitol S/TBO 2222), produced by Gary Usher and Roger Christian.

I'm Looking Through You (Lennon-McCartney)

Paul sings lead on this song, recorded in the winter of 1965 for the Beatles' sixth British LP, **Rubber Soul**.

This number is five seconds longer in mono than in stereo. The difference is in the length of the fade-out.

There are two false starts to this track on the stereo edition of the American **Rubber Soul** (Capitol ST 2442) and on all Capitol prerecorded tape issues of this album.

I'm Only Sleeping (Lennon-McCartney)

Recorded in the spring of 1966 for the Beatles' August release, **Revolver** (UK), this track actually surfaced two months earlier in America on **"Yesterday"**. . . **And Today**.

According to information gathered from Beatles collectors around the world, there are five variations to George's "backwards" guitar part that winds through the song. The greatest number of "backwards" passages are found on the British mono **Revolver** (Parlophone PMC 7009). This version contains all of the guitar "fills" heard on the British stereo **Revolver** (Parlophone PCS 7009) plus one additional one played during the lyric "lying there and staring at the ceiling."

On the British stereo **Revolver**, George's guitar comes in as John sings the word "running" in the line "running everywhere at such a speed." On the U.S. mono **"Yesterday"**. . . **And Today** (Capitol T 2553), the "backwards" guitar doesn't enter until the instrumental break begins.

The body of the guitar solo heard on a French EP (Odeon MEO 134) differs from all other pressings.

The rarest version of this recording is found on the long out-of-print U.S. stereo eight-track prerecorded tape of **"Yesterday"**. . . **And Today** (Capitol 8XT-2553). Here, the entire guitar track is delayed one second throughout the instrumental break.

The only pressings of **"Yesterday"**. . . **And Today** that contain the true stereo version of *I'm Only Sleeping* are the American Capitol Record club edition (Capitol ST-8 2553) and the Japanese issue (Apple AP-80061). (See "**Rarities** . . . And Box Sets," pp. 70, 75, 83.)

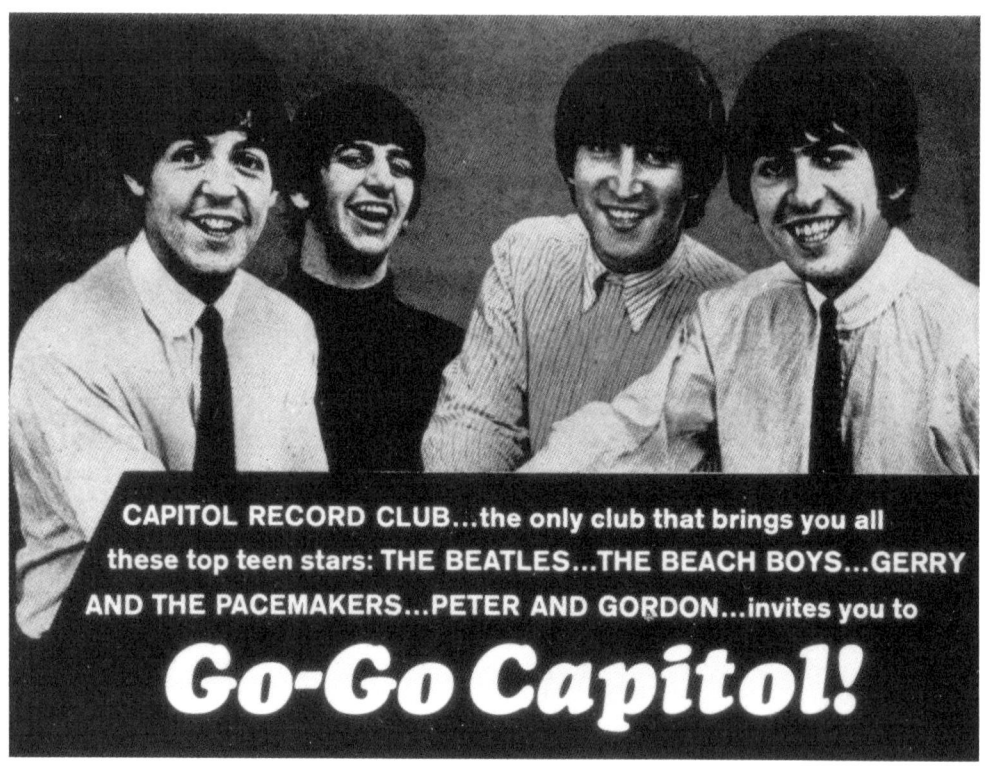

Ad for the Capitol Record Club.

Members of the Capitol Record Club were treated to separate, and sometimes superior pressings. The Capitol Record Club edition of **"Yesterday"... And Today** (Capitol ST-8 2553) featured the three new tracks in true stereo while the ordinary stock copies had these numbers in "reprocessed" stereo.

I'm So Tired (Lennon-McCartney)
(See "The White Album," p. 53.)

Inner Light, The (Harrison)
Issued in March 1968 as the B-side of *Lady Madonna*, with George singing lead. The instrumental track was recorded two months earlier in Bombay with all Indian musicians. George was there working on the soundtrack to the Indian film, "Wonderwall" (Cinecenta, 1968).

This song was issued in "reprocessed" stereo on a Japanese prerecorded cassette; all other tape configurations and record pressings contain the mono mix. (See **"Rarities . . . And Box Sets,"** pp. 65, 71, 72, 87.)

I Saw Her Standing There (Lennon-McCartney) - studio
The opening cut on the Beatles' first British LP, **Please Please Me**, recorded on February 11, 1963.

In America, VeeJay Records omitted "one, two, three" from Paul's four beat "count-off" of this song. Pressings with the shortened beginning are **Introducing The Beatles** (VJLP/S 1062), **Songs, Pictures And Stories Of The Fabulous Beatles** (VJLP/S 1092) and **The Beatles Vs. The Four Seasons** (VJDX/S-30).

In the spring of 1976, George Martin remixed a stereo version of *I Saw Her Standing There* in Los Angeles for **Rock 'N' Roll Music**. (See **Rock 'N' Roll Music**, p. 210.)

A "live" version was taped in December 1962 in Hamburg, Germany. (See "The Star Club Tape," p. 32.)

I Should Have Known Better (Lennon-McCartney)
One of seven songs written especially for the Beatles' first motion picture, "A Hard Day's Night" (United Artists, 1964).

The true stereo version contains an alternate harmonica introduction by John Lennon. Here, John's playing is sloppy and he's forced to take a breath in the middle of a phrase, leaving an unexpected silence followed by a wrong note.

In the original and much more common mono version, John phrases his four-bar harmonica opening cleanly with no breaks or fluffs. This mono version was used twice in the movie "A Hard Day's Night" and was subsequently issued on all original singles, EPS, and mono and "reprocessed" stereo LPs.

In the fade-out, the final line of the song, "you love me too," is repeated four times in stereo but only three times in mono.

The true stereo version, with John's mistake, was first issued on the British stereo **A Hard Day's Night** (Parlophone PCS 3058) as well as on other European stereo releases including **4 Garcons Dans Le Vent** (France: Odeon ZC 062-04.348) and **The Beatles' Greatest**

4 Garcons Dans Le Vent
France: Odeon 2C062-04 348 (LP)

The French edition of **A Hard Day's Night**.

(Germany: Odeon SMO 73-991/Holland: Parlophone OHMS 3001). The first American release of this version was in February 1970 on **The Beatles Again/Hey Jude** (Apple SO 385/SW 385).

During the 1970s, EMI Records used this take exclusively when reissuing this song. In March 1976, *I Should Have Known Better* was released as a single for the first time in Britain (Parlophone R 6013). Parlophone used the faulty true stereo version even though the single was pressed in mono.

In March 1982, EMI put out **Reel Music**, a collection of fourteen songs from the Beatles' five feature films. Included was a true stereo version of *I Should Have Known Better*, this time with the original clean harmonica intro.

A :47 excerpt of *I Should Have Known Better* was included in *The Beatles' Movie Medley*, edited by John Palladino of Capitol Records in America and first issued in March 1982.

It's All Too Much (Harrison)

One of two songs George wrote for the feature-length, animated cartoon "Yellow Submarine" (United Artists, 1968).

The version used in the film was shorter, restructured, and contained a verse not heard in any commercial release of the song.

All commercial pressings run 6:27; the original master tape is reputed to be twenty-five minutes long.

It Won't Be Long (Lennon-McCartney)

John sings lead on this song, the opening cut on the Beatles' second British LP, **With The Beatles**.

In mono, an extra lead vocal track was overdubbed into the final mix where John sings the last line of the song, "Till I belong to you." Here, John sings the word "belong" faster than he did on his original vocal track in the stereo version.

I Wanna Be Your Man (Lennon-McCartney)

Ringo sings lead on this song, first issued on November 1, 1963, as a cover version by the Rolling Stones. The Beatles' rendition came out three weeks later on their second British LP, **With The Beatles**. However, the Beatles' first version, which remains unreleased, had John and Paul sharing the lead vocals while Ringo sang another song on the album, *Little Child*.

In the spring of 1976, George Martin remixed a stereo version of *I Wanna Be Your Man* in Los Angeles for **Rock 'N' Roll Music**. (See **Rock 'N' Roll Music**, p. 210.)

I Want To Hold Your Hand (Lennon-McCartney)

Recorded on October 19, 1963, and issued as the Beatles' fifth

British single on Parlophone, this track also became the group's first American single on Capitol Records and was the song that established them in the United States, reaching the Number One spot three weeks after it was released.

A :58 excerpt from *I Want To Hold Your Hand* was used by Capitol Records in America in its 1964 documentary release, **The Beatles' Story** (Capitol S/TBO 2222), produced by Gary Usher and Roger Christian.

I Want You (She's So Heavy) (Lennon-McCartney)
John sings lead on this song, recorded in mid-1969 for the Beatles' final LP, **Abbey Road**.

This track was shortened slightly on a Mexican EP (Apple EPEM 10458) by fading it out early.

I Will (Lennon-McCartney)
(See "The White Album," p. 54.)

Kansas City (Jerry Leiber-Mike Stoller) - studio
Paul sings lead on this track, actually cover versions of two songs, *K. C. Loving* (Leiber-Stoller) and *Hey, Hey, Hey, Hey* (Richard Penniman, a.k.a. Little Richard). It was recorded in the fall of 1964 for the Beatles' fourth British LP, **Beatles For Sale**.

The running time is listed as 2:30, which is the actual length of the mono version. However, the true stereo version plays for 2:37.

In the spring of 1976, George Martin remixed a stereo version of *Kansas City* in Los Angeles for **Rock 'N' Roll Music**. (See **Rock 'N' Roll Music**, p. 210.)

A "live" version was taped in December 1962 in Hamburg, Germany. (See "The Star Club Tape," p. 32.)

Komm, Gib Mir Deine Hand (Lennon-McCartney-Nicolas-Hellmer)
A German version of *I Want To Hold Your Hand*, recorded on January 29, 1964, at the Pathé Marconi studios in Paris. (See "**Rarities** . . . And Box Sets," pp. 65, 76.)

Let It Be (Lennon-McCartney)
(Version 1) - Recorded in January 1969 at the Apple Recording Studios in London and produced by George Martin, this version runs 3:50 and was released worldwide as a single in March 1970. It was later reissued on **The Beatles 1967-1970** and **The Beatles Ballads**.

(Version 2) - Also recorded in January 1969 at the Apple Studios in London but "reproduced for disc" by Phil Spector in March 1970, this version runs 4:01 and was originally released on **Let It Be**. It was later reissued on **Reel Music** and in Australia on **The Essential**

Beatles (Apple TVSS-8). (See **"Rarities. . .And Box Sets,"** pp.75, 84.

Little Child   (Lennon-McCartney)
John and Paul share the vocals on this song, recorded in July 1963 for the Beatles' second British LP, **With The Beatles**. However, the first version, which remains unreleased, had Ringo singing lead while John and Paul sang another song on the album, *I Wanna Be Your Man*.

A :46 excerpt from *Little Child* was included in the five-song *Beatle Medley* created in America in 1964 by Capitol Records for its documentary release, **The Beatles' Story** (Capitol S/TBO 2222), produced by Gary Usher and Roger Christian.

Long, Long, Long,   (Harrison)
(See "The White Album," p. 56.)

Long Tall Sally   (Enotris Johnson-Richard Penniman-Robert Blackwell) - studio
Paul sings lead on this Little Richard classic, recorded in late February 1964 and first issued in April on the American compilation, **The Beatles' Second Album**.

The common mix, available on most singles, EPs and LPs (in both mono and stereo), has Paul's lead vocal echoed with additional echo and reverb added to the instrumental track. However, the version found on the U.S. mono **The Beatles' Second Album** (Capitol T 2080) has both the vocal and instrumental tracks mixed relatively flat.

A :44 excerpt from *Long Tall Sally* was included in the five-song *Beatle Medley* created in America in 1964 by Capitol Records for its documentary release, **The Beatles' Story** (Capitol S/TBO 2222), produced by Gary Usher and Roger Christian.

In the spring of 1976, George Martin remixed a stereo version of *Long Tall Sally* in Los Angeles for **Rock 'N' Roll Music**. (See **Rock 'N' Roll Music**, p. 210.)

Two "live" versions of *Long Tall Sally* have been issued. One was recorded on August 23, 1964, and is available on **The Beatles At The Hollywood Bowl**. The other dates back to December 1962 and was taped in Hamburg, Germany. (See "The Star Club Tape," p. 32.)

Love Me Do   (Lennon-McCartney)
The A-side of the Beatles' debut single on EMI/Parlophone Records, issued in England on October 5, 1962.
(Version 1) - Recorded on September 4, 1962, with Ringo Starr on drums, this version was issued on the original British "red label"

Love Me Do
UK: Parlophone R 4949 (45)

Love Me Do
Canada: Capitol 72076 (45)

England and Canada were the only two countries where "Version 1" of
"Love Me Do" with Ringo on drums was originally issued as a single.

The Original Greatest Hits by the Beatles
US: Suta 6667 (pirated LP)

Also contains "Version 1" of "Love Me Do" with Ringo on drums.

single (Parlophone R 4949), and on the original "orange and yellow label" Capitol of Canada single (Capitol 72076). It was replaced by "Version 2" on all subsequent pressings worldwide. This track also surfaced in America on **The Original Greatest Hits** (Greatest Records GRC-1001), a pirated album that appeared in 1964, and on an updated edition put out in 1967 (Suta 6667). In 1969, the Beatles' Swedish fan club issued a special, limited edition single (Odeon SD 5937) that contained the original version of *Love Me Do* backed with the original version of *Please Please Me*. Only 1,000 copies were pressed. (See "**Rarities**. . .And Box Sets," pp. 69, 72, 84, and "It Was Twenty Years Ago Today," p. 121, 125.)

(Version 2) - Recorded on September 11, 1962, this version features British session musician Andy White playing drums and Ringo on tambourine. From 1965 to 1982, this is the only recording of *Love Me Do* that EMI put out commercially.

To date, no true stereo version of this song has been released.

Love You Too (Harrison)
One of George's contributions to the Beatles' seventh British LP, **Revolver**.

The running time of this song is listed as 3:00. However, the mono version is actually 3:06 while the stereo mix is 2:58. The difference is in the length of the fade-out.

Lucy In The Sky With Diamonds (Lennon-McCartney)
Written in February 1967 for **Sgt. Pepper's Lonely Hearts Club Band**, the title was inspired by John Lennon's first son, Julian, who came home from school one day with a painting he'd made that he said showed his friend "Lucy in the sky with diamonds."

The mono version was compressed, making the voices sound as if they were electronically "phased" (see "Glossary") in the final mix. In stereo, the voices sound relatively flat.

The track was faded a few seconds earlier in mono than in stereo, thereby eliminating a bit of harmonizing by John and Paul on the final repeat of the song's title.

Magical Mystery Tour (Lennon-McCartney)
The title song to the Beatles' ill-fated 1967 Christmas television special (Apple Films).

Between the second and third verses there's an instrumental break. Near the end, John, Paul, and George sing a long, drawn-out "aaah" which lasts for eight beats. Accompanying this is a brass section playing a sustained chord. In stereo, the brass plays for all eight beats. However, in mono, the brass drops out two beats early.

It's the mono version of this song that's heard twice in the soundtrack of the TV special.

A :31 excerpt from *Magical Mystery Tour* was included in *The Beatles' Movie Medley*, edited by John Palladino of Capitol Records in America and first issued in March 1982.

Matchbox   (Carl Perkins) - studio

Ringo sings lead on this cover version of a Carl Perkins tune, recorded in late February 1964 and first issued in June on the Beatles' fifth British EP, **Long Tall Sally.**

The stereo version, first issued in America in July 1964 on **Something New** (Capitol ST 2108), but not released in England until June 1976 on **Rock 'N' Roll Music** (EMI/Parlophone PCSP 719), features two unison lead vocal tracks by Ringo. (The song was recorded a few months before engineer Ken Townsend came up with a way to electronically double-track while mixing.) One track is mixed forward while the other track is mixed down so as to echo the first. However, in mono, the second vocal track is mixed forward while the first track was omitted.

In the instrumental break, there's a slight variation to George's lead guitar solo. The first eight bars are identical in mono and stereo, but the final four bars are completely different. As the rest of the backing track is the same in both versions, one of the solos was probably edited by engineer Norman Smith.

In the spring of 1976, George Martin remixed a stereo version of *Matchbox* in Los Angeles for **Rock 'N' Roll Music.** (See **Rock 'N' Roll Music**, p. 210.)

A "live" version of *Matchbox*, with John singing lead, was taped in December 1962 in Hamburg, Germany. (See "The Star Club Tape," p. 32.)

Memphis   (Chuck Berry)

One of over a dozen songs recorded by the Beatles at their audition for Decca Records in London on January 1, 1962.

The original version runs 2:12. On **The Silver Beatles - Volume 1** (US: Phoenix-10 PHX 352), the track was artificially lengthened to 2:39.

Michelle   (Lennon-McCartney)

Recorded in late October-early November 1965 for the Beatles' sixth British LP, **Rubber Soul**, *Michelle* ranks as the second-most recorded Beatles song. *Yesterday* tops the list.

The stereo version (2:40) fades out two seconds earlier than the mono version.

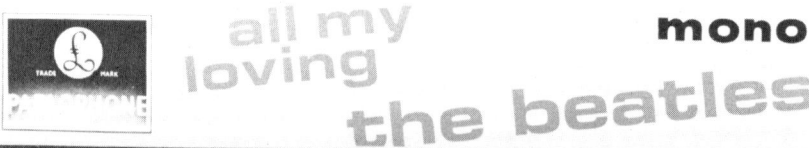

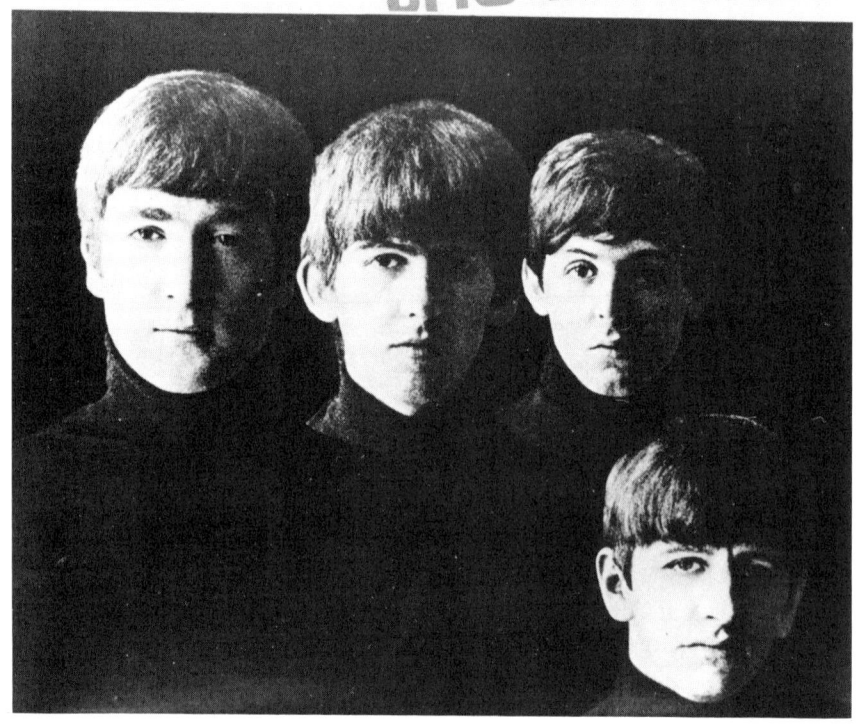

All My Loving
UK: Parlophone GEP 8891 (EP)

Contains the mono version of "Money" with the alternate piano intro
and flat mix.

Misery (Lennon-McCartney)

John and Paul share the vocals on this song, recorded on February 13, 1963, for the Beatles' first LP, **Please Please Me**.

On several pirated pressings of **Introducing The Beatles** (US: VeeJay VJLP SR 1062), the word "the" was omitted from the song's opening line, "*The* world is treating me bad . . ." (See "**Rarities** . . . And Box Sets," p. 70.)

Mr. Moonlight (Roy Lee Johnson) - studio

John sings lead on this Doctor Feelgood song, recorded in the fall of 1964 for the Beatles' fourth British LP, **Beatles For Sale**.

The track was faded earlier in mono than in stereo, thereby eliminating a bit of harmonizing by John and Paul on the final repeat of the song's title.

A "live" version of *Mr. Moonlight* was taped in December 1962 in Hamburg, Germany. (See "The Star Club Tape," p. 32.)

Money (Janie Bradford-Berry Gordy)

John sings lead on this cover version of a Barrett Strong hit.

(Version 1) - One of over a dozen songs recorded by the Beatles at their audition for Decca Records in London on January 1, 1962. The original version runs 2:18. On **The Silver Beatles - Volume 2** (US: Phoenix 10-PHX 353), the track was artificially lengthened to 2:56.

(Version 2) - Recorded in July 1963 for the Beatles' second British LP, **With The Beatles**. The original mono version contains an alternate piano introduction played by producer George Martin. The piano part is a bit different from the stereo intro and is accompanied by handclapping. It's also mixed flat. This rare mix is found only on the British mono **With The Beatles** (Parlophone PMC 1206), the British **All My Loving** EP (Parlophone GEP 8891), on a mono single from Holland (Odeon 45-0 29499), and on the Mexican **The Beatles Volume III** (Capitol SLEM O45). All other pressings, whether mono or stereo, are heavily echoed and contain a more forceful piano intro without any clapping.

In the spring of 1976, George Martin remixed a stereo version of *Money* in Los Angeles for **Rock 'N' Roll Music**. (See **Rock 'N' Roll Music**, p. 210.)

My Bonnie (J. T. Woods-H. J. Fuller)

(See "Tony Sheridan And The 'Beat Brothers'," p. 15.)

Night Before, The (Lennon-McCartney)

One of seven songs written especially for the Beatles' second motion picture, "Help" (United Artists, 1965).

In the spring of 1976, George Martin remixed a stereo version of *The Night Before* in Los Angeles for **Rock 'N' Roll Music**. (See **Rock 'N' Roll Music**, p. 210.)

Nobody's Child (Mel Foree-Cy Coben)
(See "Tony Sheridan And The 'Beat Brothers'," p. 16.)

No Reply (Lennon-McCartney)
The opening cut on the Beatles' fourth British LP, **Beatles For Sale**.

Throughout the song, John's voice is double-tracked using ADT (see "Glossary"). However, when John sings the words "in *my place*" for the first time, he overdubbed his voice again. In stereo, John's voice was tripled on the last two words; in mono, only the word "place" was overdubbed a second time.

Norwegian Wood (Lennon-McCartney)
John sings lead on this song, recorded in the fall of 1965 for the Beatles' sixth British LP, **Rubber Soul**.

In mono, someone coughs right after the lyric "She asked me to stay and she told me to sit anywhere"; the cough was edited out in stereo.

Nowhere Man (Lennon-McCartney)
Recorded in the fall of 1965 for **Rubber Soul** (UK) and issued in America as a single in February 1966 and in June on **"Yesterday"**. . . **And Today**.

The only **"Yesterday"**. . . **And Today** pressings that contain the true stereo version of *Nowhere Man* are the Capitol Record Club edition in the U.S. (Capitol ST-8 2553) and the Japanese issue (Apple AP-80061).

Ob-La-Di, Ob-La-Da (Lennon-McCartney)
(See "The White Album," p. 52.)

Only A Northern Song (Harrison)
One of two songs George contributed to the feature length animated cartoon "Yellow Submarine" (United Artists, 1968).

To date, no true stereo version of this song has been released.

Paperback Writer (Lennon-McCartney)
Recorded on April 16, 1966, and released worldwide as a single in June.

The mono version runs 2:25; the stereo version, first issued on the British stereo **A Collection Of Beatles Oldies** (Parlophone PCS

7016), was shortened to 2:14 by fading it out early.

The original mono mix, put out as a single, is heavily compressed with the percussion mixed way up and a lot of echo between verses. In contrast, the stereo mix has the voices and instruments separated and less echo. The result is that the stereo version lacks some of the force and drive of the original single.

Penny Lane (Lennon-McCartney)
Recorded in January 1967 and originally intended for **Sgt. Pepper's Lonely Hearts Club Band**, this track was issued worldwide as a single in February.

The U.S. (Capitol P-5810) and Canadian (Capitol of Canada 5810) promotional singles end with a seven-note piccolo trumpet coda played by David Mason of the London Symphony Orchestra. This final trumpet passage was omitted from all commercial pressings. (See "**Rarities** . . . And Box Sets," pp. 70, 72, 84.)

The true stereo version, first issued on the German **Magical Mystery Tour** (Horzu SHZE 327) and later put out on the British **The Beatles 1967-1970** (Apple PCSP 718) and the Australian **The Essential Beatles** (Apple TVSS-8), contains several short trumpet notes after the line "It's a clean machine" that were mixed out of the mono version. The trumpet was played by Philip Jones of London's Brass Ensemble.

On the Brazilian **Beatles For Ever**, the words "in summer" were omitted from the lyric "finger pies *in summer.*"

Piggies (Harrison)
(See "The White Album," p. 53.)

Please Please Me (Lennon-McCartney)
Recorded on November 26, 1962, and issued in January 1963 as the A-side of the Beatles' second Parlophone single, and in March as the title cut on the group's debut album.

Before the track was released, engineer Norman Smith made several edits on the vocal track to eliminate a few garbled words from John Lennon. This corrected recording was then compressed to mono and put out as a single, and later on the mono edition of **Please Please Me.**

However, the original, un-edited twin-track tape, with the mistakes intact, was used as the master for the stereo edition of **Please Please Me** and for all stereo reissues of the song.

In stereo, John sings the lyric "I know you never even try girl" in the final verse as "I know *I* never even try girl"; in mono, the correct words were spliced back into the track from the first verse so the song plays correctly.

Penny Lane
US: Capitol P-5810 (counterfeit promo 45)

A counterfeit copy of the American "Penny Lane" promotional single
with the seven-note trumpet coda.

Please Please Me
UK: Parlophone R 4983 (45)

The first pressing of the Beatles' second single for EMI, pressed on the
red Parlophone label.

Also in stereo, John sings the words "Come on, come on . . . ." in the final chorus in a raspy voice; again, with some editing, they come out cleanly in mono.

In 1969, the Beatles' Swedish fan club issued a special, limited edition single (Odeon SD 5937) that contained the mono version of *Please Please Me* backed with the original version of *Love Me Do* with Ringo on drums. Only 1,000 copies were pressed.

P. S. I Love You (Lennon-McCartney)

The B-side of *Love Me Do*, the Beatles' debut single on Parlophone Records in England.

To date, no true stereo version of this song has been released.

Revolution (Lennon-McCartney)

Recorded in July 1968 and issued in August as the B-side of *Hey Jude*, the Beatles' first single put out on their own Apple Records label.

The original mono version is heavily compressed and has John Lennon's distorted rhythm guitar mixed way up. John and George Martin achieved this incredible distortion by overloading one of the pre-amps during recording. EMI was reluctant to put out this "hot mix" for fear the public wouldn't buy it. As it turned out, *Hey Jude* b/w *Revolution* became the Beatles' biggest-selling single ever.

The true stereo version, first issued in America in February 1970 on **The Beatles Again/Hey Jude** (Apple SO/SW 385), has John's vocal and the instruments separated and the level of John's guitar reduced quite a bit. The result is a cleaner track; however, this version lacks some of the power of the original single.

In the spring of 1976, George Martin remixed a stereo version of *Revolution* in Los Angeles for **Rock 'N' Roll Music**. According to Martin, Capitol Records was still worried about the amount of distortion in the recording, eight years after its initial release. (See **Rock 'N' Roll Music**, p. 210.)

Rock And Roll Music (Chuck Berry)

The manic piano playing on this cover version of Chuck Berry's classic was provided by John, Paul, and George Martin, all sharing one keyboard.

In the spring of 1976, George Martin remixed a stereo version of *Rock And Roll Music* in Los Angeles for **Rock 'N' Roll Music**. (See **Rock 'N' Roll Music**, p. 210.)

Rock 'N' Roll Music

In June 1976, Capitol Records in America released **Rock 'N' Roll Music** (Capitol SKBO 11537), a two-record set made up of the

Ad for **Rock 'N' Roll Music.**

Beatles' most popular uptempo numbers. This new compilation spearheaded the label's summer Beatles revival.

Earlier in the year, the group's contract with EMI Records had expired. EMI no longer needed the band's permission to reissue any of their recordings. It now had complete control over all of the Beatles' material in its vaults.

Rock 'N' Roll Music was supported by a $1 million publicity campaign that included newspaper and magazine ads, radio and TV spots, plus a fourteen-minute, in-store promotional film, "Cream Of Beatles." (This short history of the group, produced in Los Angeles by Chuck Braverman and Gary Rocklen, was originally put together for "The Geraldo Rivera Special" on ABC-TV.) Record stores also received reprints of the Beatles' album covers, from **Meet The Beatles** through **Rock 'N' Roll Music**, along with forty feet of clothesline to display them from the ceiling.

Executives in the Capitol Records tower were responsible for the album's atrocious packaging. Instead of trying to evoke the "Swinging Sixties," Capitol's art director put the Beatles back in the fifties, equating Beatles music with hot rods, drive-ins, and Marilyn Monroe. Ringo called the jacket "disgusting," and said that John had offered to design a cover himself but was turned down.

The album's line-up was also chosen by the Capitol brass in Hollywood. Capitol president, Bhaskar Menon, tried to contact each of the Beatles for their final approval but was unsuccessful. Even though EMI was no longer obligated to consult with the group about reissues, it chose to do so as it still courted John, Paul, George, and Ringo as solo artists. (Only Paul had renewed his contract in 1976.)

Unable to get through the Beatles' battery of attorneys and personal assistants, Menon put in a call to George Martin, who was then living in Los Angeles where he was a partner in Chrysalis Records. Menon had studied the production side of the record business under Martin when he first joined EMI and the two had remained friends. George listened to the tapes for **Rock 'N' Roll Music** and was horrified by what he heard. The balance was all off, the stereo separation was wrong, and the recordings sounded flat and cluttered.

Long ago the Beatles had told EMI in no uncertain terms that their recordings should never be altered in any way after their original release. John was particularly worried that years later, the Beatles' tracks would be augmented as the late Buddy Holly's recordings were, with overdubbed strings and back-up vocals added. EMI took the Beatles' demand literally. When **Rock 'N' Roll Music** was assembled, direct transfers of the group's early tapes were made without any sort of equalization.

All of the Beatles' tracks made in 1962 and 1963 had been recorded in twin-track mono, without any consideration for stereo.

This meant that instead of making a true stereo mix with some of the instruments panned to the left, others panned to the right, and the voices and lead guitar put in the center, George Martin had used one track for the backing and the other for the voices. The two tracks were then compressed into a single channel. To avoid distortion when the tracks were combined, Martin compensated during the recording by reducing the volume of the instruments about seven decibels. Again, these techniques were employed to create a mono mix. The two tracks on the tape weren't supposed to be separated.

But now Capitol was doing just that. There had always been stereo releases of sorts for most of the Beatles' recordings, but this usually involved some equalization before the records were mastered. Now, Capitol was following the Beatles' instructions to the letter. The result was that all the instruments were on one side and all the voices were on the other. Also, a lot of background noise that had been picked up by the open vocal mikes, but which had been masked by the instruments in mono, was now suddenly audible. EMI was safe with the knowledge it had not gone against the Beatles' wishes but that was about all. Direct stereo dubs of the early raw tracks didn't sound anything like the originals.

George Martin couldn't bear to see the recordings go out this way knowing full well how far off they were. So, with a nod from Bhaskar Menon, George went ahead and remixed the tracks.

For the early twin-track cuts, Martin put the recordings through an equalizer where he filtered the bass out of the instrumental track and brought it into the center of the mix. Next, he raised the level of the instruments so they'd be correct in relation to the voices, which he panned into the center. Finally, he compressed each of the tracks and added a bit of echo to make them sound fuller.

With the later four-track tapes, Martin used filters and equalizers to give them a brighter, crisper feel. Somewhere in the final dubbing, the channels were also reversed.

After two days in the studio, George Martin had a product he could live with. George gave the tapes back to Bhaskar Menon who, after a brief listen, sent them to be mastered. Unfortunately, Martin's yeomanlike work wasn't met with similar approval on the other side of the Atlantic. Roy Featherstone, head of EMI Records in England, was furious with Martin for going against company policy and remixing the tapes. Featherstone ultimately refused to issue the tracks in their enhanced form and EMI never got around to paying Martin for his services. So, while **Rock 'N' Roll Music** in the United States featured the new George Martin remixes, **Rock 'N' Roll Music** (UK: Parlophone PCSP 719) in Britain consisted of direct transfers of the twenty-eight cuts.

In October 1980, EMI relegated this compilation to its budget label, Music For Pleasure, and reissued the two-record set in two single albums, **Rock 'N' Roll Music - Volume 1** (Music For Pleasure 50506) and **Rock 'N' Roll Music - Volume 2** (Music For Pleasure 50507). Ironically, EMI relented and used George Martin's remixed version for these editions. EMI also bowed to pressure and replaced the album's original artwork with cover photos of the Beatles taken on February 7, 1964, on their arrival at New York's Kennedy Airport.

> (Side One) *Twist And Shout/I Saw Her Standing There /You Can't Do That/I Wanna Be Your Man/I Call Your Name/Boys/Long Tall Sally/*(Side Two) *Rock And Roll Music/Slow Down/Kansas City/Money/Bad Boy/Matchbox /Roll Over Beethoven/*(Side Three) *Dizzy Miss Lizzy/ Anytime At All/Drive My Car/Everybody's Trying To Be My Baby/The Night Before/I'm Down/Revolution/* (Side Four) *Back In The U.S.S.R./Helter Skelter/Taxman /Got To Get You Into My Life/Hey Bulldog/Birthday/ Get Back.*

Roll Over Beethoven   (Chuck Berry) - studio
George Harrison sings lead on this early Chuck Berry hit, recorded in July 1963 for the Beatles' second British LP, **With The Beatles**.

In the spring of 1976, George Martin remixed a stereo version of *Roll Over Beethoven* in Los Angeles for **Rock 'N' Roll Music**. (See **Rock 'N' Roll Music**, p. 210.)

Two "live" versions of this song have been issued. One was recorded on August 23, 1964, and is available on **The Beatles At The Hollywood Bowl**. The other dates back to December 1962 and was taped in Hamburg, Germany. (See "The Star Club Tape," pp. 32, 37.)

Savoy Truffle   (Harrison)
(See "The White Album," p. 57.)

Searchin'   (Jerry Leiber-Mike Stoller)
Paul sings lead on this cover version of a Coasters hit. It was one of over a dozen songs recorded by the Beatles at their audition for Decca Records in London on January 1, 1962.

The original version runs 2:54. On **The Silver Beatles - Volume 1** (US: Phoenix-10 PHX 352), the track was artificially lengthened to 3:44.

September In The Rain   (Al Dubin-Harry Warren)
Paul sings lead on this 1930s pop standard. It was one of over a dozen songs recorded by the Beatles at their audition for Decca Records in London on January 1, 1962.

The original version runs 1:49. On **The Silver Beatles - Volume 2**

(US: Phoenix-10 PHX 353), the track was artificially lengthened to 2:17.

Sgt. Pepper Inner Groove

Many original pressings, and selected reissues, of **Sgt. Pepper's Lonely Hearts Club Band** have a repeated series of sounds after the fade-out of *A Day In The Life* that's pressed in the record's run-off groove. These three seconds of words and noises were created by combining various tape loops, some of which were played backwards.

A note on the log sheet from the master tape box (which appears on the special cover for the album in Mobile Fidelity's box set, **The Beatles: The Collection**) shows that the songs on Side Two are "followed by 15 khs & voices for concentric (see H. Moss for this)." The 15 khs refers to a sound that Paul McCartney suggested be put on the end of the record which could only be heard by dogs. But neither the Beatles nor anyone at EMI has ever said what, if anything, is said in the run-off groove. Two of the more popular beliefs among American Beatles fans are that the group is saying either "I never do see any other way" or "never losing an inch."

In 1969, people in America who felt that Paul McCartney may have been killed three years earlier in a car crash and had then been replaced in the group by an imposter cited this segment as a planted clue, believing the Beatles were saying "Paul will be back as Superman." (*Note*: After the senseless murder of John Lennon in 1980, we feel further discussion of the "Paul Is Dead" theory to be in extremely poor taste.)

McCartney, in an exclusive interview with music writer and critic Paul Gambaccini, said two fans had told him that when they played this track backwards, they thought the Beatles were saying "We'll fuck you like supermen." Paul admitted that he too could hear this interpretation but only after being told what to listen for.

After inspecting various copies of **Sgt. Pepper** from all over the world, we discovered that there is more than one version of the "inner groove." Four variations have been found so far; three in stereo and one in mono. The amount of sounds in the "inner groove" differs with each pressing. The whistling noise ranges from two to four seconds in length. These different versions can be distinguished by checking the matrix number stamped in the record's "dead wax." The mono pressing is numbered XEX 638-1, while the stereo tracks are listed as YEX 638-2, YEX 638-3, and YEX 638-5. The fewest sounds appear on YEX 638-2; the most are heard in mono, XEX 638-1.

On a later Japanese edition of **Sgt. Pepper's Lonely Hearts Club Band** (Apple EAS 80558), the "inner groove," which was omitted from most reissues, was spliced onto the end of *A Day In The Life*. The running time for this song was listed as 5:13 instead of the usual 5:03. (See "**Rarities** . . . And Box Sets," p. 71.)

Sgt. Pepper's Lonely Hearts Club Band (Lennon-McCartney)
The title song to the Beatles' landmark 1967 album.

In September 1978, EMI reissued this track on a maxi-single, along with *With A Little Help From My Friends* and *A Day In The Life* to "cash-in" on the Robert Stigwood movie based on characters from this LP and **Abbey Road**.

On the Australian pressing (Parlophone A-12000), the opening crowd sounds were shortened from ten seconds to two seconds, reducing the song's running time from 1:59 to 1:51. This also occured on an EP issued in Argentina, where the track was faded out early as well.

Sgt. Pepper's Lonely Hearts Club Band (Reprise) (Lennon-McCartney)
This repeat of the title song before the LP's finale, *A Day In The Life*, reinforces **Sgt. Pepper** as a "concept album."

The "link material" between *Good Morning, Good Morning* and this track is noticeably different in mono and stereo. The introduction is a few seconds longer in mono and there's also an extra guitar note after the "chicken cackle" at the beginning. Next, John mumbles a few words prior to Paul launching into his "count-off" that are audible in mono but were omitted in stereo. The "crowd sounds" are also different throughout the track, and in mono there's some laughter from the crowd before the actual start of the song that is absent in stereo. Finally, Paul's ad-lib singing in the fade-out is mixed forward in mono but remains back in the track in stereo.

On the U.S. eight-track tape cartridge of **Sgt. Pepper's Lonely Hearts Club Band** (Capitol 8XT-2653), the chorus at the end of the song is repeated one extra time compared to all other issues.

Sexy Sadie (Lennon-McCartney)
(See "The White Album," p. 56.)

She Loves You (Lennon-McCartney) - studio
The Beatles' fourth Parlophone single, and their first million-seller in England.

A :29 excerpt from *She Loves You* was included in the five-song *Beatle Medley* created in America in 1964 by Capitol Records for its documentary release, **The Beatles' Story** (Capitol S/TBO 2222), produced by Gary Usher and Roger Christian.

To date, no true stereo version of this song has been released.

A "live" version of *She Loves You*, taped on August 23, 1964, is available on **The Beatles At The Hollywood Bowl**.

She's A Woman (Lennon-McCartney) - studio

Recorded in early October 1964 and issued as the B-side of *I Feel Fine*, John and Paul actually finished the lyrics to this song just moments before the session began.

The original British single (Parlophone R 5200) is mixed flat and in the fade-out, Paul sings the words "she's a woman" five times. All other pressings are mixed with a fair amount of reverb on both the voice and the instruments, and have Paul singing "she's a woman" just three times at the end.

The true stereo version is available only on the Australian **The Beatles' Greatest Hits Volume 2** (Parlophone PSCO 7534), and on the Singapore/Malaysia/Hong Kong pressing of the same album (Parlophone LPEA 1001). However, here Paul sings "she's a woman" five times in the fade-out.

In July 1976, the true stereo version was issued as a single in Australia (Parlophone A 8133). (See "**Rarities** . . . And Box Sets," pp. 72, 76, 84, 87.)

A "live" version of *She's A Woman*, taped on August 30, 1965, is available on **The Beatles At The Hollywood Bowl**.

She's Leaving Home (Lennon-McCartney)

Paul sings lead on this song, recorded in March-April 1967 for **Sgt. Pepper's Lonely Hearts Club Band**.

The mono version was speeded-up electronically, so it plays back in a higher key than the stereo version.

Sie Liebt Dich (Lennon-McCartney-Nicolas-Montague)

A German version of *She Loves You*, recorded on January 29, 1964, at the Pathé Marconi studios in Paris. (See "**Rarities** . . . And Box Sets," pp. 65, 70, 72.)

Slow Down (Larry Williams)

John sings lead on this cover version of a Larry Williams song, recorded in late February 1964 and first issued in June on the Beatles' fifth British EP, **Long Tall Sally**.

This rousing rocker ends with John shouting a falsetto "woo." However, in stereo, John also let's loose with an "ow" just before the closing guitar riff begins. In mono, this was edited out.

The stereo version of *Slow Down* was first issued in America in July 1964 on **Something New** (Capitol ST 2108), but was not put out in England until June 1976 on **Rock 'N' Roll Music**.

A :52 excerpt from this song was used by Capitol Records in its

1964 documentary release, **The Beatles' Story** (Capitol S/TBO 2222), produced by Gary Usher and Roger Christian.

In the spring of 1976, George Martin remixed a stereo version of *Slow Down* in Los Angeles for **Rock 'N' Roll Music**. (See **Rock 'N' Roll Music**, p. 210.)

Strawberry Fields Forever (Lennon-McCartney)

Issued in February 1967 as the B-side of *Penny Lane*, recording on this track began in December 1966 when it was originally planned for **Sgt. Pepper's Lonely Hearts Club Band.**

U.S. pressings have a slightly different mix than other copies. The U.S. stereo version on **Magical Mystery Tour** (Capitol SMAL 2835) also has more echo and is about two percent slower than the British stereo version. Here the harpsichord heard in the background is put onto the left channel, while the brass and strings are panned from left to right.

In the British stereo version, first issued in April 1973 on **The Beatles 1967-1970** (Parlophone PCSP 718), there's no echo in the track and the harpsichord is panned from right to left at the end of the second and third verses.

A major difference between the mono and stereo versions is the degree of the first fade-out. In mono, the track never fades all the way out. The U.S. stereo version fades a bit more. Only the British true stereo version fades out completely.

In the final fade, John mumbles a few words. John's voice sounds slower than the rest of the track but that's not suprising since the final master of *Strawberry Fields Forever* is actually a combination of two different takes performed at different tempos and in different keys.

Neither the Beatles nor anyone at EMI has ever said what John is saying. In 1969, many Americans who felt that Paul McCartney may have been killed three years earlier in a car crash and had then been replaced in the group by an imposter, cited this segment as a planted clue, believing that John was saying "I buried Paul." (*Note*: After the senseless murder of John Lennon in December 1980, we feel further discussion of the "Paul Is Dead" theory to be in extremely bad taste.)

When questioned about this by journalists in 1969, John responded that he had said "cranberry sauce" on the record but later admitted he couldn't really remember what he'd said at the session. Another belief among collectors is that John was saying "I'm very bored."

Regardless of the words, this phrase can be heard twice in the true stereo version, available on the German **Magical Mystery Tour** (Horzu SHZE 327), on the German **The Beatles 1967-1970** (Apple

218

1C 172-05 307/08), and on the British **The Beatles 1967-1970** (Apple PCSP 718), while it can only be heard once on most other pressings. This version was later issued on a single in Japan (Apple EAR-20234).

Sure To Fall (Carl Perkins-William E. Cantrell-Quinton Claunch)
John and Paul share the vocals on this Carl Perkins number. It was one of over a dozen songs recorded by the Beatles at their audition for Decca Records in London on January 1, 1962.
The original version runs 1:55. On **The Silver Beatles - Volume 1** (US: Phoenix-10PHX 352), the track was artificially lengthened to 2:47.

Sweet Georgia Brown (Ben Bernie-Maceo Pinkard-Kenneth Casey)
(See "Tony Sheridan And The 'Beat Brothers'," p. 16.)

Take Good Care Of My Baby (Gerry Goffin-Carole King)
George sings lead on this Bobby Vee hit. It was one of over a dozen songs recorded by the Beatles at their audition for Decca Records in London on January 1, 1962.
The original version runs 2:16. On **The Silver Beatles - Volume 2** (US: Phoenix-10 PHX 353), the track was artificially lengthened to 2:50.

Take Out Some Insurance On Me Baby (Charles Singleton-Waldenese Hall)
(See "Tony Sheridan And The 'Beat Brothers'," p. 19.)

Taxman (Harrison)
Paul plays lead guitar on this George Harrison song, put out in August 1966 as the opening cut on **Revolver**.
The starting "count-off" was omitted from the French pressing of **Revolver** (Odeon CLSO-105) and from a Mexican EP (Capitol EPEM 10536).
In mono, Ringo's cowbell comes in at the end of the first line of the second verse, "Should five percent appear too small." In stereo, the cowbell enters a bit later, after the words "'Cos I'm The Taxman" in the second chorus.
In the spring of 1976, George Martin remixed a stereo version of *Taxman* in Los Angeles for **Rock 'N' Roll Music**. (See **Rock 'N' Roll Music**, p. 210.)

Tell Me Why (Lennon-McCartney)
One of seven songs written especially for the Beatles' first motion picture, "A Hard Day's Night" (United Artists, 1964).

Separate and distinct mono and stereo mixes were made. In stereo, Artificial Double Tracking (see "Glossary") was added to John Lennon's lead vocal, while in mono John's voice remains flat. Also in stereo, a fair amount of echo was added to the guitars and drums, creating the impression that the song was being performed "live" as it appears in the concert scene of the movie. Again, in mono, the instruments stay flat. Ironically, it's the mono mix of *Tell Me Why* that's heard in the finale of "A Hard Day's Night."

After the song's final chord, there's a short guitar "fall-off" in the stereo version that was omitted in mono.

Thank You Girl (Lennon-McCartney)

The B-side of *From Me To You*, the Beatles' third Parlophone single in England, recorded on March 4, 1963.

The stereo version of *Thank You Girl* contains three extra harmonica "fills" by John Lennon that are not found in mono. The stereo mix was first issued in the United States on both the mono and stereo pressings of **The Beatles' Second Album** (Capitol S/T 2080) and later on a mono U.S. single (Capitol 6064), as well as on the German stereo edition of **The Beatles Beat** (Odeon SMO 83-692). It has yet to be put out in England.

An early Japanese pressing of **The Beatles' Second Album** (Apple AP-80012) contained the mono version of *Thank You Girl* but this was replaced by the stereo version when the LP was reissued (Odeon EAR 20223).

Things We Said Today (Lennon-McCartney) - studio

In England, the B-side of *A Hard Day's Night*, the title song from the Beatles' first motion picture, although this was not a song from the film.

A :37 excerpt from *Things We Said Today* was included in the five-song *Beatle Medley* created in America by Capitol Records for its documentary release, **The Beatles' Story** (Capitol S/TBO 2222), produced by Gary Usher and Roger Christian.

A "live" version of this song, taped August 23, 1964, is available on **The Beatles At The Hollywood Bowl**.

Think For Yourself (Harrison)

George sings lead on this song, recorded in the fall of 1965 for the Beatles' sixth British LP, **Rubber Soul**.

The U.S. edition of **The Best Of George Harrison** (Capitol ST 11578) contains the American "reprocessed" stereo version of this song; the British album includes the original, true stereo version.

The Beatles sing an impromptu and unaccompanied four-second excerpt from *Think For Yourself* in the feature-length, animated cartoon "Yellow Submarine" (United Artists, 1968).

This Boy   (Lennon-McCartney)

The B-side of *I Want To Hold Your Hand*, the Beatles' fifth Parlophone single in England, recorded on October 19, 1963.

The true stereo version of *This Boy* was not released until 1976, when it appeared on a reissued single in Canada (Capitol of Canada 72144). It was later put out on a similar reissue in Australia (Parlophone A8103). (See **"Rarities** . . . And Box Sets," pp. 72, 76, 87.)

An :08 excerpt from *This Boy* was used by Capitol Records in America in its 1964 documentary release, **The Beatles' Story** (Capitol S/TBO 2222), produced by Gary Usher and Roger Christian.

Three Cool Cats   (Jerry Leiber-Mike Stoller)

George sings lead on this Coasters number. It was one of over a dozen songs recorded by the Beatles at their audition for Decca Records in London on January 1, 1962.

The original version runs 2:16. On **The Silver Beatles - Volume 1** (US: Phoenix 10-PHX 352), the track was artificially lengthened to 2:38.

Ticket To Ride   (Lennon-McCartney) - studio

One of seven songs written especially for the Beatles' second motion picture, "Help" (United Artists, 1965).

A bit of Paul McCartney's opening lead guitar riff was omitted from the German pressing of **A Collection Of Beatles Oldies** (Odeon C062-04.258).

American pressings of this song have a fair amount of reverb added to Paul's guitar, giving it a stronger, more forceful sound than on the original British releases. This is particularly noticeable during the intro.

The true stereo version, first issued in England on **Help** (Parlophone PCS 3071), contains a longer fade-out, with a longer repeated guitar riff by Paul. The true stereo mix was not released in the United States until March 1982, when it was included on **Reel Music** (Capitol SV-12199). (See "Rarities . . . And Box Sets," p. 75.)

A :31 excerpt from *Ticket To Ride* was included in *The Beatles' Movie Medley*, edited by John Palladino of Capitol Records in America and also first issued in March 1982.

A "live" version of this song, taped August 30, 1965, is available on **The Beatles At The Hollywood Bowl.**

Till There Was You   (Meredith Willson) - studio

Paul sings lead on this popular song from the 1957 musical, "The Music Man."

(Version 1) - One of over a dozen numbers recorded by the Beatles at their audition for Decca Records in London on January 1, 1962.

(Version 2) - Recorded in July 1963 for the group's second British LP, **With The Beatles**, this is the only commercial recording of *Till There Was You* that the band made.

A "live" version of this song was captured on tape in December 1962 in Hamburg, Germany. (See "The Star Club Tape," p. 32.)

Tomorrow Never Knows (Lennon-McCartney)

The closing track on the Beatles' August 1966 release, **Revolver**. Many of the lyrics to this song, originally titled *The Void*, were inspired by "The Tibetan Book of the Dead." John asked George Martin to make his voice sound as if it were coming from a mountain top in Tibet. George responded by feeding John's lead vocal through a rotating Leslie speaker. This highly experimental recording features a sitar and an assortment of tape loops created by the Beatles and cued in at different times.

Separate and distinct mono and stereo mixes were made. The mono version begins at full volume while the stereo version fades in gradually. Also, in mono the various tape loops are faded completely in and out of the track. In stereo, the tape loops play continuously but are mixed louder or softer at different points. The stereo version also contains more tape loops than the mono version does.

Twist And Shout (Bert Russell-Phil Medley) - studio

John belts out the lead on this Isley Brothers hit. It was recorded on February 13, 1963, at the end of the grueling twelve-hour session that produced the Beatles' debut LP, **Please Please Me**. By necessity, it was cut in one take.

In the spring of 1976, George Martin remixed a stereo version of *Twist And Shout* in Los Angeles for **Rock 'N' Roll Music**. To help promote this "new" Beatles two-record set in England, EMI also issued *Back In The U.S.S.R.* b/w *Twist And Shout* as a single (Parlophone R 6016). However, the original stereo versions of both songs were used, not the remixed tracks. (See **Rock 'N' Roll Music**, p.210.)

Two "live" versions of *Twist And Shout* have been released. One was recorded on August 23, 1964, but was not issued in its entirety until May 1977 on **The Beatles At The Hollywood Bowl**. However, in November 1964, Capitol Records in America included a :40 excerpt from this "live" track on its documentary release, **The Beatles' Story** (Capitol S/TBO 2222), produced by Gary Usher and Roger Christian. This abbreviated cut came straight from the original three-track master tape, produced on location by Voyle Gilmore. In 1977, prior to the issue of **The Beatles At The Hollywood Bowl**, George Martin and engineer Geoff Emerick remixed and equalized all the material to upgrade the overall sound quality.

The other "live" version of *Twist And Shout* dates back to December 1962 and was taped in Hamburg, Germany. (See "The Star Club Tape," p. 38.)

What Goes On   (Lennon-McCartney-Starkey)

Ringo sings lead on this song, recorded in the fall of 1965 for the Beatles' sixth British LP, **Rubber Soul**, and issued in America in February 1966 as the B-side of *Nowhere Man* and later on **"Yesterday"**. . . **And Today.**

The stereo version contains a lead guitar "fill" by George Harrison at the end of the song that is not found in mono.

The only pressings of **"Yesterday"**. . . **And Today** that feature the true stereo version of *What Goes On* are the Capitol Record Club edition (Capitol ST-8 2553) in America and the regular Japanese issue (Apple AP-80061).

What You're Doing   (Lennon-McCartney)

Paul sings lead on this song, recorded in the fall of 1964 for the Beatles' fourth British LP, **Beatles For Sale**.

The track opens with a four-bar drum pattern that's reminiscent of the intro to the Ronettes' *Be My Baby*. In stereo, there's also a handclap in the third bar of the intro that's absent in mono.

When I Get Home   (Lennon-McCartney)

One of four songs recorded between June 1-3, 1964, to round out the British LP, **A Hard Day's Night**, although it was not part of the soundtrack material.

In the bridge of the song, John phrases the lyric "I'll love her more, till I walk out that door . . ." differently in mono than in stereo. In mono, John pauses exactly three beats between the words "more" and "till"; in stereo, the pause is half a beat longer, with the word "till" run together with "I."

While My Guitar Gently Weeps   (Harrison)
(See "The White Album," p. 52.)

Why Don't We Do It In The Road   (Lennon-McCartney)
(See "The White Album," p. 54.)

Wild Honey Pie   (Lennon-McCartney)
(See "The White Album," p. 52.)

223

Words Of Love (Buddy Holly)

John and Paul harmonize on this early Buddy Holly number, recorded in the fall of 1964 for the Beatles' fourth British LP, **Beatles For Sale**.

In America, the running time of this song is listed as 2:10, the actual length of the mono version. However, in stereo the track was faded out at 2:01.

Yellow Submarine (Lennon-McCartney)

Ringo sings lead on this children's song, recorded in the spring of 1966 and first issued as the B-side of *Eleanor Rigby*.

In mono, John's acoustic guitar comes in right on the first beat of the song; in stereo, his guitar doesn't enter until after Ringo sings the word "town" in the opening line, "In the *town* where I was born."

In the third verse, John repeats the lyrics after Ringo. Here, John's voice is electronically "phased" (see "Glossary") to give the impression of singing through an intercom. In mono, John repeats every line of the verse; in stereo, his repetitions don't begin until the second line, "Every one of us has all we need."

The mono version was issued on all original singles and mono LPs and was also used in the soundtrack of the feature-length, animated cartoon of the same name (United Artists, 1968). However, the mono pressing of the British **Yellow Submarine** (Apple PMC 7070) was derived from the stereo master tape by simply combining the two channels. Therefore, the song *Yellow Submarine* is actually the stereo version mixed down to mono, rather than the mono mix.

Yer Blues (Lennon-McCartney)

(See "The White Album," p. 54.)

Yes It Is (Lennon-McCartney)

John, Paul, and George harmonize on this song, recorded in February 1965 and first issued in April as the B-side of *Ticket To Ride*.

To date, no true stereo version of this song has been released.

You Can't Do That (Lennon-McCartney)

First issued in March 1964 as the B-side of *Can't Buy Me Love*. The instrumental track was recorded on January 29 at the Pathé Marconi studios in Paris, while the vocals were overdubbed on February 25 at EMI in London.

A :58 excerpt from *You Can't Do That* was used by Capitol Records in America in its 1964 documentary release, **The Beatles' Story** (Capitol S/TBO 2222), produced by Gary Usher and Roger Christian.

In the spring of 1976, George Martin remixed a stereo version of this song in Los Angeles for **Rock 'N' Roll Music**. (See **Rock 'N' Roll Music**, p. 210.)

You Know My Name (Look Up The Number) (Lennon-McCartney)
The B-side of *Let It Be*, this track is actually an outtake from the **Sgt. Pepper** sessions. The number was inspired by the Bonzo Dog Doo Dah Band, with whom the Beatles later worked in their TV special, "Magical Mystery Tour." Along with the four Beatles, Brian Jones of the Rolling Stones made a guest appearance on this cut playing saxophone.

To date, no true stereo version of this song has been released.

Your Mother Should Know (Lennon-McCartney)
Paul sings lead on this song from the Beatles' ill-fated 1967 Christmas television special, "Magical Mystery Tour" (Apple Films).

In the final verse, the vocal and percussion tracks were electronically "phased" (see "Glossary") in mono; in stereo, everything was mixed flat.

You've Got To Hide Your Love Away (Lennon-McCartney)
One of seven songs written especially for the Beatles' second motion picture, "Help" (United Artists, 1965).

A :35 excerpt from *You've Got To Hide Your Love Away* was included in *The Beatles' Movie Medley*, edited by John Palladino of Capitol Records in America and first issued in March 1982.

You Won't See Me (Lennon-McCartney)
Paul sings lead on this song, recorded in the fall of 1965 for the Beatles' sixth British LP, **Rubber Soul**.

In America, the running time of this song is listed as 3:19, the actual length of the true stereo version. However, in mono the track plays for 3:21.

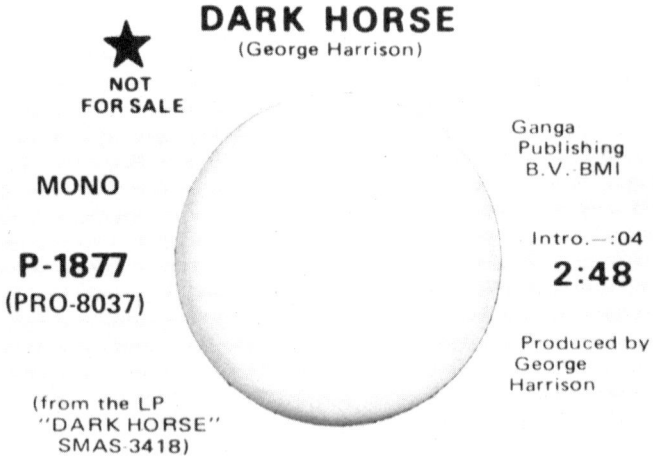

An Apple Record

DARK HORSE
(George Harrison)

NOT
FOR SALE

Ganga
Publishing
B.V.-BMI

MONO

Intro.—:04
2:48

P-1877
(PRO-8037)

Produced by
George
Harrison

(from the LP
"DARK HORSE"
SMAS-3418)

GEORGE HARRISON

℗1974 EMI Records Limited
MFD BY APPLE RECORDS, INC

Dark Horse
US: Apple S/PRO-8036/7 (promo 45)

11

George
Harrison

The variations to George Harrison's recordings are primarily album tracks that were edited for single release or for American airplay. An interesting sidelight concerns Warner Brothers Records' (US) refusal to issue the 1981 LP, **Somewhere In England**, until George revamped it to include more upbeat material.

Dark Horse   (Harrison)
The title song from George's ill-fated December 1974 LP, this cut was also issued as a single. George was suffering from laryngitis, brought on by extensive rehearsing for his U.S. tour, when he laid down the vocals for this track.
The single runs 3:52, the album version is listed as 3:50. The American promotional single (Apple S/PRO-8036/7) was shortened to 2:48 by eliminating the second verse and chorus of the song.

Ding Dong; Ding Dong   (Harrison)
Ringo Starr plays drums on this **Dark Horse** track, also issued as a Christmas single in 1974.
All commercial pressings run 3:39; the American promotional single (Apple S/PRO-8038/9) was shortened to 3:12 by omitting the second repeat of the second verse.

It's What You Value   (Harrison)
Released in November 1976 on **Thirty-Three And A Third**, George's first LP on his own Dark Horse label, and later as a single.
The album version runs 5:05; the British single (Dark Horse K 16967) was shortened to 3:46.

Love Comes To Everyone   (Harrison)
Co-produced by George and Russ Titelman, this song was issued in February 1979 on **George Harrison** and later as a single.
The album version runs 4:33; the single was shortened to 3:35.

My Sweet Lord   (Harrison) - studio

George's first solo single, taken from his November 1970 three-record set, **All Things Must Pass**. The song was inspired by the Edwin Hawkins Singers' *Oh Happy Day* but was later the subject of a law suit brought by Bright Tunes Music, which claimed George plagiarized the tune from the 1963 Chiffons' hit *He's So Fine*.

The background vocals on the single were sung by George and producer Phil Spector; on the album version, George double-tracked his own back-up vocals and credited them to the "George O'Hara-Smith Singers."

In December 1976, the single was reissued by EMI in England to help promote **The Best Of George Harrison**. EMI remastered the disc, replacing the single version of *My Sweet Lord* with the LP track. The record also came in a new picture sleeve but bore its original Apple catalog number.

A "live" version, recorded August 1, 1971, at New York's Madison Square Garden, is available on **The Concert For Bangla Desh**.

Somewhere In England

Warner Brothers Records (American distributors of George's Dark Horse label) first planned to issue **Somewhere In England** (US: Dark Horse DHK 3492) on October 29, 1980, two weeks prior to the release of John and Yoko's **Double Fantasy** on Geffen Records. The album consisted of new Harrison songs, mainly ballads, plus updated arrangements of two Hoagy Carmichael numbers, *Hong Kong Blues* and *Baltimore Oriole*. A photo and description of the LP appeared in Warner's fall 1980 catalog of new releases.

But in light of the mediocre sales of George's past few records, Warner executives began to wonder if an audience still existed for George's new material. After repeated listening, Warner Brothers postponed the album's release indefinitely and returned the finished master tape to George with polite but pointed instructions to make the LP more commercial. Warner also ordered all promotional copies destroyed.

Below is the original track listing for **Somewhere In England**:

(Side One) *Hong Kong Blues/Writing's On The Wall/ Flying Hour/Lay His Head/Unconsciousness Rules/*(Side Two) *Sat Singing/Life Itself/Tears Of The World/Baltimore Oriole/Save The World.*

George reassembled his backup musicians at his own Friar Park studio and, with percussionist Ray Cooper now acting as co-producer, recorded four additional titles. (George was listed as the sole producer on the original LP.) Once the tracks were completed, George and Ray then re-sequenced the album to better accomodate the new numbers. From the original line-up they shelved *Flying Hour*, *Lay His Head, Sat Singing* and *Tears Of The World*. In their place, they substituted *Blood From A Clone* (George's blistering attack on Warner Brothers for tampering with his music), *That Which I Have Lost* and the album's two subsequent hit singles, *All Those Years Ago* and *Teardrops*.

Here's the LP's revised running order:

(Side One) *Blood From A Clone/Unconsciousness Rules/Life Itself/All Those Years Ago/Baltimore Oriole/* (Side Two) *Teardrops/That Which I Have Lost/Writing's On The Wall/Hong Kong Blues/Save The World.*

Along with this change in content came a change in sleeve graphics. Both the front and the back covers were redesigned to give the album a brighter, happier feel. The original cover showed a solemn profile of George superimposed over a black-and-white satellite photo of England. The back cover had the song titles listed, but out of order, and contained the Universal Price Code symbol (which was deleted from the revised edition).

George sent the new package back to Warner Brothers for approval, and in June 1981 the LP was released.

An exact reproduction of **Somewhere In England** in its first state surfaced on the underground market in late 1982. This counterfeit edition featured the discarded sleeve design and presented the songs in their original sequence, complete with excellent quality, true stereo versions of the four unreleased tracks.

These four cuts first appeared in bootleg form in January 1982 on **By George** (US: Handmade Records NSU001). Excellent quality counterfeit printings of the original cover slicks also circulated about this time, often being passed off as originals.

(On September 1, 1983, a genuine unissued cover slick for **Somewhere In England** was put up for auction at Sotheby's in London where it sold for £200, or about $320.)

Teardrops (Harrison)

Released in June 1981 on **Somewhere In England** and later issued as a single.

The album version runs 4:04; the single was shortened to 3:20 by eliminating the instrumental break and a second repeat of the chorus near the end of the song.

229

Teardrops
US: Dark Horse DRC 49785 (promo 45)

This Guitar
US: Apple P-1885 (promo 45)

This Guitar (Harrison)

A follow-up to George's popular 1968 song, *While My Guitar Gently Weeps*, this track was issued in September 1975 on **Extra Texture (Read All About It)** and was also the last single put out by Apple Records.

The album version runs 4:11; the single was shortened to 3:49 by omitting about half of George's final guitar break.

This Song (Harrison)

Issued in November 1976 on **Thirty-Three And A Third** and also as a single, George composed this number as a "send-up" of the lawsuit filed against him by Bright Tunes Music for allegedly plagiarizing the melody of the Chiffons' 1963 hit *He's So Fine* for his own 1970 million-seller, *My Sweet Lord*.

The album version runs 4:11; most single pressings were shortened to 3:45 by eliminating George's final guitar break. However, the running time of the British single (Dark Horse K 16856) is 3:50.

Shaved Fish
US: Apple SW 3421 (LP)

12

John
Lennon

In the summer of 1975, John Lennon created a good many variations to his original recordings when he compiled **Shaved Fish**, a "greatest hits" package of sorts made up of his American Apple singles. John put together this album to preserve his solo tracks after he discovered that the master tapes to *Cold Turkey* and *Power To The People* had been misplaced by EMI; he was forced to settle for inferior quality dubs. Amazed by EMI's lack of regard for his post-Beatles work, John figured he'd better assemble his early cuts on one LP before any more of them were lost.

Most of John's early singles were political anthems whose strength came in the repeating of their choruses. *Give Peace A Chance, Happy Xmas (War Is Over)* and *Power To The People* all bore extended endings. Unfortunately, when these tracks were played back-to-back, the long repetitions tended to become monotonous and the individual songs lost some of their drive. To avoid this, John shortened the majority of the cuts for the album, hence the title **Shaved** Fish. Some of the recordings were faded early while others were condensed. For those who wish to hear the material on **Shaved Fish** in its entirety, they'll have to hunt up the original Apple singles.

On December 8, 1980, shortly before 11:00 p.m., John Lennon was shot and killed as he and Yoko returned home to the Dakota apartments in New York City. For an instant, it seemed as if the whole world mourned.

In the winter of 1982, EMI put together a second "greatest hits" album with the aid of Yoko, titled **The John Lennon Collection**. As part of its deal with Geffen Records, which allowed EMI to include material from John and Yoko's album, **Double Fantasy**, Geffen was given the rights to release this new compilation in the United States (Geffen GHSP 2023). Geffen managed to confuse collectors by listing different running times for all of the tracks, including those already on Geffen, even though the tracks were all the same length as when they were last issued. The new times differ anywhere from one to ten seconds. Each of these variations is noted in this chapter.

The John Lennon Collection was also one of the first American albums where the prcrecorded cassette included songs (*Happy Xmas* and *Stand By Me*) not found on the LP. This was part of a short-lived effort by major labels to cut back on the home-taping of records by offering something extra on the cassette version. It was strictly an American policy. Non-U.S. pressings of **The John Lennon Collection** contained all seventeen cuts.

Rock 'N' Roll was another album with several variations. The entire project is dealt with at length in Chapter 9, "The **Roots** of **Rock 'N' Roll**." Songs from that LP are listed here with the notation, See "The **Roots** of **Rock 'N' Roll**," followed by the appropriate page number(s).

John Lennon/Plastic Ono Band, John's first solo album, posed a few problems. Two of the songs on the LP, *Working Class Hero* and *I Found Out*, contained certain four-letter words that were not permissible on the airwaves in 1970. EMI Records issued censored versions of both numbers in Australia and in England. In Rhodesia, not only were these tracks edited but the song *God* was cut from the album altogether.

As with George Harrison's material, a few of the harder-to-find John Lennon variations have been bootlegged. Most notable are the two unreleased tracks from **Rock 'N' Roll**, *Angel Baby* and *Be My Baby*. Other bootlegged cuts include the British version of *I Found Out* with its slightly longer ending, and the extended fade-out to *(Just Like) Starting Over*, which is available only on the American 12-inch promotional single. All four recordings appear on **Limited Edition** (US: Bag 5069), a deluxe bootleg LP of John Lennon rarities. The first pressing came with a twelve-page booklet containing liner notes and a collection of John's lyrics and drawings.

Ain't That A Shame   (Antoine Domino-Dave Bartholomew)
   (See "The **Roots** of **Rock 'N' Roll**," p. 155.)

Beautiful Boy (Darling Boy)   (Lennon)
   John's song for his son Sean, issued in November 1980 on **Double Fantasy**, John and Yoko's long-awaited "comeback" album, and later as a single.
   All pressings run 4:01. On the American edition of **The John Lennon Collection**, the running time is listed incorrectly as 4:05.

Borrowed Time   (Lennon)
   The reggae-sounding third single from **Milk And Honey**, John and Yoko's final album, released three years after John's murder.

Borrowed Time
US: Polydor 821 204-7 DJ (promo 45)

All commercial pressings run 4:30; the American 7-inch promotional single (Polydor 821 204-7 DJ) contains a *Short Version* that was edited down to 3:45 by fading out the track in the middle of John's closing rap, just after he says "...does she really love me?"

Cold Turkey (Lennon) - "live"

John's harsh story about kicking heroin, written in the summer of 1969.

(Version 1) - Recorded September 13,1969, at Toronto's Varsity Stadium by the Plastic Ono Band, this version runs 3:43 and was issued in December 1969 on **Live Peace In Toronto**. (See **Live Peace In Toronto**, p. 242.)

(Version 2) - Recorded December 15,1969, at London's Lyceum Ballroom by John, Yoko and the Plastic Ono Supergroup, this version runs 7:34 and was released in 1972 on the "live" half of **Sometime In New York City**, a two-record set.

The original studio recording, with Ringo Starr on drums, was taped September 30, 1969, and was put out as a single in October.

Dear Yoko (Lennon)

John's light-hearted love song to his wife, issued in November 1980 on **Double Fantasy**.

All pressings run 2:33. On the American edition of **The John Lennon Collection**, the running time is listed incorrectly as 2:35.

Do You Want To Dance (Bobby Freeman)

(See "The **Roots** of **Rock 'N' Roll**, p. 155.)

Give Peace A Chance (Lennon-McCartney)

(Version 1) - Recorded "live" on June 1, 1969, at Montreal's Queen Elizabeth Hotel, this track was produced by John and Yoko and credited to the Plastic Ono Band. John's count-off (". . . two, one, two, three, four") was omitted from the American single (Apple 1809), shortening the cut from 4:51 to 4:49. This version wasn't available in its entirety in the United States until November 1982 when it was issued on **The John Lennon Collection** (Geffen GHSP 2023). (The liner notes on that LP cite **Shaved Fish** as the source of this recording even though John's own "greatest hits" compilation includes only a fifty-nine-second segment of this track. In fact, the only pressing of **Shaved Fish** that contains the full-length version of *Give Peace A Chance* comes from East Germany.)

(Version 2) - Recorded "live" on September 13, 1969, at Toronto's Varsity Stadium and produced by John and Yoko, this version is available only on the Plastic Ono Band's **Live Peace In Toronto**. (See **Live Peace In Toronto**, p. 242.)

(Version 3) - Recorded "live" on August 30, 1972, at New York's Madison Square Garden and produced by John, this version was aired as part of the "One to One" television special and syndicated radio broadcast. Only a fifty-second segment is available commercially, as the closing track on **Shaved Fish.**

Happy Xmas (War Is Over) (Ono-Lennon)
Recorded October 28-29, 1971, in New York and produced with the aid of Phil Spector, this holiday song features John and Yoko backed by the Plastic Ono Band and the Harlem Community Choir. The track was issued as a single in the United States in December 1971 but was not put out in England until the following winter.

The complete version of *Happy Xmas (War Is Over)* is available as a single and also on non-U.S. pressings of **The John Lennon Collection.** On **Shaved Fish**, the closing is segued into *Give Peace A Chance.*

How Do You Sleep (Lennon)
John's biting attack on Paul, written while litigation to dissolve the Beatles' partnership was in full swing. The song contains a few pointed lyrics by manager Allen Klein and was issued in the fall of 1971 on **Imagine.**

The opening ten seconds of "tuning" were omitted from the quadraphonic version, shortening the track from 5:29 to 5:19. (See **Imagine**, p. 238.)

I Don't Want To Be A Soldier Mama, I Don't Want To Die (Lennon)
Produced by John, Yoko, and Phil Spector, with George Harrison on slide guitar and King Curtis on sax, this is the final cut on Side One of **Imagine**, John's second solo album.

The quadraphonic remix has two changes in the instrumental break, and the electronic ending is also slightly different. (See **Imagine**, p. 238.)

I Found Out (Lennon)
Produced by John, Yoko, and Phil Spector, with Ringo Starr on drums, this track was issued in December 1970 on **John Lennon/ Plastic Ono Band**, John's first solo album.

The word "cock" in the line, "Some of you sitting there with your *cock* in your hand" was censored on the first British pressing of the LP (Apple PCS 7124) as well as on the Rhodesian and Australian copies.

At the end of the fade-out on the U.S. **John Lennon/Plastic Ono Band** (Apple SW 3372), John can be heard mumbling, "Well that must be my...." On most other pressings, John can clearly be

237

heard saying, "Well that must be my girl, yours, she don't look like that" before the fade-out ends. These words are actually the opening lines to Carl Perkins' 1955 song, *Gone, Gone, Gone*.

In the final verse, John sings, "No one can harm you to feel your own pain"; the album's accompanying lyric sheet reads, "Can't do you no harm to feel your own pain."

I'm Losing You (Lennon)

Another track from **Double Fantasy**, issued in November 1980.

All pressings run 3:58. On the American edition of **The John Lennon Collection**, the running time is listed incorrectly as 4:04.

I'm Stepping Out (Lennon)

The second single from **Milk And Honey**, put out posthumously in 1984, with a tongue-in-cheek spoken intro by John about the woes of being a "househusband."

All commercial pressings run 4:06, although on **Milk And Honey** the running time is listed as 4:05. The American 7-inch promotional single (Polydor 821 107-7 DJ) contains a *Short Version* that was edited down to 3:33 by eliminating John's count-off ("one, two, one, two, three, four") plus the last few repeats of the chorus, and by condensing the final instrumental break. However, both versions still end with John's "I'll be in before one, or two, or three, goodbye."

Imagine (Lennon)

The title track from John's second solo album, this is probably his most widely recognized solo composition.

The true running time of this track is 2:59 as it was listed on the original 1971 single and LP. However, for some unexplained reason, everytime the song has been reissued, the running time given on the record has increased. In 1975, John included *Imagine* on **Shaved Fish** and the time became 3:01. Then several months after John's murder, the song was put out on two different 12-inch singles in Germany (EMI/Electrola 1C052-04.940 YZ and EMI/Electrola 1C052-05.992 YZ). The running time on these two discs was listed as 3:02. Finally, in late 1982, the number was reissued on **The John Lennon Collection**. In America, the time read 3:04. (See **Imagine**, below.)

Imagine

Recorded in July 1971 at Ascot Sound, John's home studio at Tittenhurst Park, and co-produced by John, Yoko, and Phil Spector, this was John's second solo album. It proved to be far more accessible (and therefore more commercial) than his previous LP, **John**

I'm Stepping Out
US: Polydor 821 107-7 DJ (promo 45)

Imagine
Germany: EMI/Electrola 1C052-05.992 YZ (12" maxi-single)

Lennon/Plastic Ono Band, which had been written while he and Yoko were undergoing primal therapy.

After the initial release of **Imagine**, John went back into the studio and made a four-channel remix of the title track, although he didn't stay to supervise the remixing of the rest of the album. Quadraphonic pressings of **Imagine** were subsequently issued in Australia (Apple 10004), England (Apple 10004), Japan (Apple EAZ-80006) and the United States.

Instant Karma! (We All Shine On)   (Lennon)

This song by John Ono Lennon with the Plastic Ono Band was rush-released throughout Europe on February 6, 1970, just days after John had approved producer Phil Spector's final mix. However, prior to its February 20 release in America (Apple 1818), Spector went into a studio in Los Angeles where he added strings and remixed the entire track without John's knowledge. The original U.S. single also had the words "Phil + Ronnie" (Phil's wife Veronica Bennett, formerly the lead singer of the Ronettes) etched in the dead-wax.

The single runs 3:18; on **Shaved Fish**, the cut was shortened to 3:12 by fading it out early. On the American pressing of **The John Lennon Collection**, the running time is listed incorrectly as 3:21.

It's So Hard   (Lennon)

Produced by John, Yoko, and Phil Spector, this song was issued in the fall of 1971 on **Imagine**, and in America as the B-side of the title track.

The quadraphonic version features some extra sax by King Curtis in the final instrumental break. (See **Imagine**, p. 238.)

Jealous Guy   (Lennon)

Another track on **Imagine.**

All pressings run 4:10. On the American edition of **The John Lennon Collection,** the running time is listed incorrectly as 4:17.

(Just Like) Starting Over   (Lennon)

The first single, and also the opening cut, from **Double Fantasy**, John and Yoko's much-heralded 1980 "comeback" album, produced by John, Yoko, and Jack Douglas.

The American 12-inch promotional single (Geffen PRO A 919) runs 4:17; all commercial pressings were shortened to 3:55 (album) and 3:54 (single) by fading them out early. On the American edition of **The John Lennon Collection**, the running time is listed incorrectly as 3:59.

Live Peace In Toronto

A "live" recording of the Plastic Ono Band's performance at the "Toronto Rock 'n' Roll Revival," held September 13, 1969, at Varsity Stadium. The album was rush-released in December by Apple Records after *Rolling Stone* reported that a bootleg version had surfaced in Ann Arbor, Michigan.

The U.S. pressing (Apple SW 3362) fades out slowly at the end of Side One and then back in again at the beginning of Side Two; the British pressing (Apple CORE 2001) ends and restarts abruptly.

Love (Lennon)

This track, with Ringo Starr on drums and Klaus Voorman on bass, was issued in December 1970 on **John Lennon/Plastic Ono Band**, John's first solo album.

The original version runs 3:17. In late 1982, two years after John's murder, the song was reissued on **The John Lennon Collection.** In America, the time was listed incorrectly as 3:22. A British single (Parlophone R 6059), released simultaneously with the LP, was shortened to 3:12 by fading out the closing piano sooner.

The album version was produced by John, Yoko, and Phil Spector, with Spector also playing piano, and is basically a heavily compressed, mono mix. The lone piano fades in gradually during the first thirty seconds of the song; at the end of the number, it again fades in and out. John's vocal is also double-tracked during the "middle eight," which begins "Love is you." Due to the use of a newly-cut lacquer, the track is not quite as compressed on **The John Lennon Collection** as it is on **John Lennon/Plastic Ono Band**.

The single version, which carries the same production credits, turns out to be a previously unissued, true stereo mix. John's acoustic guitar is heard only on the left channel while Spector's piano is panned to the right; on the album version, both instruments come through both channels. The piano on the single is also heard at full volume at both the beginning and end of the song. In addition, John's vocal is much clearer and echoed slightly, but never double-tracked.

Meat City (Lennon)

Produced by John, this song was issued in November 1973 as the closing track on **Mind Games** and as the B-side of the *Mind Games* single.

On the single, the "backwards" voice heard in the middle of the song says "check the album"; on the LP, it says "fuck a pig."

Mind Games (Lennon)

The title track of John's November 1973 LP on Apple Records,

Love
UK: Parlophone R 6059 (45)

and also a single.

The running time of the original track is 4:10. The song was reissued in 1975 on **Shaved Fish** where the time was given as 4:12 even though the cut still ran just 4:10. Then in late 1982, the number was included on **The John Lennon Collection**. In America, the running time was listed incorrectly as 4:20 but the track actually did last for 4:12.

Money (Janie Bradford-Berry Gordy)

Available only as a "live" recording from the Plastic Ono Band's appearance at the "Toronto Rock 'n' Roll Revival," held on September 13, 1969, at Varsity Stadium.

The original mix by filmmaker D. A. Pennebaker included background vocals by Yoko Ono that were edited out of the track by John and Yoko before they released it on **Live Peace In Toronto**. (See **Live Peace In Toronto**, p. 242.)

This raw version has never been issued commercially. It first appeared in the soundtrack of Pennebaker's "Sweet Toronto" (Pennebaker, Inc., 1971), a documentary about the entire rock event that featured much of the Plastic Ono Band's performance. Due to contractural problems, this footage was cut from the film before it went into general release under its new title, "Keep On Rockin'."

In 1982, this track was played during a weekly syndicated radio program in America called "Retro Rock." It appeared in a show that spotlighted the work of D. A. Pennebaker. Also included were other film outtakes by the Who (from "Monterey Pop") and by Bob Dylan (from "Don't Look Back"). "Retro Rock" was distributed on LPs to several hundred radio stations across the United States.

Mother (Lennon)

John's anguished song to his mother Julia, who was killed in an automobile accident when he was only seventeen. It was written while John and Yoko were undergoing primal therapy with American psychologist Arthur Janov and was issued in December 1970 on **John Lennon/Plastic Ono Band** and in the United States as a single.

The original album version runs 5:29; the single was shortened to 3:55 by eliminating most of John's hair-raising screams for his mother and father in the latter part of the song. A second edited version, on **Shaved Fish**, runs 5:03 although it's listed as 5:06.

The bell heard in the introduction was omitted from the Spanish (Apple 3C006-04.726) and Italian (Odeon 1J006-04.726) singles.

 # 9 Dream (Lennon)

The second single from **Walls And Bridges**, John's fall 1974 LP recorded in New York at Record Plant East.

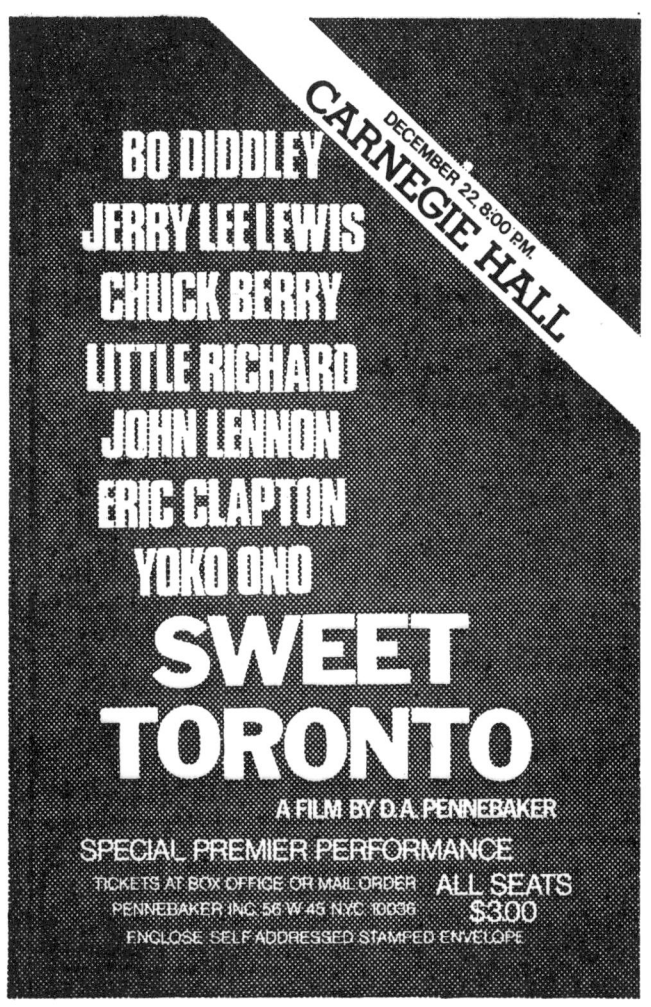

Ad for "Sweet Toronto."

All original commercial pressings run 4:44; the American promotional single (Apple PRO-8029) was shortened to 2:58. On **Shaved Fish**, the track is listed as 4:46 even though it plays for just 4:44, and on the American edition of **The John Lennon Collection**, the time is also given as 4:46 when the cut actually fades out at 4:42.

Power To The People   (Lennon)
Produced by John, Yoko, and Phil Spector, with Bobby Keys on sax, this political anthem was first issued as a single in March 1971.

The longest version of this song, found on an Italian single (Apple 1J006-04.766), runs 3:20; all other single pressings are 3:15. The difference is in the length of the fade-out.

On **Shaved Fish**, the track was shortened to 3:04 although the time was given as 3:07, and on the American pressing of **The John Lennon Collection** the cut also plays for 3:04 but is listed as 3:05.

In compiling **Shaved Fish**, John found out that EMI still could not locate the master for *Power To The People*, so he was forced to settle for an inferior-quality dub.

Slippin' And Slidin'   (Richard Penniman-Edwin J. Bocage-Albert
          Collins-James Smith)
(See "The **Roots** Of **Rock 'N' Roll**," p. 155.)

Stand By Me   (Ben E. King-Elmo Glick)
(See "The **Roots** Of **Rock 'N' Roll**," p. 156.)

Watching The Wheels   (Lennon)
The third single from **Double Fantasy**, released on Geffen Records.

The album version contains one last bass-drum beat at the end of the song that was omitted from the single. The song itself runs 3:30. However, on **Double Fantasy**, the track is linked with Yoko's *I'm Your Angel* by a series of "city sounds" (random voices, cars, footsteps), making its total time 3:59.

On the American edition of **The John Lennon Collection**, which contains just the song, the running time is listed incorrectly as 3:34.

Whatever Gets You Through The Night   (Lennon) - studio
Elton John joined John Lennon in this rollicking duet, released in the fall of 1974 on **Walls And Bridges** and also as a single.

On **Shaved Fish**, the track was shortened to 3:04; all other pressings run 3:24. On the American edition of **The John Lennon Collection**, the running time is listed incorrectly as 3:28.

A "live" version featuring John as a suprise guest with the Elton John Band was recorded November 28, 1974, at New York's Madison Square Garden. In March 1981, three months after John's murder, this "live" rendition was issued in England, Europe, and Japan by DJM Records on both a 7-inch and 12-inch maxi-single but has yet to be issued in the United States. (See *I Saw Her Standing There*, p. 248.)

Woman (Lennon)

The second single from **Double Fantasy**.

All pressings run 3:30. On the American edition of **The John Lennon Collection**, the running time is listed incorrectly as 3:37.

Woman Is The Nigger Of The World (Lennon-Ono)

Produced in New York by John, Yoko, and Phil Spector and banned by radio stations everywhere, this rousing "womens' rights" number was issued in 1972 as the opening cut on **Sometime In New York City** and as a single in America. The recording features John Lennon backed by the Plastic Ono Band, Elephant's Memory and the "Invisible Strings."

On **Shaved Fish**, the track was shortened to 4:37 by cutting Stan Bronstein's second sax solo in half and by omitting the second verse of the song that follows. All other pressings run 5:15.

In April 1977, Capitol Records in the United States reissued this song b/w *Stand By Me* on a double-A sided single (Capitol Starline 6244). This newly-mastered disc sounds clearer than previous pressings.

Working Class Hero (Lennon)

John's embittered attack on society written while he and Yoko were undergoing primal therapy with American psychologist Arthur Janov. It was issued in December 1970 on **John Lennon/Plastic Ono Band** and in October 1975 in England as the B-side of *Imagine*.

The word "fucking" in the lines "Till you're so *fucking* crazy you can't follow their rules" and "But you're still *fucking* peasants as far as I can see" was censored on the first British pressing of **John Lennon/Plastic Ono Band** (Apple PCS 7124) as well as on the Rhodesian and Australian copies.

Ya Ya (Morris Levy-Clarence Lewis)

(Version 1) - Recorded in the summer of 1974 at New York's Record Plant East with John singing and playing piano and son Julian on drums, this 1:06 rehearsal tape was included as the final cut on **Walls And Bridges**.

(Version 2) - Recorded in October 1974 at Record Plant East

with John backed by many of the musicians from **Walls And Bridges**, this version runs 2:17 and was put out on **Rock 'N' Roll**. (See "The **Roots** Of **Rock 'N' Roll**," pp. 142, 147.)

You Can't Catch Me   (Chuck Berry)
(See "The **Roots** Of **Rock 'N' Roll**," p. 156.)

with DAVID BOWIE

Fame   (John Lennon-David Bowie-Carlos Alomar)
Recorded in January 1975 in New York with John playing guitar and singing background vocals, this track was first issued in March on Bowie's **Young Americans** and later as a single.
The album version runs 4:12; the single was shortened to 3:30.

with ELEPHANT'S MEMORY

Liberation Special   (Rick Frank-Stan Bronstein)
Produced by John and Yoko, this is the opening cut on the band's only Apple LP, **Elephant's Memory** (put out in the winter of 1972), and was later issued as a single.
Most pressings run 5:28; the American single (Apple 1854) was shortened to 3:30. (Incidentally, the first pressing of the single, released on November 13, 1972, featured *Madness* as the B-side. Then on December 4, it was reissued with *Power Boogie* on the flip.)

with ELTON JOHN

I Saw Her Standing There   (Lennon-McCartney)
This was the last of three songs John performed "live" in a surprise appearance with the Elton John Band at New York's Madison Square Garden on November 28, 1974. (The other two were *Whatever Gets You Through The Night* and *Lucy In The Sky With Diamonds*). At the end of the number, with the applause and yells from the sold-out crowd at an almost ear-splitting level, Elton shouted "John Lennon," to which John replied "alright." On the original issue, put out as the B-side of Elton's February 1975 Top 20 hit *Philadelphia Freedom*, both remarks were mixed forward. However, in March 1981, three months after John's murder, all three tracks were remixed and issued on both a 7-inch and a 12-inch maxi-

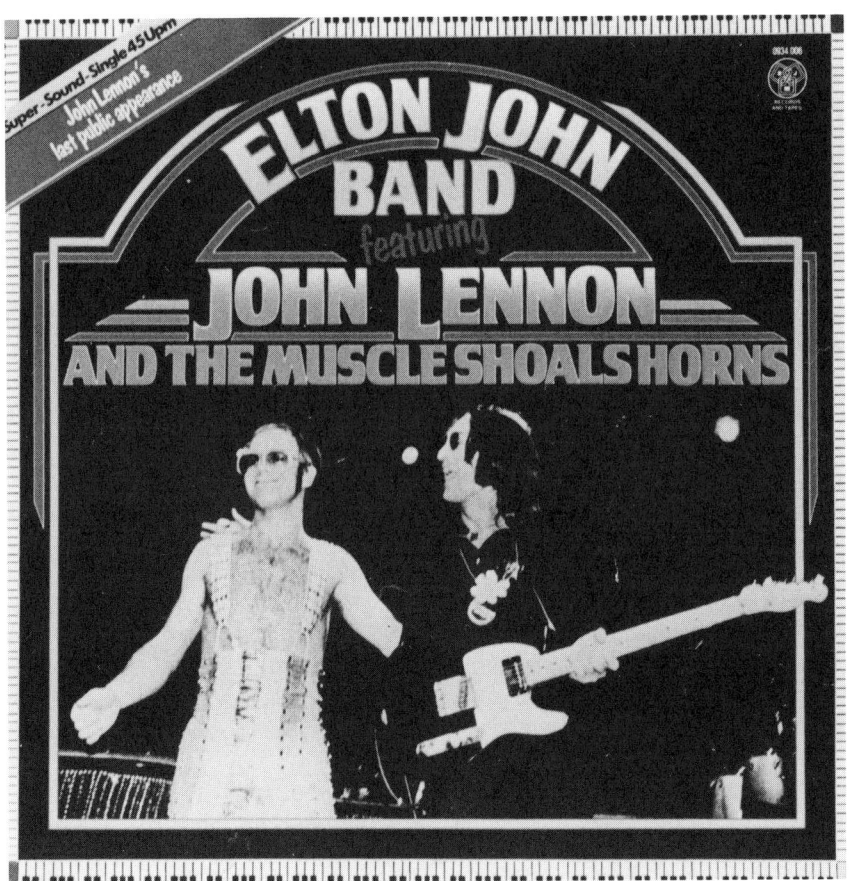

Elton John Band featuring John Lennon
and the Muscle Shoals Horns
Germany: DJM 0934 006 (12" maxi-single)

single, and on a European and Japanese album of highlights of Elton's Madison Square Garden show. This time, John's "alright," although still audible, was mixed way down.

with YOKO ONO

Death Of Samantha (Ono)
Produced by John and Yoko for Yoko's early 1973 two-record set, **Approximately Infinite Universe**, and later issued as a single. The album version runs 6:23; the single was condensed to 3:40.

Don't Worry Kyoko (Mummy's Only Looking For A Hand In The Snow) (Ono) - "live"
(Version 1) - Recorded September 13,1969, at Toronto's Varsity Stadium by the Plastic Ono Band, this version runs 4:44 and was issued in December 1969 on **Live Peace In Toronto**. (See **Live Peace In Toronto**, p. 242.)
(Version 2) - Recorded December 15,1969, at London's Lyceum Ballroom by John, Yoko, and the Plastic Ono Supergroup, this version runs 17:12 and was released in 1972 on the "live" half of **Sometime In New York City**, a double-album.
The original studio recording, first put out in October 1969 as the B-side of the Plastic Ono Band's *Cold Turkey*, runs 4:52.

Hirake (Ono)
The alternate title of *Open Your Box*, it was used by Yoko on her second solo LP, **Fly**, issued in the winter of 1971. This is actually the original recording of the song with the uncensored lyrics, "Open your trousers. . . skirts. . . legs. . . thighs." (See *Open Your Box*, p. 251.)

I'm Your Angel (Ono)
Produced by John, Yoko, and Jack Douglas for **Double Fantasy**, this 1930s-style song was also put out as the B-side of *Watching The Wheels*, the album's third single, under the title *Yes I'm Your Angel*.
The song itself runs 2:50. On **Double Fantasy**, *Watching The Wheels* is linked to *I'm Your Angel* by a series of "city sounds" (random voices, honking horns, footsteps). Part of these noises are considered the end of John's number while the others are meant as an intro to Yoko's. Here, the total running time of *I'm Your Angel* is listed as 3:08.

Mind Train (Ono)
Produced by John and Yoko (with John on guitar) for Yoko's

1971 release, **Fly**, and later issued as a single.

The album version runs 16:52; the British single (Apple 41) was condensed to 4:45.

Never Say Goodbye (Ono)

Produced by Yoko in mid-1982 and issued around the second anniversary of John's murder on **It's Alright**, this solo composition incorporates a tape of John screaming "Yoko!" during the instrumental break.

The album version runs 4:25. The American 7-inch single (Polydor 810 556-7) was shortened to 3:25 while the American 12-inch single (Polydor 810 575-1) was remixed and artificially lengthened to 4:27.

Open Your Box (Ono)

Recorded in February 1971 (with John playing guitar) and produced by John and Yoko, this track first appeared in England as the B-side of *Power To The People* (Apple R 5892). The song originally bore the lyrics, "Open your trousers. . . skirts. . . legs. . . thighs." Prior to release, EMI demanded that the offending lines be removed. On March 4, Yoko re-cut her lead vocal, replacing the questionable words with "Open your houses. . . churches. . . lakes. . . eyes."

In America, Capitol Records chose to avoid all controversey and substituted *Touch Me* from **Yoko Ono/Plastic Ono Band**, Yoko's first solo album.

Toward the end of the year, Yoko included the original, uncensored recording on **Fly**, her second solo release. Here, the song went unnoticed under an alternate title, *Hirake*. (See *Hirake*, p.250.)

Walking On Thin Ice (Ono)

John and Yoko finished remixing this song at New York's Hit Factory the night of December 8, 1980, just half an hour before John was murdered. The track was an outtake from the **Double Fantasy** sessions.

John was ecstatic that Yoko had finally received critical acclaim for her writing and performance on **Double Fantasy**. He now wanted her to share the joy of having a Number One record and felt *Walking On Thin Ice*, with its heavy dance beat and New Wave synthesizers, was just the cut to take her to the top of the charts.

During the first week of December, John and Yoko worked at a fever pitch to finish the track and get it out. On December 4, John laid down his guitar overdubs; on December 7, Yoko had a rough version, and on December 8, John and Yoko completed the final mix. John, Yoko, and producer Jack Douglas were so sure this track was going to be a hit, they decided to meet at New York's Sterling Sound

(7YCE.21528)

R 5892

Ono Music

Mfd. In U.K.

Produced by:

JOHN & YOKO

℗ 1971

45 r.p.m

OPEN YOUR BOX

(Yoko Ono)

YOKO ONO/PLASTIC ONO BAND

Open Your Box
UK: Apple R 5892 (45)

first thing in the morning to supervise the cutting of a lacquer. But the next morning never came....

Following John's tragic death, it was several months before Yoko could face going back into the studio. But since this was her final collaboration with John, she decided it was best to finish the project, which also included designing a picture sleeve for the single and completing a promotional video clip. On February 1, 1981, *Walking On Thin Ice* was issued.

All commercial pressings run 5:58; the American promotional version (12-inch Geffen PRO-A935; 7-inch Geffen 49683) was shortened to 3:23. Yoko also put together a 7:32 disco version but that remains unreleased.

Yes I'm Your Angel (Ono)
(See *I'm Your Angel*, p. 250.)

Give My Regards To Broad Street
US: Columbia SC 39613 (LP)

13

Paul
McCartney

Among the ex-Beatles, Paul McCartney holds the record for having the most singles edited for American airplay. Beginning in 1971 with *Uncle Albert/Admiral Halsey*, Paul has had thirteen edited promotional singles distributed by Apple, Capitol and Columbia Records. Two of the more widely known promo cuts are *Jet* and *Band On The Run*, which were chosen for release and edited by Capitol Records promotion man Al Coury in early 1974. In the fall of 1975, Paul remixed and resequenced two tracks from **Venus And Mars** for commercial singles, *Letting Go* and *Venus And Mars/Rock Show*. Both versions of these songs were made from the same basic recordings, yet the singles are noticeably different from the album tracks.

The October 1984 release of "Give My Regards To Broad Street" (Twentieth Century Fox), Paul's first major motion picture, provided fans with three new McCartney songs plus re-recordings of six Beatles numbers, one Wings track and four other solo efforts. For the collector, it also offered a wealth of new McCartney variations.

The soundtrack album was issued in three configurations: on standard LP, cassette and compact disc. However, the packages were not identical. The LP contained edited versions of *Good Day Sunshine, Wanderlust, Ballroom Dancing, Eleanor Rigby, Eleanor's Dream* and the "playout version" of *No More Lonely Nights*. Full-length recordings were found on the cassette and CD. The cassette was put out in Dolby stereo on high quality, chromium-dioxide tape and included a "bonus track" from the movie not found on the LP, *So Bad*. This song also appeared on the compact disc along with *Goodnight Lonely Princess*, an instrumental available only on the CD.

Ballroom Dancing (McCartney)
(Version 1) - Produced in 1982 by George Martin with Paul

singing and playing piano, drums, bass, guitar and percussion, this version runs 4:06 and is available on **Tug Of War** and on the 12-inch promotional maxi-single put out in America and Canada, **A Sample From "Tug Of War"** (Columbia AS-1444; pressed on white vinyl).

(Version 2) - Also produced by Martin, the song was re-recorded for "Give My Regards To Broad Street" (Twentieth Century Fox, 1984) with an all-star line-up that included Ringo Starr, Dave Edmunds and Chris Spedding. The complete film version runs 6:06 and is available only on the "Broad Street" home videocassette (US:CBS Fox Video-Beta HiFi/VHS Stereo 1448). It also contains an extra verse not heard in the original recording.

(Version 3) - For the **Broad Street** soundtrack album, Paul and George Martin shortened the film version to 4:36 by omitting the first instrumental break, the third verse, which begins "Well the kids have flown to a better life. . .," and the chorus that follows. The **Broad Street** cassette (US: Columbia SCT 39613) lists the running time of *Ballroom Dancing* as 4:51 but this also includes the dialog at the end of the track plus the sound effects that precede the start of the next cut, *Silly Love Songs*. (See **Give My Regards To Broad Street**, p. 256.)

Band On The Run   (McCartney) - studio
The title song from Paul McCartney and Wings' 1973 Grammy Award-winning album, and later a single.

All commercial pressings run 5:09; the American promotional single (Apple PRO-6825) was shortened to 3:50 by Capitol Records promotion man Al Coury. This version was also issued in England (Apple R 5997 DJ).

A "live" version, recorded during Wings' 1976 U.S. tour, is available on **Wings Over America**.

Band On The Run
Recorded during September 1973 in Lagos, Nigeria and London by Paul, wife Linda and guitarist Denny Laine, this critically acclaimed album stayed in the British charts for sixty-five weeks and earned gold discs in England, the United States, Australia, Norway and Sweden.

When Odeon Records in Germany cut the lacquers to press the album there, they accidentally accelerated the playback speed of the master tape, making every song two to eight seconds faster than its true running time. Below is a list of each song followed by 1) its original running time and 2) its slightly faster German time:

Band On The Run	5:09	5:01
Jet	4:08	4:00

Bluebird	3:22	3:17
Mrs. Vanderbilt	4:40	4:33
Let Me Roll It	4:51	4:44
Mamunia	4:51	4:45
No Words	2:36	2:28
Picasso's Last Words (Drink To Me)	5:48	5:46
Nineteen Hundred And Eighty Five	5:30	5:23

Helen Wheels was added to the American pressing of **Band On The Run** at the suggestion of Capitol Records promotion man Al Coury so the album could benefit from the success of this recent Wings' Top Ten single. Coury was also responsible for selecting *Jet* and *Band On The Run* as subsequent singles in America and for making edited promotional copies of both to generate more airplay. Paul credits Coury's aggressive marketing of **Band On The Run** for its reaching the Number One spot on the American charts on three separate occasions during 1974.

Beware My Love (McCartney) - studio
Released in the spring of 1976 on **Wings At The Speed Of Sound** and as the B-side of *Let 'Em In*.

The album version runs 6:25; the single was shortened to 6:05 by eliminating twenty seconds of organ chords from the beginning of the track. However, Odeon Records in Germany used the full-length album cut for its single pressing.

A "live" version, recorded during Wings' 1976 U.S. tour, is available on **Wings Over America**.

Coming Up (McCartney) - "live"
(Version 1) - Subtitled "(*Live at Glasgow*)," this version by Paul McCartney and Wings was recorded on either December 16 or December 17, 1979, at the Apollo Theater in Glasgow, Scotland, the final city on the group's U.K. tour. The track runs 3:51 and is available commercially on a 7-inch single (US: Columbia 1-11263) as well as on a 12-inch promotional single (US: Columbia AS 775). In America, it was also included with **McCartney II** on a bonus, one-sided 7-inch disc (Columbia AE7 1204). This limited edition release was pressed at 33 1/3 rpm.

(Version 2) - Also by Wings, this version was taped some two weeks later, on December 29, 1979, at London's Hammersmith Odeon Theater during a benefit performance for the Cambodian refugees. The track runs 4:08 and was issued only on **Concerts For The People Of Kampuchea**.

A studio version, actually the demo, features just Paul singing and playing all the instruments (with wife Linda on back-up vocals)

Ebony And Ivory
US: Columbia 44-02878 (12" maxi-single)

Contains both the hit version of the McCartney-Wonder duet as well as
Paul's original solo recording of the song.

and contains a verse that was omitted from all subsequent recordings. The cut runs 3:49 and was first put out in April 1980 as a single (US: Columbia 1-11263) and later on **McCartney II**.

Ebony And Ivory   (McCartney)

Recorded in 1981 at George Martin's AIR Studio in Montserrat with Paul and Stevie Wonder playing all the instruments.

(Version 1) - This track, with vocals by Paul and Stevie, is avail– able as a 7-inch single, as the title cut on a commercial 12-inch maxi- single (US: Columbia 44-02878) and is included on **Tug Of War** and on the 12-inch promotional maxi-single put out in America and Canada, **A Sample From "Tug Of War"** (Columbia AS-1444; pressed on white vinyl).

(Version 2) - Sung by just Paul, this version is available only on the B-side of the commercial 12-inch maxi-single (US: Columbia 44- 02878).

Eleanor Rigby   (Lennon-McCartney)

First recorded in 1966 with the Beatles and put out as a single and on **Revolver**, Paul re-recorded this song for "Give My Regards To Broad Street" (Twentieth Century Fox, 1984). In the movie, the song lasts 4:08. Paul sings for the first 2:07 and is followed by another 2:01 of orchestration. The number then segues into *Eleanor's Dream*, an extended instrumental composed by Paul based on the original melody and arranged by producer George Martin.

On the **Broad Street** cassette and compact disc, *Eleanor Rigby* appears in its entirety. However, on the LP, the song was shortened to 2:07, ending just after Paul stops singing. (See *Eleanor's Dream* (below) and **Give My Regards To Broad Street**, p. 261.)

Eleanor's Dream   (McCartney) - instrumental

An extended orchestration based on the melody of *Eleanor Rigby*, composed by Paul and arranged by producer George Martin for "Give My Regards To Broad Street" (Twentieth Century Fox, 1984).

In the movie, this number follows Paul's new rendition of *Eleanor Rigby*. It serves as background music to the fantasy chase through Victorian London. The scene in the film actually runs 6:27 but the musical passages add up to only 4:59.

Eleanor's Dream appears in its entirety on the **Broad Street** cassette and compact disc. On the LP, this track was shortened to 1:01. In fact, Paul and George Martin just condensed the remaining instrumental music from the end of *Eleanor Rigby* to 1:01 and labeled it *Eleanor's Dream* for the LP and CD. (See *Eleanor Rigby*

Girls' School
US: Capitol SPRO-8747 (promo 45)

and **Give My Regards To Broad Street**, below.)

Every Night   (McCartney) - studio

Paul sings and plays acoustic guitar, drums, bass and electric guitar on this cut off his first solo album, **McCartney**, released in April 1970.

An edited version found on a Mexican EP (Apple EPEM 10603) was shortened to 1:50 by fading it out just before the extended ending; all other pressings run 2:27. This edited track was also incorrectly identified on both the record label and picture sleeve as *Valentine Day*, another cut off the same LP.

A "live" version by Paul McCartney and Wings, recorded December 29, 1979, at London's Hammersmith Odeon theater during a benefit performance for the Cambodian refugees, is available on **Concerts For The People Of Kampuchea.**

Girls' School   (McCartney)

In England, this McCartney rocker was the B-side of the multi-platinum *Mull Of Kintyre*. In America, Capitol Records made it the A-side of Paul's winter 1977 single.

All commercial pressings run 4:34; the American promotional single (Capitol SPRO-8747) was shortened to 3:19 by condensing the closing instrumental break and fading the track out early.

Give My Regards To Broad Street

The soundtrack album to Paul's first major motion picture, this 1984 release was issued simultaneously in three formats: standard LP, cassette and compact disc. However, Paul and producer George Martin made each of the compilations unique. Since cassettes and compact discs offer a longer playing time than LPs and do not necessitate any extra limiting or compression for extra material, the **Broad Street** cassette and CD contain longer versions of five songs. The cassette also includes *So Bad* as a "bonus track" not found on the LP. Likewise, the compact disc features an instrumental not found on either the LP or cassette, *Goodnight Lonely Princess.*

Besides these real differences, Columbia Records in America created more confusion for collectors by printing different running times for songs that were identical in length in all three modes. *Ballroom Dancing* is listed as 4:36 on both the LP and CD but 4:51 on the cassette.

Some of the confusion stems from the method used to compute running times. On the LP, songs were timed from the first note in each track (even if it was a bit of the film's background music) to the final note of the song.

In contrast, song lengths on the cassette and CD were figured by elapsed time, i.e. starting a clock at the beginning of the first track (in fact, at the beginning of the leader tape on Side One of the cassette) and marking the time at the end of each song, then subtracting the two figures. In this way, all incidental material between songs, including dialog and sound effects, was also added in, hence the slightly longer running times given for most songs on the **Broad Street** cassette and compact disc.

To compound matters, there are also some blatant errors in certain times on the cassette. *Silly Love Songs* runs 4:59, as listed on both the LP and CD. The same cut is timed at only 3:35 on tape.

Finally, Columbia in America borrowed the cover art, sleeve graphics and liner notes, including timing information, for the compact disc from the LP. Since five of the tracks are longer on CD than on LP, the figures are useless. On CD, *Eleanor Rigby* and *Eleanor's Dream* are listed as one composite track with a total running time of 1:01. In fact, these two cuts combine to over 9:12. Luckily for CD owners, the running time of each track is encoded in the disc, and when played is displayed on the front of the CD player. Therefore, true running times can finally be discovered. But again, Columbia was sloppy in deciding whether "link material" should be computed as the end of one track or the beginning of the next. In the encoded information, *No Values* is considered over after Paul says "Finish it this time," while the coda of the song with guitar solos by Chris Spedding and Dave Edmunds is calculated as the beginning of *No More Lonely Nights* (ballad reprise). The only times that match are *Silly Love Songs* (reprise), which is listed both on the jacket and on the disc read-out as :36, and *The Long And Winding Road* at 3:47.

Below is a track-by-track comparison of running times from the **Give My Regards To Broad Street** LP, cassette and compact disc. True differences are in italics. The other discrepancies are due to alternative methods of computation, not actual differences in the length of a particular song. (CD times are those that are encoded on the disc, and not the times from the liner notes, which are identical to the LP.)

	LP	Cass	CD	7"	12"
No More Lonely Nights (ballad)	4:50	5:00	4:57	4:38	4:38
Good Day Sunshine	*1:43*	2:26	2:28		
Corridor Music*	:17	:19	:18		
Yesterday	1:43	1:43	1:42		

* Incidental music.

262

	LP	Cass	CD	7"	12"
Here, There And Everywhere	1:44	1:43	1:43		
Wanderlust	2:48	4:00	3:58		
Ballroom Dancing	4:36	4:51	4:49		
Silly Love Songs	4:29	3:35	4:38		4:29
Silly Love Songs (reprise)*	:36	1:01	:36		
Not Such A Bad Boy	3:19	4:25	3:43		
So Bad		3:10	3:17		
No Values	4:06	3:58	3:54		
No More Lonely Nights (ballad reprise)*	:13	:27	:29		
For No One	1:56	2:10	2:11		
Eleanor Rigby	2:07	4:08			
Eleanor's Dream	1:01	4:59	9:12		
The Long And Winding Road	3:47	3:42	3:47		
No More Lonely Nights (playout version)	4:17	5:11	5:16		8:10
Goodnight Lonely Princess			3:58		
No More Lonely Nights (special dance mix)				4:14	6:53 promo
No More Lonely Nights (mole mix)					x

Good Day Sunshine   (Lennon-McCartney)

First recorded in 1966 with the Beatles and put out on **Revolver**, Paul re-recorded this song for "Give My Regards To Broad Street" (Twentieth Century Fox, 1984). On this new rendition, Paul plays all the instruments except for the piano, which was played as it was eighteen years before by producer George Martin.

In the movie, this new version is presented as if it were the Beatles' original. Paul is stuck in traffic in his limousine, late for a meeting at his office on a wet, rainy morning. With the radio on, Paul begins to daydream when the disc jockey says "This should help you take your mind off the gloom . . . remember the summer of '66 . . . ." as the new recording of *Good Day Sunshine* fades in.

The complete version, as heard in the film, was issued on the **Broad Street** cassette and compact disc. The running time is given as 2:26 (and 2:28), although the first sixteen seconds are actually dialog. For the LP, the song was shortened to 1:43 (not including

*Incidental music.

263

Goodnight Tonight
US: Columbia 23-10940 (12" single)

The disco version, available only as a 12" single, contains an extra verse
not heard on 7" pressings.

Jet
US: Apple PRO-6827 (promo 45)

Let 'Em In
US: Capitol PRO-8423 (promo 45)

dialog) by omitting the third verse, which begins "Then we lie beneath a shady tree . . . ." and the preceding chorus.

Even though the **Broad Street** cassette and CD contain *Good Day Sunshine* in its entirety, the third verse is omitted on the accompanying lyric sheets. (See **Give My Regards To Broad Street**, p. 261.)

Goodnight Tonight (McCartney)
Paul's first single on Columbia Records (US) after signing with the label in 1979 for what was then the most lucrative contract in music history: a guaranteed $2 million per album for five albums, plus 22% of the royalties.

The original disco version, released in the United States (Columbia 23-10940) and in England (Parlophone 12Y R 6023) on a limited edition, 12-inch single, runs 7:25; the 7-inch single was shortened to 4:18. The disco version contains an additional verse not heard on the 7-inch pressing.

Jet (McCartney) - studio
Named after a puppy of Paul's, this straight ahead rocker was the second U.S. single taken from **Band On The Run.**

All commercial pressings run 4:08; Al Coury of Capitol Records shortened the American promotional single (Apple PRO-6827) to 2:49 by condensing the intro, omitting several instrumental breaks and resequencing the track.

A "live" version, recorded during Wings' 1976 U.S. tour, is available on **Wings Over America.**

Junior's Farm (McCartney)
Recorded in Nashville during the summer of 1974 with new Wings members Jimmy McCulloch (guitar) and Geoff Britton (drums).

All commercial pressings run 4:20; the American (Apple PRO-6999) and British (Apple R 5999 DJ) promotional singles were shortened slightly.

Let 'Em In (McCartney) - studio
Issued in the spring of 1976 on **Wings At The Speed Of Sound** and as a single.

All commercial pressings run 5:08; the American (Capitol PRO-8423) and British (Parlophone R 6015 DJ) promotional singles were shortened to 3:43 by eliminating the final verse, chorus and snare drum break and by fading the track out early and not bringing it back up for the final chord.

A "live" version, recorded during Wings' 1976 U.S. tour, is available on **Wings Over America.**

Letting Go
US: Capitol PRO-8225 (promo 45)

Maybe I'm Amazed
US: Capitol S/PRO-8570/l (promo 45)

Letting Go   (McCartney) - studio

Recorded in November 1974 in London, this song was issued in May 1975 on Wings' **Venus And Mars** and in September as a single.

The album version runs 4:36; the single was shortened to 3:30, remixed and resequenced, and one second of electric organ, not heard on the LP, was added to the introduction.

A "live" version, taped during Wings' 1976 U.S. tour, is available on **Wings Over America**.

London Town   (McCartney)

The title track from Wings' 1978 album, their last new LP for Capitol Records in the United States.

All commercial pressings run 4:10; the American promotional single (Capitol PRO-8908) was shortened to 3:48.

Mary Had A Little Lamb   (Paul & Linda McCartney)

Recorded in early 1972 with Wings members Denny Seiwell (drums), Denny Laine (guitar) and Henry McCullough (lead guitar).

The background vocals sung by Paul's children were mixed out of the German single (Odeon 1C006-05.598).

Maybe I'm Amazed   (McCartney) - "live"

Recorded during Wings' 1976 U.S. tour, this version was issued on **Wings Over America** and as a single.

All commercial pressings run 5:11; the American 7-inch promo-- tional single (Capitol S/PRO-8570/1) was shortened to 3:43 by eliminating the first guitar solo, the third verse of the song, and by editing out the track's false ending.

Capitol Records (US) also put out a 12-inch promotional EP (Capitol S/PRO-8574/7) that contained four copies of the song. Each side had both the long and short versions with one side in stereo and the other in mono.

The original studio version, released in 1970 on **McCartney**, features Paul singing and playing every instrument.

McCartney Interview, The

A transcription recording of author Vic Garbarini's interview with Paul, published in the August 1980 issue of *Musician: Player & Listener.*

The interview, conducted in Paul's Soho Square office in London, proved so successful that Columbia Records in America decided to issue it to radio stations on a promo album. The resulting double-LP (Columbia A2S-821/AS 822 and AS 823) consisted of two versions of the interview: one with the complete tapes and the other "open-ended," with the questions edited out for local disc

Mull Of Kintyre
US: Capitol SPRO-8746 (promo 45)

jockeys. The two-record set also came with a copy of the magazine.

Interest in the album was strong enough to warrant its commercial release, so in December 1980, Columbia in the U.S. issued a limited edition, commercial version (Columbia PC 36987). This single record had the questions intact and bore the same cover art as the promo copy.

On February 23, 1981, EMI in England put out the album (Parlophone CHAT 1) and guaranteed its immediate "collectable" status by deleting it the same day.

Mull Of Kintyre   (Paul McCartney - Denny Laine)

Paul and Denny's attempt to write an authentic Scottish folk song became England's biggest-selling single of all time, with 2.5 million copies reported sold in the U.K. alone.

All commercial pressings run 4:42; the American (Capitol SPRO-8746) and British (Parlophone R 6018 DJ) promotional singles were shortened to 3:31 by eliminating one chorus, one of the bagpipe solos by the Campbeltown Pipe Band and the third verse of the song.

No More Lonely Nights - ballad   (McCartney)

The featured song in "Give My Regards To Broad Street" (Twentieth Century Fox, 1984). Two versions were released on record, one with an introduction and the other without. The intro is made up of incidental material from the film soundtrack and begins with the sound of rain, then a cloudburst, a variation of the melody played on an electric bass and repeated three times, and strings.

The album track, with the intro, is available on the LP, cassette and compact disc editions of **Give My Regards To Broad Street**. Although the same version appears on all three configurations, the times are given as follows: LP-4:50, cassette-5:00, compact disc-4:57.

The single version, minus the intro, runs 4:38 and was issued on a standard 7-inch pressing (US: Columbia 38-04581) and on two 12-inch maxi-singles, one a regular release (US: Columbia 44-05077) and the other a picture disc (US: Columbia 39927). Several thousand copies of the original British 7-inch single (Parlophone R 6080) had the title misspelled as *No More **Lonley** Nights*.

In the movie, *No More Lonely Nights* was shortened to 3:25. Here, the first chorus and second verse, which begins "May I never miss the thrill . . . . ," were omitted. This version is available commercially on the home videocassette of "Give My Regards To Broad Street" (US: CBS Fox Video-Beta HiFi/VHS Stereo 1448).

Incidentally, the song's introduction was condensed from the first few moments of the movie and therefore does not precede

No More Lonely Nights
US: Columbia 38-04581 (45)

No More Lonely Nights (playout version)/Silly Love Songs/
No More Lonely Nights (ballad)
US: Columbia 39927 (12" picture disc)

No More Lonely Nights on screen. The song turned out to be the next-to-the-last number in the picture. However, for the soundtrack album, Paul chose this highlighted tune (and hit single) as the opening cut. Otherwise, the rest of the material is arranged in the order it appeared in the film. (See **Give My Regards To Broad Street**, p. 261.)

No More Lonely Nights - mole mix (McCartney)

The eighth and final variation of this song was issued only to British disc jockeys on a one-sided, 12-inch disc (Parlophone 12R 6080 DJ). The records were numbered and just 300 copies were pressed.

No More Lonely Nights - playout version (McCartney)

Paul played all the instruments except horns in this uptempo rendition, recorded for use behind the close credits in "Give My Regards To Broad Street" (Twentieth Century Fox, 1984).

Paul and producer George Martin created three different versions of this track. The longest one runs 8:10 and is available only as the A-side of the 12-inch *No More Lonely Nights* maxisingle. This was issued both as a regular release (US: Columbia 44-05077) and as a picture disc (US: Columbia 39927). In England, the original 12-inch maxi-single (Parlophone 12R 6080) was deleted two months after release and replaced by a second edition in which the "extended special dance mix" was substituted for the "playout version."

In the movie, the song actually runs 4:43 from the opening horn riff. This same track, coupled with an intro of dialog and incidental music, was issued on the **Broad Street** cassette and compact disc.

The version on the LP was shortened to 4:17 (not counting the intro) by omitting an instrumental break along with one repeat of a verse and chorus.

As with the maxi-single in England, the "playout version" of *No More Lonely Nights* that appeared on the B-side of the original 7-inch single was replaced two months after release by the "special dance mix." (See **Give My Regards To Broad Street**, p. 261.)

No More Lonely Nights - special dance mix (McCartney)

Remixed in America by Arthur Baker from the "playout version," these two tracks contain different percussion and synthesizer parts throughout the song.

The "special dance mix," available only as the B-side of the re-issued 7-inch single of *No More Lonely Nights* - ballad (US: Columbia 38-04581), runs 4:14.

275

The "extended special dance mix" runs 6:53 and was not commercially released in the United States. It was put out only on a 12-inch promotional single (US: Columbia AS 1990) coupled with the shorter version of the same track. However, in England, it appeared on the reissued 12-inch maxi-single, replacing the "play-out version" of *No More Lonely Nights*. (See **Give My Regards To Broad Street**, p. 261.)

No Values (McCartney)

According to Paul, he once had a dream in which the Rolling Stones were singing this song. Later realizing that the Stones had never done such a number, Paul scribbled down the lyrics and melody and included it in "Give My Regards To Broad Street" (Twentieth Century Fox, 1984).

The complete version, as heard in the film, runs 5:16 and is available only on the home videocassette of the movie (US: CBS Fox Video-Beta HiFi/VHS Stereo 1448). The album version was shortened to 4:06. The difference is in the length of Chris Spedding and Dave Edmunds' guitar work in the fade-out. In the film, their extended solos serve as background to Paul's fantasy about Harry the roadie (Ian Hastings) selling the master tape of Paul's latest album to Big Bob the bootlegger (Luke McMasters, a.k.a. "Giant Haystacks"). Both tracks end with feedback caused when Paul cupped his hands around a microphone.

On the **Broad Street** cassette, the running time is listed as 3:58. The recording is identical to the LP and CD versions but here the master tape was played back at a slightly faster speed in order to squeeze all the soundtrack material on one tape. (See **Give My Regards To Broad Street**, p. 261.)

Oh Woman, Oh Why (McCartney)

Released in February 1971 as the B-side of Paul's first solo single, *Another Day*.

The original version, available only on the American promotional single (Apple PRO-6194), contains the sound of cannon shots mixed in with the normal percussion.

Rock Show (McCartney) - studio

Recorded at Sea Saint studios in New Orleans with Allen Toussaint on piano, this track was issued in May 1975 on Wings' **Venus And Mars** and was later put out as a single.

The album version runs 5:32; the single (which is linked with *Venus And Mars*) was shortened to 2:34 by condensing the entire track and by omitting the end of Paul's closing rap, ". . . place your wig on straight . . . ."

Silly Love Songs
US: Capitol SPRO-8365 (promo 45)

A "live" version, recorded during Wings' 1976 U.S. tour, is available on **Wings Over America.**

Sally G (McCartney)

Recorded by Wings at Sound Shop studios in Nashville with country music legends Chet Atkins and Floyd Cramer joining in on electric guitar and piano, this track was issued in the winter of 1974 as the B-side of *Junior's Farm.* In early 1975, Apple Records reversed the A and B-sides and *Sally G* entered the country charts in America.

Paul's three taps on his guitar at the end of this song were omitted from the German single (Odeon Records).

Silly Love Songs (McCartney) - studio

(Version 1) - Produced by Paul and released in March 1976, two months prior to the start of Wings' record-breaking U.S. tour, this song became the biggest-selling single of the year in America. All commercial pressings run 5:54; the American (Capitol SPRO-8365) and British (Parlophone R 6014 DJ) promotional singles were shortened to 3:28 by eliminating two horn breaks and two vocal refrains in the middle of the song. A "live" version, recorded on tour, is available on **Wings Over America.**

(Version 2) - Produced by George Martin and re-recorded for "Give My Regards To Broad Street" (Twentieth Century Fox, 1984). The complete version, as heard in the film, runs 4:50 and is available only on the home videocassette of the movie (US: CBS Fox Video-Beta HiFi/VHS Stereo 1448). The commercial recording was shortened to 4:29 by condensing the opening tape loops and Paul's "I love you"s. This version is available on the standard LP and compact disc editions of **Give My Regards To Broad Street** and on the B-side of the 12-inch *No More Lonely Nights* maxi-single, which was issued as a regular release (US: Columbia 44-05077) and as a picture disc (US: Columbia 39927). On the **Broad Street** cassette, the running time is incorrectly listed as 3:35 when in fact it's the same recording, although it was speeded up slightly to playback in 4:25. The commercial recording was also remixed to include a jet airplane roar between the intro and the start of the first verse, and extra keyboards behind the lyrics "What's wrong with that, I need to know . . ." These effects are not heard in the film version. (See **Give My Regards To Broad Street**, p. 261.)

Smile Away (McCartney)

The closing cut on Side One of Paul and Linda McCartney's **Ram**, issued in May 1971.

Paul's count-off ("one, two, three, four") was omitted from the

Take It Away
Japan: Toshiba-EMI EPS-10004 (12" maxi-single)

German single (Odeon 1C006-04.864).

So Bad (McCartney)

(Version 1) - Issued in the winter of 1983 on **Pipes Of Peace** and later as a single, this version runs 3:18 and features Ringo Starr on drums and Eric Stewart on guitar, with George Martin producing.

(Version 2) - Also produced by Martin with largely the same personnel, this song was re-recorded for "Give My Regards To Broad Street" (Twentieth Century Fox, 1984). Due to space limitations, the track was omitted from the **Broad Street** soundtrack LP. Instead it was released on the cassette (US: Columbia SCT 39613) as a "bonus track" even though it was also included on the compact disc (US: Columbia CK 39613). Although the tracks are identical, the running time of *So Bad* is listed as 3:10 on the cassette while it's given as 3:12 on the compact disc. (See **Give My Regards To Broad Street**, p. 261.)

Soily (McCartney)

Performed by Wings as a second encore during their 1976 sold-out tour of the United States, this song is available only as a "live" recording. It was issued later that year on **Wings Over America** and in February 1977 as the B-side of another "live" cut off the same album, *Maybe I'm Amazed*.

Paul's closing remark ("See you next time, alright, thank 'yous' ") was omitted from the Dutch single.

Take It Away (McCartney)

Produced by George Martin, with Ringo Starr sharing the drumming chores with session man Steve Gadd, this track was issued in the spring of 1982 on **Tug Of War**, Paul's landmark LP, and was later put out as a single.

The album version runs 4:13; the single was shortened to 4:00 by eliminating the final chorus of horns in the fade-out.

Tug Of War (McCartney)

The title track from Paul's much-heralded 1982 LP. Also released as a single.

The album version runs 4:21; the single was shortened to 4:00 by omitting most of the grunting "tug of war" sounds at the beginning of the track.

Uncle Albert/Admiral Halsey (Paul & Linda McCartney)

In America, the featured single from **Ram**, Paul and Linda's 1971 collaboration.

The album version runs 4:50; the American promotional single

Uncle Albert/Admiral Halsey
US: Apple S/PRO-6278/9 (promo 45)

(Apple PRO-6278) and the version on **Wings Greatest** (US: Capitol S00-11905) were shortened to 4:47 by fading the track out early.

Venus And Mars (McCartney) - studio
Recorded at Sea Saint studios in New Orleans, this is the title track of Wings' May 1975 LP and was later issued as a single.

The album version runs 1:16; the single (which is linked with *Rock Show*) was shortened to 1:05.

A "live" version, taped during Wings' 1976 U.S. tour, is available on **Wings Over America.**

Wanderlust (McCartney)
The title of the song came from the name of a trimaran that Paul, Linda and their family stayed aboard in the Virgin Islands in May 1977 while recording **London Town.**

(Version 1) - Produced by George Martin, this version runs 3:49 and was issued in April 1982 on the widely acclaimed **Tug Of War.**

(Version 2) - Also produced by George Martin and featuring Ringo Starr on drums, the song was re-recorded for "Give My Regards To Broad Street" (Twentieth Century Fox, 1984). The complete version, as heard in the film, runs 4:00 (including eight seconds of dialog by Paul at the end of the cut) and was issued on the **Broad Street** cassette, compact disc and home videocassette. On the soundtrack LP (US: Columbia SC 39613), the cut was shortened to 2:48 (without dialog) by omitting the first instrumental break with the Philip Jones Brass Ensemble, the first bridge of the song, which begins "Oh where did I go wrong my love . . ." and the second chorus. (See **Give My Regards To Broad Street**, p. 261.)

Waterfalls (McCartney)
The second single taken from **McCartney II**, Paul's May 1980 solo effort.

All commercial pressings run 4:41; the American (Columbia 1-11335 promo) and British (Parlophone R 6037 DJ) promotional singles were shortened to 3:22. However, once the song became a hit in Europe, Parlophone Records (UK) and Odeon Records (Germany) replaced the full-length recording on their commercial singles with the shorter, promotional version.

Wild Life (Paul & Linda McCartney)
The title track of the first Wings' LP, produced by Paul and Linda McCartney for Apple Records and issued in December 1971.

With A Little Luck
US: Capitol S/PRO 8812/3 (promo 45)

This song was edited into two parts on a Venezuelan single with the A-side running 3:20 and the B-side lasting 3:10.

With A Little Luck (McCartney)

The first single from **London Town**, Wings' March 1978 LP recorded both in London and in the Virgin Islands.

Most commercial pressings run 5:45; the American (Capitol S/PRO-8812/3) and British (Parlophone R 6019 DJ) promotional singles were shortened to 3:13 by eliminating the fourth verse of the song and the extended instrumental break that follows. This abbreviated version was issued for a limited time in Poland (Tonpress/EMI S-131) where the running time on the single was listed as 3:13 even though it was really 3:10.

With MICHAEL JACKSON

The Girl Is Mine (Michael Jackson)

Produced in 1982 by Quincy Jones, this was the first single released from Michael Jackson's **Thriller**, the biggest-selling album in recording history.

The original version runs 3:41. However, when the song reached the Number One spot on the American charts, Epic Records issued a second promotional single with Paul and Michael's closing rap omitted, shortening the track to 3:32. The disc bore the same catalog number as the first pressing but was labeled as a "new edited version."

Epic in America also released *The Girl Is Mine* as a commercial, one-sided single (Epic ENR 03372), part of a short-lived attempt to boost the sales of forty-fives by making the top hits available at a less expensive price. And in England, there was a limited edition 7-inch picture disc of the song (Epic EPC A 11-2729).

Say Say Say (McCartney-Jackson)

The 1983 million-selling duet by pop's most successful composer and the record industry's top star of the eighties.

(Version 1) - Produced by George Martin, this recording runs 3:55 and was issued as a 7-inch single and on **Pipes Of Peace** .

(Version 2) - Available only as the title track of a commercial 12-inch maxi single (US: Columbia 44-04169), this is a special remix of "Version 1" made in America by John "Jellybean" Benitez, who artificially lengthened the track to 5:40 by adding instrumental breaks between each verse.

(Version 3) - This 7:00 instrumental was also created by Benitez from the original recording. It was put out only on the B-side of the commercial 12-inch maxi single (US: Columbia 44-04169).

Say Say Say
US: Columbia 44-04169 (12" maxi-single)

This 12" maxi-single contains two extended remixes of "Say Say Say,"
both created by John "Jellybean" Benitez. However, the original hit
single version is not included. Instead, a previously unreleased Paul
McCartney track, "Ode To A Koala Bear" rounds out side two.

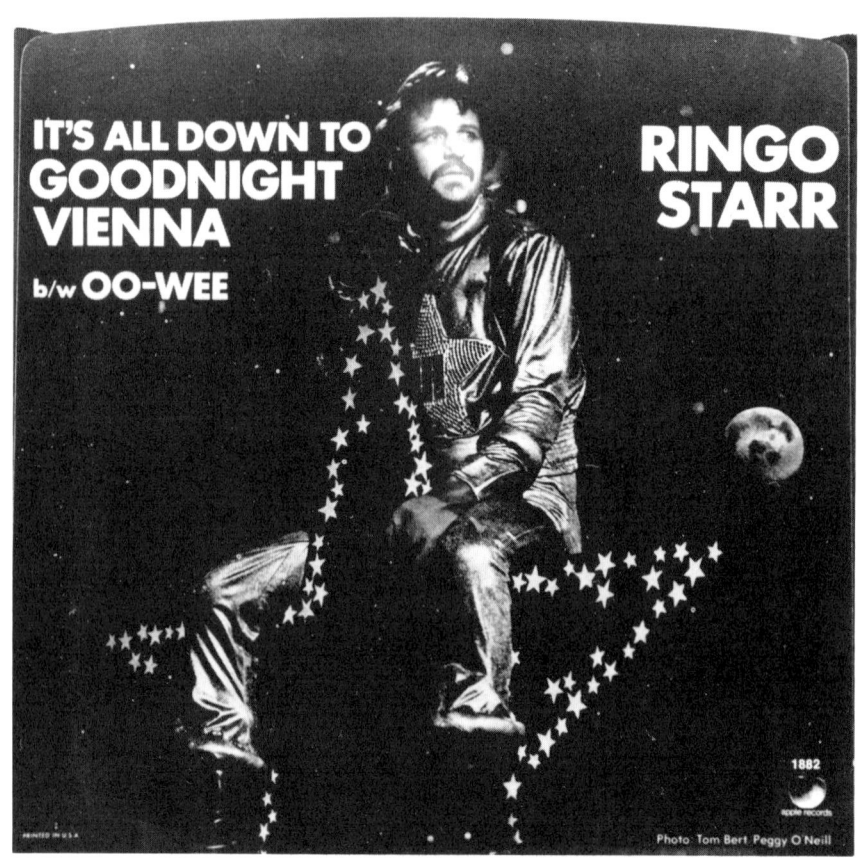

(It's All Down To) Goodnight Vienna
US: Apple 1882 (45)

14

Ringo
Starr

Most of the variations to Ringo Starr's records are tracks that were edited for singles and/or for American radio. The only true oddity is *Six O'Clock*, Paul and Linda McCartney's contribution to the much-heralded 1973 LP, **Ringo**, produced by Richard Perry. The 1:21 ending on the original tape was deleted from the commercial pressings of the album although it had been pressed on the promotional copies. Today, the full-length version is available only on the American prerecorded cassette of **Ringo**. Because of its rarity, this track has surfaced on several bootlegs including **Down And Out?** (US: Melvin MS 10) and on **Ognir Rrats Greatest Hits** (US: Wibble Records WR 91825).

Back Off Boogaloo (Starkey)
(Version 1) - Produced by George Harrison and first issued as a single in March 1972, this recording runs 3:21.
(Version 2) - Produced by Harry Nilsson as the closing track on Ringo's winter 1981 LP, **Stop And Smell The Roses**, this cut is 3:16. This new rendering, arranged by composer Van Dyke Parks, incorporates musical snatches from six other tunes by the Beatles and Ringo. The idea was similar to Nilsson's 1967 version of *You Can't Do That*, which wove together lyrics from at least twelve different Beatles songs. In fact, it was that recording that caught the ear of Derek Taylor, the Beatles' press officer, and led to the first meeting between Nilsson and the group in London in 1968.

Coochy-Coochy (Starkey)
In America, the B-side of Ringo's October 1970 single, *Beaucoups Of Blues*. Never issued in England.
The original recording, produced in Nashville by Pete Drake on June 30-July 1, 1970, was twenty-eight minutes long. Three different edited versions were issued on singles, the longest being the American release (Apple 2969), which was 4:48.

ATLANTIC

45 R P M

3412
Publisher,
Assorted Music,
BMI
SHORT VERSION
Time: 3:39
PROMOTION COPY
NOT FOR SALE

VOCAL
ST-A-33871 MO
STEREO

DROWNING IN THE SEA OF LOVE
(Kenny Gamble & Leon Huff)
RINGO STARR
PRODUCED BY ARIF MARDIN
From Atlantic LP 19108
℗ 1977 Atlantic

MFG. BY ATLANTIC RECORDING CORP. 75 ROCKEFELLER PLAZA N.Y. N.Y.

A WARNER COMMUNICATIONS COMPANY

Drowning In The Sea Of Love
US: Atlantic 3412 (promo 45)

Dose Of Rock 'N' Roll, A (Carl Grossman)

Issued in September 1976 both as a single and as the opening cut on **Ringo's Rotogravure**, this track was produced by Arif Mardin and marked Ringo's first release after leaving Apple Records.

The American promotional single (Atlantic 3361 promo) contains two versions of this song: the complete track (3:24) and the same track minus the intro (3:17). This second version was used for the commercial British single (Polydor 2001 694).

Drowning In The Sea Of Love (Kenny Gamble - Leon Huff)

Produced by Arif Mardin and issued both as a single and as the opening track on the September 1977 LP, **Ringo The 4th**.

All commercial pressings run 5:08 as does the American 12-inch promotional single (Atlantic DSKO 3375S PR). The 7-inch U.S. promo (Atlantic 3412 promo) contains the full-length track on one side; on the other is a "short version" that was edited down to 3:39 by condensing the instrumental break at the end of the song.

Have You Seen My Baby (Randy Newman)

A 1970 composition that was covered by Ringo on his first solo rock 'n' roll LP, **Ringo**, issued in November 1973. However, on the first pressing of the album, this song was listed by an alternate title, *Hold On*.

Heart On My Sleeve (Benny Gallagher - Graham Lyle)

Produced by Vini Poncia and issued in the summer of 1978 on **Bad Boy** and as a single in the United States.

The album version runs 3:20; the American single (Portrait 6-70018) was shortened to 3:07 by fading out the track early.

Hold On (Randy Newman)
See *Have You Seen My Baby*.

(It's All Da-Da-Down To) Goodnight Vienna (Lennon)

Produced by Richard Perry at Sunset Sound studios in Los Angeles with John Lennon playing piano, this song was issued in November 1974 as the opening cut on **Goodnight Vienna** and in June 1975 as a single in America.

The single consisted of a specially edited version created by combining the body of *(It's All Da-Da-Down To) Goodnight Vienna* with the closing of *Goodnight Vienna-Reprise*, both of which appear in their original form on **Goodnight Vienna**.

Oh My My (Vini Poncia - Richard Starkey)

The third American single taken from the 1973 million-selling

Publisher:
Rondor Music
(London) Ltd.
All Rights
Administered
In U.S. and
Canada by Almo
Music Corp.
(ASCAP)
Produced by:
Vini Poncia
for Mad Vincent
Productions

MONO

6-70018
ZSP 164383
℗ 1978 CBS Inc.
Intro. :09
3:07

HEART ON MY SLEEVE
-B. Gallagher · G. Lyle- Taken From The
Portrait Lp: "BAD BOY" JR 35378
RINGO STARR

Heart On My Sleeve
US: Portrait 6-70018 (promo 45)

Oo-Wee
US: Apple PRO-8140 (promo 45)

LP, **Ringo**.

The album version runs 4:17; most single pressings were shortened to 3:39 by fading out the track early. However, the German single (Apple 05617) contains the full-length album cut.

Oh My My wasn't issued as a single in England (Apple R 6011) until January 1976 when an edited version was paired with the *No No Song* to help promote Ringo's "greatest hits" compilation, **Blast From Your Past**.

Old Time Relovin' (Vini Poncia-Richard Starkey)

Produced by Vini Poncia and released in the summer of 1978 on **Bad Boy** and as the B-side of the album's first single, *Lipstick Traces (On A Cigarette)*. (In England this combination of songs was withdrawn prior to release. *Old Time Relovin'* came out as the B-side of *Tonight*.)

The album version runs 4:16; the single was shortened to 3:29.

Oo-Wee (Vini Poncia-Richard Starkey)

Produced in Los Angeles by Richard Perry in the summer of 1974 for his second LP with Ringo, **Goodnight Vienna**, and later issued as a single.

The album version runs 3:42; the American single (Apple 1882) was shortened to 3:15 by eliminating a repeat of the first part of the second verse and by fading out the track early.

Six O'Clock (Paul & Linda McCartney)

Paul McCartney's contribution to the highly successful November 1973 LP, **Ringo**, the Richard Perry-produced project that also contained songs and performances by George Harrison and John Lennon.

The original version runs 5:26 and can be found on **Ringo** test pressings, advance copies and an extremely limited number of store stock that had been pressed for promotional use. However, prior to the commercial release of **Ringo**, this track was shortened to 4:05 by eliminating the elongated coda with Paul's ad-lib background vocal. Despite the change, **Ringo** record labels still list the length of this song as 5:26.

The original recording was issued in England in the fall of 1981 on a limited edition cassette single but today is available only on the American prerecorded cassette of **Ringo** (Apple 4XW-3413).

Wings (Richard Starkey-Vini Poncia)

Produced by Arif Mardin, this song was first issued on the September 1977 LP, **Ringo The 4th**.

The album version runs 3:24; the American single (Atlantic

3429) was shortened to 3:03 by fading out the track early.

Wrack My Brain (Harrison)
Written and produced by George Harrison, this song was issued in the winter of 1981 on **Stop And Smell The Roses** and also as a single.

The Canadian single (RCA 01253) contains a different mix than other pressings.

You Don't Know Me At All (Dave Jordan)
Produced by Arif Mardin, this track was released in September 1976 on **Ringo's Rotogravure** and later as a single in Europe.

The album version runs 3:15; the single was shortened a few seconds by omitting the final words in the fade-out, " . . . at all, you don't . . . ."

Wings
US: Atlantic 3429 (promo 45)

Reel Music
US: Capitol SV 12199 (LP)

And In The End

"Collecting every release, alternate version, and variation can be an unending process, but then Beatles fans don't really ever want to run out of items to collect!"

Barbara Fenick
Collecting The Beatles
(Ann Arbor: Pierian
Press, 1982)

A word of caution to newer collectors: just because you've picked up a Beatles single or EP, don't assume you automatically have mono mixes of the songs. In March 1976, EMI Records in England repackaged its entire Beatles singles catalog, issuing the discs as a complete set in full-color picture sleeves. At first, the move seemed purely cosmetic, as all the singles were still in print and the new pressings were still in mono. However, on closer inspection, both *Yellow Submarine* and *All You Need Is Love* turned out to be stereo mixes. The matrix numbers on the record labels and in the "dead wax" indicated that these were mono tracks, so the source of these new pressings had to be the mono LP master of **Yellow Submarine** which, as mentioned earlier, was merely the stereo version with the two channels combined.

In September 1979, EMI in Australia reissued eleven of its Beatles EPs. Again the discs were pressed in mono but, prior to release, many of the tracks were remastered from stereo albums. In the case of non-LP cuts, "reprocessed" stereo versions from America were used. *Long Tall Sally, I Call Your Name, Slow Down,* and *Matchbox* were derived from **Rock 'N' Roll Music** for the new pressings of the EPs **Requests** and **More Requests**. The result was that George Martin's 1976 stereo remixes of these tracks replaced the original mono versions, which came from the 1964 British EP **Long Tall Sally**.

EMI-Odeon Records in Japan now reissues some of its Beatles singles in stereo, with true stereo mixes. To the best of our knowledge, no "reprocessed" stereo or remixed tracks from **Rock 'N'**

Roll Music have appeared.

More stereo substitutions have taken place around the world. As we were going to press, we received an urgent letter from Ross Klein, a contributor and fellow collector. Ross had recently purchased a new American pressing of **Beatles VI** on Capitol Records. Much to his surprise, when he played the disc the mix turned out to be mono! Capitol deleted its mono Beatles catalog in 1969 and since then has only re-pressed its Beatles LPs in "New Improved Full Dimensional Stereo." What makes this story even stranger is that the matrix number in the "dead wax" is for a stereo master. A quick purchase of this album in San Francisco yielded the same results: a mono copy of **Beatles VI**, listed as stereo and manufactured in the 1980's.

* * *

Despite all of the editing and cross checking of record numbers, promo pressings and foreign issues that we did for this book, there are undoubtedly still several errors and omissions. For this reason, we would like to hear from you. Feel free to contact us at the addresses below.

One final note. It's obvious with the amount of records we listened to that we have *ears*. We also have *eyes*. More on this soon . . .

William McCoy
P.O. Box 5072
Richmond, CA 94805

Mitchell McGeary
P.O. Box 3393
Lacey, WA 98503

Additions
1985 - 1986

The issuing of Beatles recording variations has continued unabated these past few years and shows no signs of letting up. The following is a chapter-by-chapter update on the relevant new releases.

Chapter 1. Tony Sheridan and the "Beat Brothers"
Each year, a handful of new compilations appear, mainly on budget reissue labels. So far, all these collections have had to offer was new packaging. In Japan, a recent 10-inch edition of **The Savage Young Beatles** (Overseas Records) featured a hologram of the "Silver Beatles" on the front cover and came with a bonus single of *Sweet Georgia Brown*.

Only one significant release of these early tracks has come out, a compact disc titled **The Beatles-First**, put out by Polydor Records in Germany. (See Chapter 5.)

Chapter 2. The Star Club Tape
Like the Tony Sheridan recordings, each year brings a few new releases of the Star Club tape. Again, there's only one new edition we'd advise picking up and that's a compact disc from Japan, **Live! At The Star Club In Hamburg, Germany; 1962.** (See Chapter 5.)

Chapter 3. The White Album
Following the promotional flexi-disc of *Rocky Raccoon* and *Why Don't We Do It In The Road* in April 1982, there have been no other reissues or variations from this album. The only hint of any new material was the inclusion of the original version of *Not Guilty* on **Sessions**, a proposed LP of unreleased and alternate Beatles tracks compiled in 1984 by Brian Southall, EMI's general manager of public relations. However, Paul, George, Ringo and Yoko (representing the estate of John Lennon) were strongly opposed to

this particular compilation and it was not put out.

Chapter 4. "RARITIES" . . . and Box Sets

All the permutations of Beatles box sets seem to have been exhausted. There are already collections of the Beatles' singles, EPs, and LPs (both on vinyl and cassettes). The only box set still in print is **The Beatles Collection** (UK: EMI/Parlophone BC 13) from Britain. It's currently being exported to the United States, where it sells for about $120.

The October 1986 issue of *Beatles Monthly Book* reported on the release of **The Beatles Box** (8 LPs) in France by Pathe Marconi. This would be strictly a mail-order item as it was in England and Australia. The liner notes were being corrected and updated and would then be translated into French by Jacques Volcouve.

Chapter 5. Audiophile Records

In the past two years, the compact disc has taken the record industry by storm. The durability, superior sound quality and total lack of surface noise caught the public's fancy. Compact disc pressing plants cannot keep up with the demand for the little silver-colored discs. Many feel the popularity of the CD has signalled the demise of the LP. Certainly in the area of audiophile pressings, the success of the CD has overshadowed the merits of the half-speed mastered album.

MOBILE FIDELITY

Following the release of **The Beatles: The Collection** (Mobile Fidelity BC-1), Mobile Fidelity continued issuing each of the Beatles albums individually in their customary jackets. The label also put out a half-speed mastered edition of John Lennon's **Imagine** to coincide with the 1986 home video release of "Imagine - The Film."

Half-Speed Mastered Albums

Beatles
   SGT. PEPPER'S LONELY HEARTS CLUB BAND   Mobile
      Fidelity MFSL 1-100
   HELP Mobile Fidelity MFSL 1-105
   REVOLVER Mobile Fidelity MFSL 1-107

John Lennon
IMAGINE   Mobile Fidelity MFSL 1-153

Chromium Dioxide Cassettes

Beatles
SGT. PEPPER'S LONELY HEARTS CLUB BAND   Mobile
Fidelity MFSL C-100
HELP   Mobile Fidelity MFSL C-105
REVOLVER   Mobile Fidelity MFSL C-107

John Lennon
IMAGINE   Mobile Fidelity MFSL C-153

OTHER LABELS

Teldec Schallplatten of West Germany, one of the leading European makers of disc mastering equipment, invented yet another means of manufacturing high quality LPs. Although its method, known as Direct Metal Mastering, yielded similar results to half-speed mastering, it was more economical. Direct Metal Mastering involves using a copper-plated blank disc onto which the sound information is cut with a diamond stylus, thus eliminating several steps in normal disc mastering and improving overall sound. In 1985, two Beatles compilations were issued in Germany using Direct Metal Mastering:

THE BEATLES 1962-1966   Apple 1C 172-05 307/08 (pressed
on red vinyl).
THE BEATLES 1967-1970   Apple 1C 172-05 309/10 (pressed
on blue vinyl).

Compact Discs

The rapid growth of the CD industry has brought a wealth of Beatles-related titles to the market in the past two years. (As we go to press, EMI has just announced that the Beatles' twelve original British studio albums will be issued on compact disc, beginning in February 1987.)

The earlier lack of Beatles titles in compact disc form left the door wide-open for the non-copyrighted material. In Japan, CDs were issued featuring the Star Club tracks and most of the Beatles audition tape for Decca Records. Even an American album of two uncut radio interviews surfaced in Japan on CD.

The one compact disc that does merit a mention is the Polydor release in Germany of **The Beatles-First** made up of the Tony

Sheridan tracks. Not only was this CD derived from the original master tapes, which resulted in excellent sound quality, but for the first time Polydor dug out the log sheets from the original sessions and printed them along with the liner notes. They show exactly when and where these legendary recordings were made and once and for all separate fact from fiction. Bill Harry, the founder and editor of *Merseybeat*, wrote a new history of these tracks, although it contradicts the log sheets several times. Finally, **The Beatles-First** is in true stereo and *My Bonnie* is preceded by Tony Sheridan's English spoken introduction.

Beatles
THE BEATLES-FIRST Germany: Polydor 823 701-2YH
The Tony Sheridan-Beatles recordings, in true stereo; *My Bonnie* begins with the English spoken intro.

THE GOLDEN BEATLES Japan: Teichiku Records 30CP-56
Two unedited radio interviews: one was conducted on location in the Bahamas during the filming of "Help" by American disc jockey Wink Martindale; the other was the complete Kenny Everett interview of John Lennon done during the making of the White Album. Unfortunately, the rest of the disc is padded with commentary and amateurish Beatles novelty songs.

LIVE! AT THE STAR CLUB IN HAMBURG, GERMANY; 1962
Japan: Teichiku Records 38CP-44
All thirty tracks off the Star Club tape plus *Hully Gully* by "Kingsize" Taylor and the Dominoes together on one disc.

THE SILVER BEATLES Japan: Teichiku Records 30CP-55
Twelve of the fifteen tracks from the Beatles' audition tape for Decca Records. The three missing numbers are *Hello Little Girl*, *Like Dreamers Do*, and *Love Of The Loved*, all Lennon-McCartney songs. Presumably, the manufacturers could not get copyright clearance.

George Harrison
GREENPEACE US: A&M Records
This charity compilation for Greenpeace International contains George's remix of *Save The World*, originally issued in 1981 on **Somewhere In England**.

John Lennon
DOUBLE FANTASY Geffen 2001-2

LIVE IN NEW YORK CITY   Capitol CDP 7 46196-2

MILK AND HONEY   Polydor 817 160-2

Paul McCartney
   (In America, Columbia Records, Paul's label since 1979, issued six McCartney titles on compact disc, including the two-record set **Wings Over America**):

BAND ON THE RUN   Columbia CK 36482

GIVE MY REGARDS TO BROAD STREET   Columbia
   CK 39613

PIPES OF PEACE   Columbia CK 39149

TUG OF WAR   Columbia CK 37462

VENUS AND MARS   Columbia CK 36801

WINGS OVER AMERICA (2 discs)   Columbia C2K 37990

   (In 1986, Paul left Columbia and returned to Capitol Records. In the rest of the world, he had always been part of EMI. Paul's first new work to be issued by Capitol was **Press To Play**. Capitol also reissued a CD edition of **Band On The Run**. The original Columbia compact disc was derived from the American LP master and therefore includes the U.S. hit single *Helen Wheels*, which was not found on other pressings of the album. However, the new CD was derived from the English master so *Helen Wheels* was not included. Capitol also put out **Wings Greatest** on compact disc. Until then, it had only been available on CD in England and Japan. Under Paul's new agreement, the rest of his earlier work will revert to Capitol Records during 1986-1987.)

BAND ON THE RUN   Capitol CDP 7 46055-2
   No longer includes *Helen Wheels*.

PRESS TO PLAY   Capitol CDP 7 46269-2
   The CD edition contains three tracks not found on the LP or cassette: *It's Not True, Tough On A Tightrope*, and *Write Away*.

WINGS GREATEST   Capitol CDP 7 46056-2
   Available for the first time in America on compact disc.

Various Artists

Beach Boys
THE BEACH BOYS Caribou ZK 39946
Includes *California Calling* with Ringo Starr on drums.

David Bowie
CHANGESONEBOWIE RCA PCD1 1732
Includes *Fame*, co-written by John Lennon, David Bowie and Carlos Alomar.

YOUNG AMERICANS RCA PCD1 0998
Includes *Across The Universe* with John Lennon on guitar, and *Fame*.

David Bromberg
THE BEST OF DAVID BROMBERG Columbia CK 34467
Includes *The Holdup*, co-written by George Harrison and David Bromberg.

Collections

HITS ON CD, VOLUME 3 Mercury 824 704-2
Includes *On The Wings Of A Nightingale* by the Everly Brothers. The song was written especially for the duo by Paul McCartney, who also plays guitar on the track.

ROCK FOR AMNESTY Mercury 830617-2
This compilation album, put together in honor of Amnesty International's twenty-fifth anniversary, includes *Pipes Of Peace* by Paul McCartney.

Elton John
GREATEST HITS-VOLUME 2 MCA MCAD 37216
Includes *Lucy In The Sky With Diamonds*, with John Lennon singing backup and playing guitar.

Harry Nilsson
HARRY NILSSON'S GREATEST HITS UK: RCA PD 89081
Ringo Starr plays drums on *Kojak Columbo* and *Spaceman*.

Yoko Ono
EVERY MAN HAS A WOMAN Polydor 823 490-2
Includes John Lennon's recording of the title track, *Every Man Has A Woman Who Loves Him*, written by Yoko.

JAMES BOND: 13 ORIGINAL THEMES Capitol CDP 7
46079-2
Includes *Live And Let Die* by Paul McCartney and Wings.

Chapter 6. Back To Mono

Once EMI in England and Japan released, then deleted, the mono versions of the Beatles LPs, no more was done with the mono masters. However, one rumor suggests that when EMI does eventually issue the Beatles material on compact disc, the early recordings will be put out in mono as they were originally intended.

Chapter 7. It Was Twenty Years Ago Today

EMI Records in England is continuing with its twentieth anniversary celebration of the Beatles by reissuing each of the group's original singles approximately twenty years from its initial release. A limited edition picture disc is also put out to mark each reissue. Of special note is the picture disc for *Paperback Writer* b/w *Rain*. The artwork used was the infamous "Butcher Cover" photo. American fans may not know that this shot first appeared in England in 1966 as part of a trade ad for *Paperback Writer*. Despite being featured in a three-quarter page ad in the *New Musical Express*, it caused no fuss.

United Kingdom

April 1985 *Ticket To Ride/Yes It Is*
   (Parlophone R 5265)

April 1985 *Ticket To Ride/Yes It Is*
   picture disc (Parlophone RP 5265)

July 1985 *Help/I'm Down*
   (Parlophone R 5305)

July 1985 *Help/I'm Down*
   picture disc (Parlophone RP 5305)

December 1985 *Day Tripper/We Can Work It Out*
   (Parlophone R 5389)

December 1985 *Day Tripper/We Can Work It Out*
   picture disc (Parlophone RP 5389)

June 1986 *Paperback Writer/Rain*
(Parlophone R 5452)

June 1986 *Paperback Writer/Rain*
picture disc (Parlophone RP 5452)

August 1986 *Yellow Submarine/Eleanor Rigby*
(Parlophone R 5493)

August 1986 *Yellow Submarine/Eleanor Rigby*
picture disc (Parlophone RP 5493)

Chapter 8. Beatles Records Most Collectors Will Never Own

The discovery of rare, one-of-a-kind Beatles records has been an infrequent occurrence lately. However, two much sought-after acetates were featured in back-to-back auctions held in London in the summer of 1986.

The Beatles (January 1, 1962): *Hello Little Girl* (Lennon-McCartney) b/w *Like Dreamers Do* (Lennon-McCartney)

This is an original Decca Records acetate from the Beatles' fabled audition session. Decca a&r man Dick Rowe used it to determine whether he should sign the group to a contract or not. His negative decision followed him the rest of his life.

These two cuts, along with the other thirteen from the session, first surfaced on private pressings in the United States in the mid-seventies. Several legal battles ensued to determine the true ownership of the tapes. Surprisingly, the Beatles never tried to take them off the market. By now the tracks have joined the Tony Sheridan recordings and the Star Club tape as some of the most reissued Beatles material around.

On August 29, 1986, the Beatles' original audition disc was put up for auction at Christie's in London, where it sold for £2,500 ($3,837.50).

The Beatles (January 1969): *The Long And Winding Road* (Lennon-McCartney)

This acetate, on the Apple Custom Pressing label, contains an early run through of *The Long And Winding Road* recorded at the Apple Studios by Glyn Johns. This version shows the song without the string and choir overdubs put on by producer Phil Spector prior to its inclusion on **Let It Be.**

304

On August 28, 1986, the Beatles' original acetate was put up for auction at Sotheby's in London where it sold for £400 ($614).

In 1985, Paul McCartney was involved in the production of an hour-long television special for BBC2 honoring the late Buddy Holly. During the program, Paul aired eighty-six seconds from the Quarrymen's 1958 recording of *That'll Be The Day*. In 1986, Paul expanded the show by twenty-five minutes and in August issued it on home videocassette in England (UK: Picture Music International MVN 991126 2-VHS; MXN 99 126 4-Beta). The initial release came in a special gatefold package that also included two audio cassettes filled with twenty-eight original Buddy Holly recordings. As yet, the home video has not been put out in the United States.

Chapter 9. The ROOTS of ROCK 'N' ROLL

In 1986, Yoko compiled **Menlove Avenue**, a collection of John Lennon outtakes, which EMI issued worldwide in November. Side One is made up of tracks recorded during the **Rock 'N' Roll** sessions, while Side Two features John's original studio runthroughs of five songs from **Walls And Bridges.**

The **Rock 'N' Roll** tapes originate from the legendary Phil Spector sessions in Los Angeles. An excellent quality version of *Angel Baby* is finally available after being deleted from **Rock 'N' Roll** by John. The number first surfaced illegally in the United States in 1975 on **Roots**. The other rarity from **Roots**, John's cover of the Ronettes' *Be My Baby* remains "in the can." This new collection also contains the only other known outtake from the Spector sessions, *My Baby Left Me*, the Arthur Crudup number.

Yoko managed to unearth two songs not known to exist: John's version of Spector's first hit, *To Know Her Is To Love Her*, plus an unreleased song written in the studio by John and Phil, *Here We Go Again*. The tracks are rounded out by John's original recording of *Rock And Roll People*, a song he gave to blues guitarist Johnny Winter in 1974 for his LP, **John Dawson Winter III.**

For information on the songs off **Walls And Bridges**, see Chapter 12.

Chapter 10. The Beatles

With all the flurry of activity involving compact discs, and the release of two LPs of unissued John Lennon material, there was only one release to note of any Beatles songs during the past few years.

In July 1986, Heineken beer in England began a special co-promotion with EMI Records. If you collected four specially-marked tabs from Heineken cans and mailed them to Whitbread Brewers (the parent company) along with £2.99, you would receive a unique 12-track Beatles "greatest hits" cassette. Included on the tape was the first-ever British release of *This Boy* in true stereo. (Remember, the version on the "bonus EP" in **The Beatles E.P.s Collection** that was purported to be in true stereo turned out to be a "reprocessed" track instead.)

Two weeks after this promotion began, Apple sought an injunction against Whitbread, claiming it had never given EMI the approval to market the cassette.

Chapter 11. George Harrison

In 1985-1986, George did not release any new recordings, deciding instead to concentrate on various projects at Handmade Films, his movie company. George did, however, make a triumphant return to "live" performing, first by appearing with Ringo on the TV special "Blue Suede Shoes: Carl Perkins and Friends," and then by joining a host of artists from Birmingham, including the Moody Blues, to sing *Johnny B. Goode* as part of the "Heartbeat '86" charity concert.

Save The World (Harrison)

(Version 1) - The closing track on **Somewhere In England**, George's ill-fated 1981 LP co-produced by himself and percussionist Ray Cooper.

(Version 2) - In 1985, George remixed his vocals and donated this new version to Greenpeace International, the environmental organization, for use on its charity compilation titled **Greenpeace**. In addition, a "Greenpeace: Non-Toxic" home video was issued made up of promo clips for the songs on the album. It was released in Beta HiFi and VHS Stereo as well as on LaserDisc.

Chapter 12. John Lennon

The year 1986 saw the release, by Yoko, of two LPs of previously unreleased John Lennon material. **Live In New York City**, issued in February, features highlights from John and Yoko's two charity concerts held on August 30, 1972 at New York's Madison Square Garden. (This is *not* the same show that aired on ABC-TV as the "One-To-One Special.") The tracks were put out on LP, cassette, and compact disc. Film from the show was also put out on home video, under the same title, with Hi-Fi sound, and on LaserDisc.

Here is the complete track listing for **Live In New York City**:

(Side One) *New York City/It's So Hard/Woman Is The Nigger Of The World/Well, Well, Well/Instant Karma/*(Side Two) *Mother/Come Together/Imagine/Cold Turkey/Hound Dog/Give Peace A Chance.*

The second LP, **Menlove Avenue**, is made up of studio outtakes. Side One consists of tracks from the **Rock 'N' Roll** sessions in Los Angeles in late 1974 while Side Two collects together five run-throughs of songs that appear on **Walls And Bridges**: *Sacred, Nobody Loves You (When You're Down And Out), Old Dirt Road, Steel And Glass* and *Bless You.* Here, John works out rough arrangements of the songs with Klaus Voorman (bass), Jesse Ed Davis (guitar), and Jim Keltner (drums).

A bootleg of these and more practice sessions for **Walls And Bridges** surfaced in America in August 1986. Comparing the two, you can hear the work Yoko did in preparing these tracks for commercial release. A fair amount of editing, fade-ins and fade-outs were used to make these rough tapes more palatable to the general public.

with YOKO ONO

Walking On Thin Ice (Re-edit) (Ono)
In November 1985, Yoko issued a 12-inch maxi-single with two remixes of *Cape Clear* (US: Polydor 883 872-1), the featured track from her new solo album, **Starpeace**. On the B-side, Yoko included a "re-edit" of *Walking On Thin Ice*, the track she and John finished the night he was murdered. This new version runs 7:17 and was created by Joseph Watt.

Chapter 13. Paul McCartney
The release of **Press To Play** in September 1986 brought Paul back into the limelight. And, as with **Give My Regards To Broad Street**, record buyers had a wealth of material to sift through. No less than six versions of the title track *Press* were issued. And, as with **Broad Street**, the CD contained more tracks than the LP or cassette.

In mid-1985, Paul wrote and recorded the title tune to the Chevy Chase-Dan Aykroyd movie "Spies Like Us" (Warner Bros.). A bonus for collectors was the use of *My Carnival*, a 1975 outtake from **Venus And Mars**, as the B-side. Not surprisingly, 7-inch, 12-inch and picture disc singles were issued, resulting in three versions of *Spies Like Us* and two of *My Carnival*.

Angry   (Paul McCartney-Eric Stewart)

(Version 1) - Co-produced by Paul and Hugh Padgham, this track runs 3:35 and was first released in September 1986 on **Press To Play**.

(Version 2) - Remixed by Larry Alexander, this radically different version was issued in October 1986 on the B-side of the British 12-inch maxi-single of *Pretty Little Head* (Parlophone 12R 6145). In November, these same three cuts were put out in England on a limited edition cassette single (Parlophone TCR 6145). Only 2,000 copies were made.

It's Not True   (McCartney)

(Version 1) - Co-produced by Paul and Hugh Padgham, this track runs 4:27 and was first released in August 1986 on the B-side of the 7-inch single of *Press*. However, it was not included on the LP or cassette of **Press To Play**, although it can be found on the compact disc.

(Version 2) - Remixed by Julian Mendelsohn, this punchier and extended version runs 5:50 and is available on both the 12-inch **Press** maxi-EP and the limited edition British 10-inch maxi-single of *Press* (Parlophone 10R 6133). Only 6,000 copies of the latter disc were made.

My Carnival   (McCartney)

Recorded in 1975 with Wings during the **Venus and Mars** sessions in New Orleans, this song - inspired by the Mardi Gras - remained unreleased for ten years before it was issued as the B-side of *Spies Like Us*. The track runs 3:56 and is available both on a 7-inch single and on the English *Spies Like Us* shaped picture disc (Parlophone RP 6118).

My Carnival - party mix   (McCartney)

The original recording was artificially lengthened to 6:00. It was issued only on the A-side of the 12-inch **Spies Like Us** EP (US: Capitol V-15212). In England, this limited edition collection was also put out as a picture disc (Parlophone 12RP 6118).

Only Love Remains   (McCartney)

Recorded at Hoghill, Paul's new 48-track studio, with an arrangement by veteran producer Tony Visconti.

(Version 1) - Co-produced by Paul and Hugh Padgham, this track runs 4:16 and was first released in September 1986 on **Press To Play**.

(Version 2) - Remixed by Jim Boyer, this new version was issued in England in December 1986 as a 7-inch single (Parlophone R 6148).

(Version 3) - This is an extended version of Jim Boyer's earlier mix. It was only put out in England, as the title track of a 12-inch maxi-single (Parlophone 12R 6148).

Press (McCartney)

The title song from Paul's September 1986 release, **Press To Play**, and the first number to be issued as a single.

(Version 1) - Co-produced by Paul and Hugh Padgham, this track runs 3:57 and is available only on the first pressing of the British 7-inch single (Parlophone R 6133), which was put out on August 14. The length is listed incorrectly on the sleeve as 4:20. This version is extremely rare. On the day of its issue, Parlophone began a second pressing and replaced this cut with *Press-Video Edit*.

(Version 2) - Mixed by Bert Bevans and Steve Forward, this version runs 4:41 and is available on the A-side of the 12-inch **Press** maxi-EP (UK: Parlophone 12R 6133) and on the compact disc of **Press To Play**. Beginning with the second pressing of the British maxi-EP, and on most foreign issues, this track was designated as the *Press-Video Soundtrack*. (See *Press* - Video Soundtrack, p.310.)

An edited version, cut to 4:37, was also issued on the first British pressing of **Press To Play** (Parlophone PCSD 103). The matrix number for Side Two is PCSD 103 B-7-1-1. Only about 45,000 copies were made. The second pressing contains yet another version of this song.

(Version 3) - Remixed by co-producer Hugh Padgham, this track runs 4:20 and was first issued in England on August 18 on the A-side of the limited edition 10-inch maxi-single of *Press* (Parlophone 10R 6133). Here the lead guitar is more prominent throughout and the cut ends with the same repeated guitar lick that's heard in the introduction. Only 6,000 copies of the 10-inch disc were made.

Several weeks later, this cut was substituted for the 4:41 mix by Bert Bevans and Steve Forward on the second British pressing of **Press To Play**. The matrix number for Side Two is PCSD 103 B-3U-1-2-1. However, the jacket still lists this as the earlier, and slightly longer, Bevans/Forward mix.

Press - Dub mix (McCartney)

Mixed by Bert Bevans and Steve Forward, this extended version, minus Paul's lead vocal, runs 6:28 and is available only on the B-side of the 12-inch **Press** maxi-EP (UK: Parlophone 12R 6133).

Press - Video edit (McCartney)

A condensed version of the *Press-Video Soundtrack*. Also mixed by Bert Bevans and Steve Forward, this version was shortened to 3:35 by omitting an instrumental break, a second guitar solo and a percussion and synthesizer refrain, all from the latter part of the song. (See *Press* - Video Soundtrack.)

In England, the 7-inch single (Parlophone R 6133 - second pressing) actually runs for 3:42. The *Video Edit* was also issued in Britain on the B-side of a limited-edition 10-inch maxi-single of *Press* (Parlophone 10R 6133). Only 6,000 copies were made. Here the length is the usual 3:35.

Press - Video Soundtrack   (McCartney)

The complete recording heard in the promotional videoclip for *Press*, directed by Phillip Davey. Mixed by Bert Bevans and Steve Forward and running 4:41, this version is available on the A-side of the 12-inch **Press** maxi-EP (UK: Parlophone 12R 6133), and without the *Video Soundtrack* subtitle on the compact disc of **Press To Play**, where it replaces co-producer Hugh Padgham's mix of *Press* that's found on both the LP and cassette.

Press To Play

Paul's first collection of all-new material since the release of **Pipes Of Peace** in the winter of 1983. Like **Give My Regards To Broad Street** in 1984, this album was issued on LP, cassette and compact disc. Similarly, the CD contains three songs not found on the other formats: *It's Not True, Tough On A Tightrope*, and *Write Away*. In England, these numbers were subsequently put out on vinyl, on either 7-inch or 12-inch singles.

Timing continues to be a problem for record companies. The given times for the ten tracks on LP and cassette all differ by a few seconds from the times encoded in the compact disc, even though no real differences exist.

Pretty Little Head   (Paul McCartney-Eric Stewart)

(Version 1) - Co-produced by Paul and Hugh Padgham, this track runs 5:13 and was first released in September 1986 on **Press To Play**.

(Version 2) - Remixed by Larry Alexander, with some additional re-recording as well, this dramatically new version was issued in England in October as a 7-inch single (Parlophone R 6145).

(Version 3) - Another radical remix, this time by John Potoker, this third version runs 6:56 and is available only in England as the title track on a 12-inch maxi-single (Parlophone 12R 6145). In November 1986, these same three cuts were put out in Britain on a limited edition cassette single (Parlophone TCR 6145). Only 2,000 copies were made.

Spies Like Us   (McCartney)

The theme song from the motion picture "Spies Like Us"

(Warner Bros., 1985), starring Chevy Chase and Dan Aykroyd. The track runs 4:40 and is available both on a 7-inch single and on the English *Spies Like Us* shaped picture disc (Parlophone RP 6118).

Spies Like Us - Alternative mix (known to his friends as Tom)
        (McCartney)
Remixed in London by Art of Noise, this track runs 3:56 but is radically different from other versions. Most of the vocals were omitted except for the "spies like us" chorus, Paul's scat singing and some background sounds. It is available only on the A-side of the 12-inch EP of **Spies Like Us** (US: Capitol V-15212). In England, this limited edition release was also put out as a picture disc (Parlophone 12RP 6118).

Spies Like Us - DJ version   (McCartney)
The same recording as the original version, this track fades out at 3:56. It was released on a 7-inch promotional single and was also issued commercially in America where it was included on the B-side of the 12-inch **Spies Like Us** EP (Capitol V-15212). Foreign pressings of this limited edition collection do not include this shortened cut.

Spies Like Us - Party mix   (McCartney)
Remixed in New York by John Potoker, this version runs 7:10. It was created from the original recording of *Spies Like Us* but also includes dialogue from the movie with Chevy Chase and Dan Aykroyd. The track is available only on the B-side of the 12-inch **Spies Like Us** EP (US: Capitol V-15212). In England, this limited edition collection was also put out as a picture disc (Parlophone 12RP 6118).

Talk More Talk   (McCartney)
(Version 1) - Co-produced by Paul and Hugh Padgham, this track runs 5:16 and was first released in September 1986 on **Press To Play**.
(Version 2) - Remixed by Jon Jacobs and Paul, this new version runs 5:56 and is available only on the B-side of the British 12-inch maxi-single of *Only Love Remains* (Parlophone 12R 6148) put out in December.

Tough On A Tightrope   (McCartney)
(Version 1) - Co produced by Paul and Hugh Padgham, this track runs 4:41 and was issued in September 1986 on the compact disc of **Press To Play**. However, in December it was given a wider release in England on the B-side of the 7-inch single of *Only Love Remains* (Parlophone R 6148).
(Version 2) - Remixed by Julian Mendelsohn, this extended

version runs 7:03 and can be found only on the B-side of the British 12-inch maxi-single of *Only Love Remains* (Parlophone 12R 6148).

with LINDA McCARTNEY

Seaside Woman   (Linda McCartney)
(Version 1) - First released in the United States in May 1977 as a 7-inch single (Epic 8-50403) under the pseudonym "Suzy and the Red Stripes," this recording was produced by Paul and runs 3:36.
(Version 2) - Issued in July 1986 and available only on the B-side of a 12-inch single (UK: EMI 12EMI 5572), this extended version was remixed by Alvin Clarke.

Chapter 14. Ringo Starr
Like George, Ringo's recording output was extremely limited in 1985-1986. His most visible work was joining his son Zak to participate in the anti-apartheid record *Sun City*, spearheaded by Steve Van Zandt, former lead guitarist for Bruce Springsteen.

with ARTISTS UNITED AGAINST APARTHEID

Sun City   (Little Steven)
Produced by Little Steven and Arthur Baker, this charity record featured over fifty top rock, pop and jazz musicians who banded together to protest the political conditions in South Africa. Ringo and Zak did not attend the mammoth recording sessions in New York. Instead, they recorded their drum tracks at Ringo's Startling Studio in Ascot, England.
(Version 1) - The opening cut on the album (US: Manhattan ST-53019), this track runs 7:10.
(Version 2) - The kickoff to Side Two, this edited version was shortened to 5:42.
Between the 7-inch and 12-inch singles and the LP, there are four versions of *Sun City*. One is a spoken track interspersed with segments of speeches by Desmond Tutu.

Glossary

For those of you who may not be familiar with the language of the recording industry, here is a glossary of the terms used throughout this book.

Acetate - an aluminum disc, coated with acetate and cut directly from the master tape. Used for reference by artists, producers and music publishers. In recent years, several acetates of unissued Beatles tracks, including *Bad To Me* and *One And One Is Two*, have fetched large sums when put up for auction at Sotheby's in London.

Alternate mix - on a multi-track recording, a different balance between the voices and instruments than on the common version of the cut. The mono version of *Can't Buy Me Love* has Ringo's drums mixed way up, while in stereo the percussion track was reduced in volume quite a bit.

Alternate take - a similar but different recording of a song, usually taped at the same session as the original. The mono and stereo mixes of *Help* actually turned out to be different takes.

Analog recording - the traditional method of sound recording, invented by Thomas Edison. Sound waves are picked up by microphones and captured on magnetic tape. A cutting stylus approximates the patterns of the waves and etches them in the grooves of a disc. For playback, a needle traces the grooves, and with an amplifier, turns them back into sound.

Artificial Double Tracking (ADT) - an electronic method of *double-tracking* voices (and instruments), invented in early 1964 by Ken Townsend, an engineer at EMI's Abbey Road studios in London. On a tape machine, the tape travels first past the recording head, then on over the playback head. Ken devised a way to pick up the voice off both the recording and playback head simultaneously during remixing, thereby getting two voices, with one slightly delayed. By manually adjusting the distance between the two heads, different degrees of delay were possible. Artificial Double Tracking was introduced on the stereo mix of **A Hard Day's**

313

Night. Tracks that received a heavy dose of ADT were the stereo versions of *If I Fell, And I Love Her* and *Tell Me Why*. Prior to this invention, a singer had to go back and match his or her voice to the original recording.

Backwards guitars/voices - one night in early 1966, John Lennon was listening to some recordings on his home tape machine. Not being too technically minded, he had threaded the tape through the recorder backwards and proceeded to play it that way. Liking the garbled sound he heard, he persuaded George Martin to incorporate this effect into the new record the Beatles were working on. The result was that the ending of the final mix of *Rain* featured John's lead vocal played backwards. Intrigued by the results, the Beatles experimented with "backwards" guitar sounds on another track, *I'm Only Sleeping*. At least five separate mixes of this cut have been issued, each with a different amount of backwards guitar fills.

Bootleg recording - an unauthorized recording, usually of a "live" concert, packaged and sold without the consent of the artists, their record company or music publisher. The first Beatles bootleg dates back to the fall of 1962 in Liverpool and was an "off-the-air" recording of *Some Other Guy* made at the Cavern in August and later broadcast by Granada TV. Also called an **underground record**.

Compact disc (CD) - a 4.72-inch plastic record in which all sound information is represented by a series of pits beneath the surface that are "read" by a laser beam. The CD represents the future of audio with its unparalleled sound reproduction and lack of any surface noise. The first Beatles compact disc was a 1983 reissue of **Abbey Road**, put out in Japan by Toshiba-EMI. Unfortunately, the necessary clearances had not been given by Apple Records and the title was soon withdrawn.

Compatible stereo - a patented process, developed in 1968 by Columbia Records in America, whereby the grooves of a stereo disc were modified to also accept the larger mono stylus and play back in mono without any distortion or serious damage to the record. Most major labels, including Capitol, adopted it. The "White Album" was the first Beatles LP issued in America only in stereo.

Compilation album - an accumulation of previously released material, usually a "greatest hits" package. The first Beatles compilation issued in England was **A Collection Of Beatles Oldies**, put out in December 1966.

Compression - during remixing, two or more tracks are reduced in volume and combined, creating a dense, thundering sound. The single version of *Revolution* was heavily compressed and was a

314

"hotter" mix than the true stereo album version later issued on **Hey Jude.**

Counterfeit record - an unauthorized pressing of a published work where the manufacturer has reproduced the cover art and record label in an attempt to pass it off as an original. In 1970, a glut of counterfeit copies of **Let It Be** filled American record stores.

Dead wax - the blank part of a disc between the sound information and the label over which the run-off groove is pressed. The record's matrix number is also stamped here. On the first American pressing of John's 1970 single, *Instant Karma! (We All Shine On)*, producer Phil Spector had the words "Phil + Ronnie" etched in the dead wax in a secret show of love for his wife Veronica (Ronnie of the Ronettes).

Demo - a demonstration disc. Usually a rough recording by a song-writer to show how his or her song should be performed. The late Dick James, the Beatles' music publisher, had a treasure trove of the group's demos, not only for the tracks they released them-selves, but also for the dozen-and-a-half songs that John and Paul gave to other artists.

Digital recording - as sound waves are processed by a computer, each sound is converted into a binary number representing frequency, volume and timbre. For true digital playback, the numbers are then stamped as bits below the surface of a compact disc and are scanned by a laser beam. To date, the surviving Beatles have chosen to continue to make analog recordings, although Paul has transferred his last four solo LPs to digital prior to remixing.

Dolby noise reduction - a patented method of reducing tape hiss by cutting out the top-end sound and boosting the slightly lower frequencies. The prerecorded cassette of Paul's **Give My Regards To Broad Street** benefitted by being issued on high-quality, chromium-dioxide tape with Dolby-encoded sound.

Double-tracking - recording a voice or instrument twice on the same tape to create a "duet." George Martin introduced the Beatles to double-tracking during the making of their first album, **Please Please Me**, where Paul double-tracked the lead vocal to the group's cover version of *A Taste Of Honey*. In 1964, Ken Townsend, an engineer at EMI, discovered a way to artificially double-track (ADT) sound electronically so the artist would only have to perform his or her part once.

Dub - a tape that is copied from another tape or disc. It doesn't originate from the master. When the first version of *Love Me Do*, with Ringo on drums, was included on **Rarities** (US) in 1980, Capitol Records had to settle for a dub made from a clean copy of the original single since the master tape could no longer be located in EMI's vaults.

Echo - can be introduced electronically or through the use of acoustic chambers where sound is fed in through a speaker and then re-recorded through a microphone as it bounces off the walls. George Martin used echo sparingly on the original Beatles mixes. Unfortunately, Capitol Records added some echo to just about every American Beatles LP from **Meet The Beatles** to **"Yesterday" . . . And Today.**

Editing - taking different sections from one or more tapes and rearranging them to make a finished recording. In analog form, this is done by cutting the master tape with scissors, then rejoining it with splicing material. The Beatles' first two singles, *Love Me Do* and *Please Please Me*, went through quite a bit of editing at the hands of engineer Norman Smith to come up with the perfect takes. The unedited version of *Please Please Me* later surfaced on the stereo edition on the group's debut LP.

Equalize (EQ) - the balance between the bass, treble and midrange frequencies. These are checked and adjusted prior to the cutting of a lacquer.

Feedback - the piercing, high-frequency sound that results when a microphone or electric instrument is placed in front of a speaker. John Lennon introduced the use of feedback on a rock 'n' roll record in November 1964 when he employed it in the opening of *I Feel Fine.*

Final mix - the ultimate balance of all tracks in a multi-track recording, which are then combined to form a two-track stereo master. In 1966, an early mix of *I'm Only Sleeping* appeared in America two months before the finished track was issued in England.

Flexi-disc - usually a promotional record that is pressed on thin plastic or cardboard. The Beatles' official fan club Christmas singles (1963-1969) were issued in England and later in America on flexi-discs.

Half-speed mastering - a method of creating a superior vinyl disc by playing back the master tape at half the normal speed while rotating the lacquer at halfspeed, giving the cutting stylus four times as long to accurately etch sound information in the grooves. Mobile Fidelity Sound Lab in California championed this process and has, by now, made available all of the Beatles' original British studio albums in high-quality editions.

Lacquer - a disc cut directly from the master tape and used to make stampers from which vinyl records are pressed. The accuracy with which the lacquer is cut dictates how good the commercial disc will sound. In the 1970s, Paul McCartney provided finished lacquers for his solo records to EMI and Columbia (US) to guarantee a certain standard of excellence.

Leslie speaker - a top brand of speaker with a rotating cone that creates a swirling effect. In *Tomorrow Never Knows*, George Martin fed John Lennon's lead vocal through a Leslie speaker in an attempt to meet John's request that his voice sound as if it were coming from a mountain top in Tibet.

Limiting - an electronic means of reducing the volume of a recording once it reaches a certain level so that the stylus won't jump out of the grooves when a lacquer is cut. Only Mobile Fidelity's half-speed mastered albums are manufactured without any limiting.

Mastering - cutting the lacquer from which stampers are made to press vinyl discs. The Beatles opened Apple Records in 1969 partly to be able to cut their own masters. The Apple cutting crew, which came over from EMI, gained quite a reputation for producing the best lacquers in England and many other artists sent their material to No. 3 Savile Row to be mastered.

Master tape - the final version of a particular recording once it has been remixed. Over the years, several Beatles master tapes have disappeared from EMI's vaults, including the original version of *Love Me Do* with Ringo on drums.

Matrix number - a record's complete catalog number, which is stamped into the dead wax.

Maxi-single - a 7-inch, 10-inch, or 12-inch disc comprised of three songs. In 1982, Paul McCartney issued a 12-inch maxi-single from **Tug Of War** featuring the two tracks from the 7-inch single, *Take It Away* and *Dress Me Up As A Robber*, plus one additional track from the same sessions that was unavailable elsewhere, *I'll Give You A Ring*.

Mellotron - an early form of synthesizer, it housed a wide variety of sounds on tape loops that could be played back on a keyboard. The Beatles experimented with a Mellotron on *I Am The Walrus*.

Mixing - the selection of the proper balance between the voices and instruments and the proper degree of stereo panning for each track. On the Beatles' first album, **Please Please Me**, there was very little actual mixing. Once a balance had been found, most everything was recorded directly onto tape. **Rubber Soul** was a turning point as far as time spent on mixing, and by the release of the "White Album" in 1968, it was not uncommon for the Beatles to spend as much as six hours remixing a particular song.

Mono - a monaural recording consists of just one channel of sound. Despite the fact that the Beatles recorded on two or more tracks at EMI, the following songs remain available only in mono: *Love Me Do; P.S., I Love You; She Loves You; I'll Get You; Yes It Is; Only A Northern Song;* and *You Know My Name (Look Up The Number)*.

Moog synthesizer - the brand name of a sophisticated electronic device that can be programmed to play back most any sound. George Harrison purchased one of the early models and used it on **Abbey Road**. George also issued a solo LP of synthesizer material in May 1969 titled **Electronic Sound**.

Open-reel tape - otherwise known as reel-to-reel. Prerecorded tapes were issued in four configurations in the late sixties: open-reel four-track cartridge, eight-track cartridge, and cassette. Today only the cassette remains for commercial use. Beatles material was put out on both sides of the Atlantic in various open-reel packages. In fact, in England both **Abbey Road** and **Let It Be** were released in mono on open-reel, while every other issue was in stereo.

Overdubbing - adding material to an already completed basic record-ing. The Beatles learned about overdubbing at their very first commercial session at EMI. Since they were such a loud band, George Martin found it best to record the instrumental track first, then overdub the vocals after. At their first session for *Love Me Do*, they cut the backing track over a dozen times before they were ready to lay down the vocals.

Phasing - an electronic effect which creates a swirling sensation by continually changing the equalization of a given voice or instru-ment. John's lead vocal on *Lucy In The Sky With Diamonds* sounds "phased" in mono, although in stereo it is clean.

Pirated album - an LP of copyrighted works where no attempt was made to duplicate the original cover art and/or label. The first known pirated Beatles album appeared in America in 1964 under the title **The Original Greatest Hits**.

Pocket discs - a very short-lived attempt by Americom at marketing records teenagers could carry around in their pants pockets. Two Beatles singles were licensed by Apple for this format: *Hey Jude* and *Get Back*, along with Mary Hopkin's *Those Were The Days*.

Promotional copy - a record or tape given away to radio stations and music critics in return for free publicity in the form of airplay and, hopefully, good reviews. No royalties are paid on promo-tional copies. Over the years, Apple Records has called for complete accountings by Capitol Records in America concerning its distribution and accounting practices in regards to Beatles promo albums.

Quadraphonic sound - a short-lived, four-channel home playback system for records and tapes, introduced by the major labels in the early 1970s. John Lennon went back in the studio and remixed the song *Imagine* in quad for a four-channel reissue of the LP, but left the work on the remaining tracks to the studio engineers.

Reissue - a record or tape that a label remanufactures and promotes, usually after it has been out-of-print for some time. The Beatles tracks that have been reissued most often are the eight songs they cut with Tony Sheridan, followed closely by Ted Taylor's Star Club material.

Remaster - to re-cut new lacquers from the master tape before re-pressing new records. In Australia, Parlophone remastered its Beatles singles and EPs catalog in 1976 and used stereo and "reprocessed" stereo tracks in place of the original mono recordings.

Remixing - to re-balance a multi-track recording. Most often, remixing occurs before a particular cut is issued. However, in 1976, George Martin remixed the early Beatles tracks for the American compilation **Rock 'N' Roll Music** to give the original twin-track tapes a cleaner, more modern sound.

Reprocessed stereo - an electronic means to simulate the ambience of a true stereo recording through the use of equalizers, echo and reverb. There are several ways to achieve this. On the early American Beatles records, it meant splitting the frequency spectrum, panning the bass signals to the left and the treble to the right, and then adding echo or reverb to the individual channels.

Reverb - a form of electronic echo capable of enhancing a recording without necessarily giving it the ambience of a concert hall.

Run-off groove - the lone groove on a record that follows the normal sound information and spirals across the dead wax into the label. The groove is designed to eject the tonearm of an automatic record changer. In 1967, the Beatles decided to surprise their listeners by putting sound on the run-off groove at the end of Side Two on **Sgt. Pepper**.

Second- or third-generation tape - a copy of a copy (of a copy) of an original master recording. Since tapes lose definition and frequency response with each duplication, and at the same time build up noise, it is not desirable to master a disc from such a recording. Many early American Beatles records were pressed from such tapes, however.

Stampers - two metal plates, molded from the lacquer, that are used to press a vinyl record.

Stereo - two channels of audio, designed to reproduce three-dimensional sound. The Beatles, George Martin and the engineers at EMI were at the forefront of stereo recording in the sixties. Their imaginative stereo imaging on **Sgt. Pepper**, the "White Album" and **Abbey Road** set a standard for pop records that still stands today.

Tape loop - a continuous section of tape that, when played on a

319

tape machine where the erase head has been removed, can repeat its collection of sounds indefinitely. The use of tape loops grew out of the avant-garde electronic music of the sixties. The Beatles began experimenting with them during the making of **Revolver**. In fact, tape loops are an integral part of the closing track, *Tomorrow Never Knows.*

Test pressing - the first few vinyl discs made from the stampers. They usually bear a white or generic company label and are used by the technicians to check the quality of the product. Copies then go to the artists and producer to listen to for musical merit. Only after all parties have signed their approval can the initial pressing begin.

True stereo - a three-dimensional-sounding recording. The various background instruments are panned toward the left or right while the lead instruments and voices are put on both channels to sound as if they were coming out of the center. In England, the first Beatles album available in true stereo was **A Hard Day's Night**. However, in America, the United Artists soundtrack LP was "reprocessed" from a mono tape.

Twin track recording - a convenient way of getting a well-balanced mono master. First the instruments are recorded on one channel, then the voices are overdubbed on the other. The two channels are then compressed, creating one powerful sound. This is how all of the Beatles' early singles, and their first LP, were recorded. The two channels were never intended to be divided to provide a stereo mix, which is exactly what happened to many of these tracks.

Underground record - see *Bootleg recording.*

Virgin vinyl - a record made from one hundred percent polyvinyl chloride. Today, the only country where discs are manufactured from virgin vinyl is Japan. Since the Arab oil embargo of 1973, the compound has been in short supply. Records in America now contain a large quantity of recycled vinyl, derived by melting down unsold records, labels and all, and reusing the raw material.

Bibliography

The following is a detailed bibliography of the works used to research this book. Included are books, magazines and newspaper articles about the Beatles and their recordings plus a cross section of material about the recording industry in general.

General

Bacon, David and Norman Maslov, *The Beatles' England* (San Francisco: 910 Press, 1982).

Carr, Roy and Tony Tyler, *The Beatles: An Illustrated Record* (New York: Harmony Books, 1975).

Castleman, Harry and Walter J. Podrazik, *All Together Now* (Ann Arbor: Pierian Press, 1975).

-----------, *The End Of The Beatles?* (Ann Arbor: Pierian Press, 1985).

Davies, Hunter, *The Beatles: The Authorized Biography* (New York: McGraw-Hill, 1968).

Glemser, Kurt, ed., *Hot Wacks: Book X* (Kitchener, Ontario: Blue Flake Productions, 1983).

Hamlin, Bruce, comp., *The Beatles Records in Australia* (Australia, 1981).

Harry, Bill, ed., *Mersey Beat: The Beginnings of the Beatles* (London: Omnibus Press, 1977).

The Lennon Tapes (London: BBC Publications, 1981).

McGeary, Mitchell, *The Beatles Discography* (Olympia, WA: Ticket to Ryde, 1975).

Nite, Norm N., *Rock On: The Illustrated Encyclopedia of Rock N' Roll* (New York: Thomas Y. Crowell, 1974).

Norman, Philip, *Shout! The Beatles in Their Generation* (New York: Simon & Schuster, 1981).

Prakel, David, "It Was Twenty Years Ago Today Sgt. Pepper Taught the Band To Play — and the band, of course, was the Beatles," *Practical Hi-Fi*, December 1982.

Russell, J.P., *The Beatles on Record* (New York: Charles

Scribner's Sons, 1982).

Schaffner, Nicholas, *The Beatles Forever* (Harrisburg: Cameron House, 1977).

Shepherd, Billy, *The True Story of the Beatles* (New York: Bantam Books, 1964).

Southall, Brian, *Abbey Road* (Cambridge: Patrick Stephens Limited, 1982).

Williams, Allan and William Marshall, *The Man Who Gave the Beatles Away* (New York: Macmillan, 1975).

Chapter 1. Tony Sheridan and the "Beat Brothers"

Carr, Roy, "If you'd been in Hamburg's Top Ten Club in 1961, this guy would need no introduction from us," *New Musical Express*, September 6, 1975.

Epstein, Brian, *A Cellarful of Noise* (New York: Doubleday, 1964).

Kirk, Cynthia, "European Singer Sues Beatles, Lennon Estate, Labels for $1-Bil.," *Variety*, August 25, 1982.

"Pretty Purdie – Li'l Ole Hitmaker," *Rolling Stone*, June 22, 1972.

Roxon, Lillian, *Rock Encyclopedia* (New York: Grosset & Dunlap, 1969).

Vollmer, Jurgen, *Rock 'n' Roll Times* (New York: Google Plex Books, 1981).

Weinberg, Max with Robert Santelli, *The Big Beat: Conversations With Rock's Great Drummers* (Chicago: Contemporary Books, 1984).

Weinstein, Robert, "The Man Who Really Discovered the Beatles," *The World of John Lennon and the Beatles* (New York: Graybar Publishing, Inc., 1980).

Weitzman, Steve, "Bernard Purdie: The Real Fifth Beatle?," *Gig*, February 1978.

Chapter 2. The Star Club Tape

Blanche, Ed, "Butcher May Have Fortune in Beatle Tape," *San Francisco Examiner*, July 13, 1973.

Brinkman, Howard, liner notes on **The Historic First Live Recordings** (LP) (US: Pickwick PTP-2098).

Evans, Mike, "Beatles Films," *Melody Maker*, February 14, 1976.

McCoy, William, "1962 Hamburg Beatles Recordings Uncovered," *Strawberry Fields Forever*, #4.

Miller, Jim, ed., *The Rolling Stone Illustrated History of Rock & Roll* (New York: Rolling Stone Press, 1976).

Repka, Charles, "Resurrecting the Beatles: Star Club to Stereo,"

High Fidelity, August 1977.

"Teazers," *New Musical Express*, April 24, 1976.

White, Chris, liner notes on **The Beatles—Live! At The Star Club In Hamburg, Germany, 1962** (LP) (US: Atlantic-Lingasong 7001).

Chapter 3. *The White Album*

Alverson, Charles, "The OBE: Lennon's Soul Redeemed," *Rolling Stone*, #49, December 27, 1969.

"Beatles' Record-Busting LP May be All-Time Biggest," *Rolling Stone*, #24, December 21, 1968.

Brigitta, "Mother Nature's Synthesizers," *Hit Parader*, July 1969.

Bugliosi, Vincent with Curt Gentry, *Helter Skelter: The True Story of the Manson Murders* (New York: W. W. Norton, 1974).

Doerfler, Marilyn, "Analyzing the Beatles," *Tiger Beat*, April 1969.

Evans, Mal, "George's U.S. Visit," *Beatles Monthly Book*, #66, January 1969.

Tapebook, Volume 1, Number 1, February/March/April 1969.

Wenner, Jann, "Beatles," *Rolling Stone*, #24, December 21, 1968.

Chapter 4. *"RARITIES"... and Box Sets*

Atkinson, Terry, "Beatles: Once More," *Los Angeles Times*, "Calendar," June 1, 1980.

Callahan, Mike, "Both Sides Now: The Story of Stereo Rock & Roll — Part Three: The Reprocessed Stereo Blues," *Goldmine*, December 1979.

Callahan, Mike, "Both Sides Now: The Story of Stereo Rock & Roll — Part Four: The British Invasion," *Goldmine*, January 1980.

"Made in Taiwan," *Hot Wacks*, #10.

"$160 Tag on Beatles Set," *Billboard*, July 14, 1979.

Schaffner, Nicholas, "Every Little Thing: The Story Behind 'Rarities,' the 'New' Beatles LP," *Trouser Press,* #51, June 1980.

Smeltzer, Dave, "Box Sets," *Hot Wacks*, #8, Fall 1981.

Chapter 5. *Audiophile Records*

Audiophile Buyer's Guide, Spring 1983 (New York: Hampton International Communications).

"Compact Disc Digital Audio: A Special Report Sponsored by Philips, Polygram, Sony," *Billboard*, November 5, 1983.

Digital Audio, September 1984 (premier issue).

Fantel, Hans, "Digital Recordings-Beautiful Music by the Numbers," *New York Times*, February 18, 1979.

Hanley, Charles J., "Carribean Studio Offers More Than Music-making," *Chicago Sun-Times*, August 4, 1984.

Nightingale, Anne, "Desert Island Discs," *Sunday Express Magazine*, April 15, 1984.

Rockwell, John, "For $325, A Chance to Assess the Legacy of the Beatles," *New York Times*, October 24, 1982.

Sutherland, Sam, "Do CDs Sound Better?," *High Fidelity*, March 1984.

Tircuit, Heuwell, "The Tiny Disc with a Big Future," *San Francisco Sunday Examiner and Chronicle*, "Review," March 13, 1983.

Chapter 6. Back To Mono

Martin, George and Jeremy Hornsby, *All You Need Is Ears* (London: Macmillan London Limited, 1979).

Chapter 7. It Was Twenty Years Ago Today

Blanche, Ed, "A Beatles' Bash in Britain," *Oakland Tribune*, October 6, 1982.

Cutner, Naomi, Nancy Griffin, Gail Cameron and Celia Waters, "The Beatles," *Life*, February 1984.

Grein, Paul, "Beatles' Invasion Remembered," *Billboard*, February 11, 1984.

Howlett, Kevin, *The Beatles at the Beeb* (London: BBC Publications, 1982).

Ochs, Ed, ed., "The Beatles 20th Anniversary in America: A Billboard Retrospective," *Billboard*, February 11, 1984.

Pond, Steve, "20th Anniversary Beatles Blitz: Recall the Mania," "Calendar," *Los Angeles Times*, February 5, 1984.

Rolling Stone, "Special Beatles Anniversary Issue," #415, February 16, 1984.

Sylva, Bob, "Remembering the Beatles: 20 Years Since They Hit the U.S.," *Sacramento Bee*, February 5, 1984.

Chapter 8. Beatles Records Most Collectors Will Never Own

Braun, Michael, *Love Me Do: The Beatles' Progress* (London: Penguin Books, 1964).

Brown, Mick, "Lot 66," *Sunday Times Magazine*, August 28, 1983.

Grant, Mike, "Star Beat," *Rave*, #3, April 1964.

"Quarry That Weight," *Trouser Press*, #67, November 1981.

Rense, Rip, "The First Beatles Recordings," *Los Angeles*

Herald Examiner, March 3, 1982.

Rhode, H. Kandy, ed., *The Gold of Rock & Roll 1955-1967* (New York: Arbor House, 1970).

Sotheby Parke Bernet Group, *Important Rock & Roll Memorabilia 1955-1975*, Wednesday, December 22, 1982, Catalogue No. 1136A.

Sotheby Parke Bernet Group, *Rock & Roll Memorabilia 1956-1983*, September 1, 1983, Catalogue No. 3661A.

Chapter 9. The *ROOTS of ROCK 'N' ROLL*

Carr, Roy, "The Phil Spector Story," *New Musical Express*, March 6, 1976.

Charlesworth, Chris, "Rock On!," *Melody Maker*, March 8, 1975.

Cott, Jonathan and Christine Doudna, eds., *The Ballad of John and Yoko* (New York: Rolling Stone, 1982).

Fawcett, Anthony, *John Lennon: One Day at a Time* (New York: Grove Press, 1976).

Flippo, Chet, "Lennon in Court Again: $42 Million of Old Gold," *Rolling Stone*, #210, April 6, 1976.

Hamill, Pete, "Long Night's Journey into Day," *Rolling Stone*, #188, June 5, 1975.

"Phil Spector in Mystery Mishap," *Rolling Stone*, #158, April 11, 1974.

Sheff, David and G. Barry Golson, ed., *The Playboy Interviews with John Lennon & Yoko Ono* (New York: Playboy Press, 1981).

Chapter 10. The *Beatles*

Hodenfield, Chris, "George Martin Recalls the Boys in the Band," *Rolling Stone*, #217, July 15, 1976.

Lawrence, Paul, " . . . I am a Very Nervous Character: An Interview with George Martin about Producing the Beatles and Other Things," *Audio*, May 1978.

McGeary, Mitchell, "Every Little Thing," *Strawberry Fields Forever*, #30.

----------, "Here, There and Everywhere" (Parts One through Three, *Goldmine*, 1978.

---------- and William McCoy, *Every Little Thing: The Beatles on Record* (Lacey, WA: Ticket to Ryde, 1979).

Mills, Paul, "Capitol Records: Number Three and Counting," *Fusion*, August 1973.

Piercey, Nick, "The Beatles–The Alternate Takes," *Record Collector's Magazine*, October 1982.

Remmerswaal, Jos, "Here There and Everywhere" (Parts One

through Eight), *Beatles Unlimited,* #10, #11, #12, #14, #15, #18, #20, #23.

Chapter 11. George Harrison

Harrison, George, *I Me Mine* (New York: Simon & Schuster, 1982).

Michaels, Ross, *George Harrison: Yesterday & Today* (New York: Flash Books, 1977).

Chapter 12. John Lennon

Christgau, Robert, "Leacock-Pennebaker: The MGM of the Underground?," *Show*, January 1970.

Occhigrosso, Peter, "John, Yoko: The Last Project," *San Francisco Sunday Examiner & Chronicle*, March 1, 1981.

Tremlett, George, *The John Lennon Story* (London: Futura Publications Limited, 1976).

Williams, Richard, *Out of His Head: The Sound of Phil Spector* (New York: Outerbridge and Lazard, 1972).

Chapter 13. Paul McCartney

Gambaccini, Paul, *Paul McCartney: In His Own Words* (New York: Flash Books, 1976).

Gelly, David, *The Facts About a Rock Group Featuring Wings* (New York: Harmony Books, 1977).

Give My Regards To Broad Street (London: MPL Communications/Pavilion Books, 1984).

Tremlett, George, *The Paul McCartney Story* (London: Futura Publications Limited, 1975).

Chapter 14. Ringo Starr

Garbarini, Vic, "Ringo," *Musician/Player & Listener*, February 1982.

Mewborn, Brant, "Ringo in the Afternoon," *Rolling Stone*, April 30, 1981.

"Ringo: An Interview with a Forgotten Beatle," *Rock*, October 25, 1971.

Song & Record Title
Index

327

Label & Record Number Index

About The Authors

William McCoy

A graduate of the University of California at Berkeley with a B.A. in English, William has been an ardent Beatles fan since February 9, 1964, when he saw the group debut on "The Ed Sullivan Show." He was only in the second grade then, but was soon trading Beatles bubblegum cards with his classmates during recess. A serious collector of Beatles memorabilia since 1967 (actually from the night NBC-TV aired "A Hard Day's Night" for the first time), he still has the first two Beatles singles his aunt gave him in 1964 as an Easter present, although regrettably he later threw away the "Authentic Beatles Wig" he received along with them.

William began writing about the Beatles while in high school, and had several articles on collecting published in early issues of the fanzine *Strawberry Fields Forever*. His Beatles knowledge served him well in school. In college, he received an "A" for a survey he wrote about the Beatles' business firm, Apple Corps Ltd. The grade entitled him to an unlimited "stack pass" to the U.C. Berkeley library system for the four years he attended. Extensive Beatles research followed.

Today, William works as the television production coordinator for Roller Derby/Rollermania in San Francisco, as well as handling local advertising and publicity for the World Wrestling Federation in California.

Mitchell McGeary

Mitch is known to Beatles collectors across the United States and in many foreign countries through Ticket To Ryde Ltd., his mail-order company that deals exclusively in Beatles records and related memorabilia. Begun in 1974, TTR now boasts a permanent mailing list of 1,000 customers.

Despite his success as a dealer, Mitch considers himself to be first and foremost a Beatles fan/collector. Over the years, he has discovered, bought, and sold some of the most rare of all Beatles memorabilia. His search for material has also led to several lengthy meetings (both in America and England), with drummer Pete Best, manager Allan Williams,

Apple "house hippie" Richard DiLello, photographer Iain McMillan (who shot the **Abbey Road** cover), and many other people close to the Beatles.

Mitch has always been happy to share his knowledge of the Beatles, and his impact on Beatles fandom should not be underestimated. In the mid-1970s, he was resident Beatleologist for *Goldmine*, America's largest record collecting magazine. In 1975, he published the first "Beatles Discography" to cover foreign pressings, and in the intervening years he has made ongoing contributions to record and memorabilia price guides by Jerry Osborne, Barb Fenick, and Perry Cox.

Throughout the 1970s, Mitch worked as a journeyman carpenter. In the months when business was slow, the earnings from Ticket To Ryde came in handy as supplementary income for himself, his wife Lois, and their two children. In 1978, he sold half his immense Beatles collection and used the capital to open one of the first home video stores in the United States. Today, although Mitch has also branched out into independent video production, he always finds time for his favorite hobby.